An Iraq of Its Regions

Cornerstones of a Federal Democracy?

Reidar Visser and Gareth Stansfield

editors

HURST & COMPANY, LONDON

First published in the United Kingdom by
HURST Publishers Ltd,
41 Great Russell Street, London, WC1B 3PL
© Reidar Visser, Gareth Stansfield
and the Contributors, 2007
All rights reserved
Printed in India

A catalogue data record for this volume is available
from the British Library.

ISBNs
978-1-85065-874-0 *casebound*
978-1-85065-875-7 *paperback*

www.hurstpub.co.uk

AN IRAQ OF ITS REGIONS

CONTENTS

THE CONTRIBUTORS

Hashem Ahmadzadeh is Lecturer in Kurdish Studies at the University of Exeter and co-director of its Centre for Kurdish Studies. He was previously Lecturer in Iranian Studies at the University of Uppsala. His publications include *Literature and Nation: A Study of Persian and Kurdish Narrative Discourse* (2003).

Liam Anderson is Associate Professor of Political Science at Wright State University in Dayton, Ohio. He is co-author of *The Future of Iraq: Dictatorship, Democracy or Division* (2005), and has written numerous book chapters and journal articles on federalism in Iraq and the politics of the Iraqi Kurds.

James Denselow is a doctoral candidate in geopolitics at King's College, London. He is researching the political geography of the Syrian–Iraqi borderlands, which he has visited extensively. He worked as a researcher at Chatham House, and is currently working with Richard Schofield on *New Iraq, Old Neighbours: Borders, Territoriality and Region* (forthcoming, Hurst & Columbia University Press, 2007).

Fanar Haddad is a doctoral candidate at the Institute of Arab and Islamic Studies at the University of Exeter. His focus is on Iraqi national identity and state formation. After completing his M.Phil. at Cambridge University, Darwin College, in 2004, he worked as an Iraq analyst in London.

Alastair Northedge is Professor of Islamic Art and Archaeology at Université de Paris 1 (Panthéon-Sorbonne). He has worked in Syria, Jordan, Saudi Arabia, Kazakhstan and Turkmenistan, and conducted field projects at Amman in Jordan, and Ana in Iraq, in addition to Samarra. He is author of *The Historical Topography of Samarra* (2005), *Studies on Roman and Islamic Amman* (1992) and joint author of *Excavations at Ana* (1987).

Sajjad Rizvi is Senior Lecturer in Islamic Studies at the Institute of Arab and Islamic Studies at the University of Exeter. He is a specialist on Islamic intellectual history having published on philosophical and exegetical traditions. He is currently researching messianism and the Sadr movement in Iraq.

Richard Schofield is Lecturer in Boundary Studies at King's College, London. He has written extensively on territorial aspects of Arabia and the Persian Gulf region, and is currently writing (with James Denselow) *New Iraq, Old Neighbours: Borders, Territoriality and Region* (forthcoming, Hurst & Columbia University Press, 2007) He is the author of several books on Iraq's boundaries, including *Evolution of the Shatt al Arab Boundary Dispute* (1986), *The Iran–Iraq Border: 1840–1958* (1989) and *Kuwait and Iraq: Historical Claims and Territorial Disputes* (1991).

Gareth Stansfield is Associate Professor in Middle East Politics in the Institute of Arab and Islamic Studies at the University of Exeter, and Associate Fellow of the Middle East Programme at Chatham House. He is co-director of Exeter's Centre for Kurdish Studies. His publications include *Iraq: People, History, Politics* (2007); *Iraqi Kurdistan: Political Development and Emergent Democracy* (2003); and, with Liam Anderson, *The Future of Iraq: Dictatorship, Democracy or Division?* (2005).

Reidar Visser is a Research Fellow at the Norwegian Institute of International Affairs and editor of the Iraq website historiae.org. He has a background in history and comparative politics from the University of Bergen and completed his doctorate in modern Middle Eastern studies at the University of Oxford. His latest book is *Basra, the Failed Gulf State: Separatism and Nationalism in Southern Iraq* (2005).

Ronen Zeidel teaches Iraqi history at the University of Haifa and at the Hebrew University of Jerusalem, and is a Research Fellow at the Truman Institute in Jerusalem and at the Miriam and Meir Ezri Centre for Iran and Persian Gulf Studies at the University of Haifa. His Ph.D. thesis, 'Tikrit and the Tikritis: A Provincial Town, Regional Community and State in Twentieth Century Iraq', focuses on the question of regional identity in the Iraqi context.

LIST OF ACRONYMS

ADM	Assyrian Democratic Movement
IKF	Iraqi Kurdistan Front
ITF	Iraqi Turkmen Front
KDP	Kurdistan Democratic Party
KDPI	Democratic Party of Iranian Kurdistan
KNA	Kurdish National Assembly
KRG	Kurdistan Regional Government
PUK	Patriotic Union of Kurdistan
PKK	Kurdistan Workers' Party
SCIRI	The Supreme Council for the Islamic Revolution in Iraq
TNA	Turkmen National Association
UIA	The United Iraqi Alliance

The historical Iraq in the early Islamic age.

Iraq in Ibn Hawqal, *Kitab Surat al-Ard* (967–88).

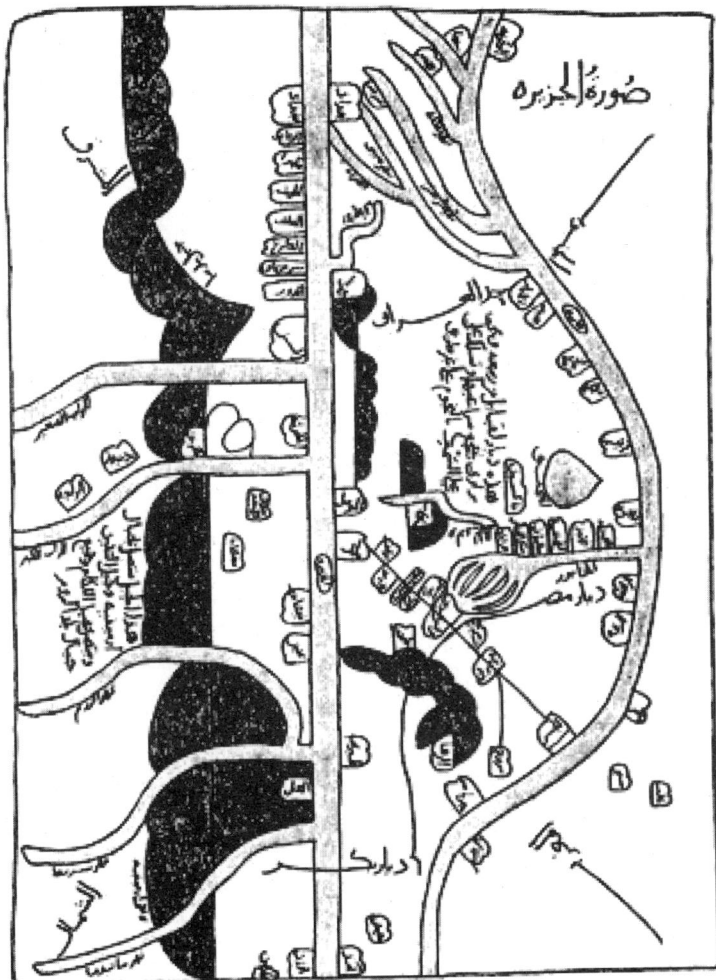

Jazira in Ibn Hawqal, *Kitab Surat al-Ard* (967–88).

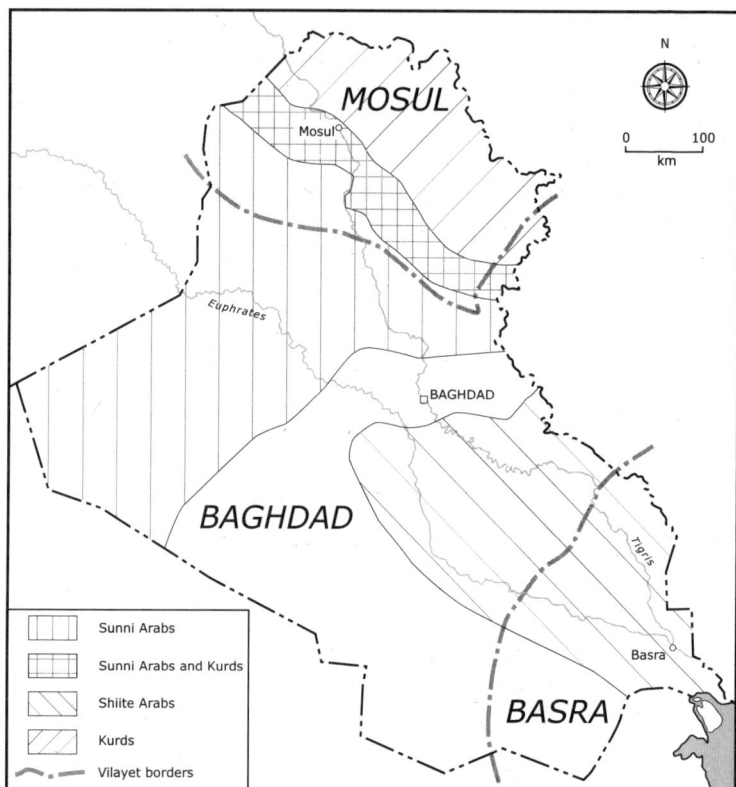

Iraq in late Ottoman times.

Administrative map of Iraq 2007 showing existing governorates and historical regions.

Iraq south of Baghdad.

Western Iraq.

Northern Iraq.

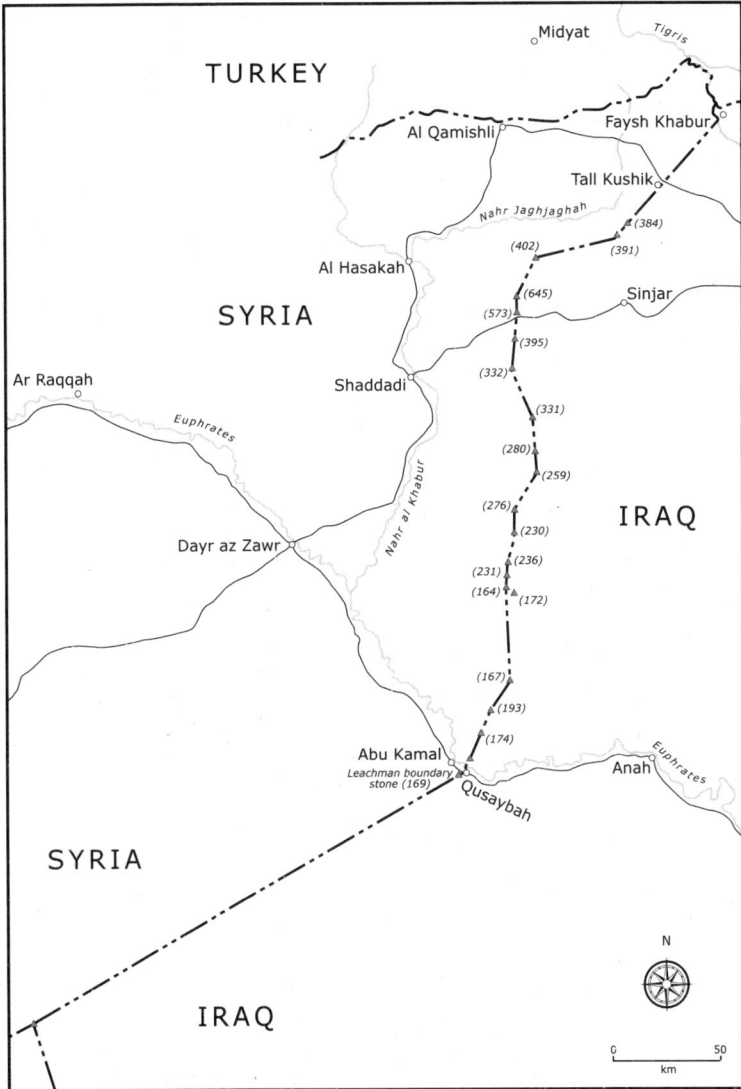

Syria-Iraq boundary and borderlands.

Head of the Persian Gulf.

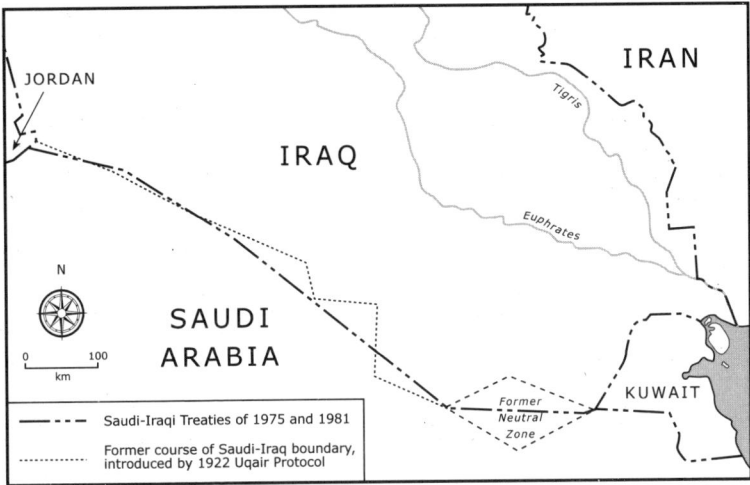

The evolving Iraq-Saudi Arabia boundary.

The Perso-Ottoman borderlands, 1914.

1
INTRODUCTION

Reidar Visser

This book focuses on a subject which al-Qaida supporters hope will never come on the agenda, and one which the Bush administration and much of international public opinion has yet to discover: Iraqi regionalism. Regionalism is an approach that puts geography centre stage. It is a sentiment that brings together citizens of a given territory despite other social factors that may set them apart, like language or religious sect. To regionalists, it makes more sense to co-operate closely with people from their own area, regardless of ethnicity, than with co-religionists or speakers of their own language living further afield. In this way, regionalism constitutes a mode of thinking that can serve to defuse ethnic and sectarian conflict in societies where there is a high degree of ethno-religious complexity.

Many will be surprised to learn that regionalism exists in Iraq at all. Journalists reporting from Iraq after 2003 have overwhelmingly employed ethnic lenses for reading Iraqi politics: Iraq is supposedly made up of three 'main groups'—the Shiite Arabs, the Sunni Arabs, and the Kurds. Growing indications of tension between these communities after 2003 have been taken as evidence that these groups are indeed the basic components of Iraqi society, and that any viable political system would need to build upon them to ensure future stability. Even though the Kurds are the only group in Iraq that has in fact made consistent demands for ethnic autonomy, many western observers jumped to conclusions as soon as a small group of Shiites

1

in the summer of 2005 announced that they aimed at a 'single Shiite federal region'. Instantly, this was construed this as a 'massive' Shiite demand for federalism along sectarian lines, and many analysts went on to demand that Iraqi Sunnis should start 'thinking in terms of federalism'.

Iraqi realities are however far more complex than this. To many Iraqis, the ethno-religious community is but one of several possible foci of identity. Historically, in many parts of the country, it has also been a rather marginal one. Instead, villages, towns and regions have shaped identities: people of southern Iraq, for instance, often think of themselves as 'Qurnawis' or 'Basrawis' or just 'Southerners' rather than as 'Shiites' or 'Sunnis'. Similar patterns prevail in many parts of western Iraq, where imported concepts from the international media like 'the Sunni triangle' have only limited resonance among a population whose habit is to use terms like 'Tikritis' or 'Fallujis' or 'Rawis' (all references to local town names) to describe their own identity. Even in the Kurdish areas—frequently highlighted for the strength of the ethnic component in local identity politics—there is an interesting dualism between ethnic and regional approaches to the definition of Kurdistan, with some Kurdish elites keen to stress their apartness from the wider Kurdish world which also encompasses areas in Syria, Turkey and Iran.

A closer look at the politics of Iraq since 2003 reveals the fascinating pervasiveness of regional identities in Iraq, even in the face of an increasingly hostile environment where foreign forces such as al-Qaida have sought to maximise the drive towards sectarianism. Among the Shiites, for instance, the first tentative pro-federal efforts followed precisely a regionalist formula—not a sectarian one. Based in the triangle of Basra, Maysan and Dhi Qar in the extreme south of Iraq, a project was launched in 2004 to amalgamate these three (mainly Shiite) provinces into an oil-rich federal entity that would have left the vast majority of Iraq's Shiites (who live to the north) without much oil. The project has continued to flourish, and it formed an important but often overlooked dimension of the internal

Shiite struggle that prompted Iraqi premier Nuri al-Maliki (himself a Shiite from central Iraq) to send troops to Basra as one of his first ministerial actions in May 2006. Similarly, in the area often described by Westerners as the 'Sunni heartland', attempts by US think tanks and advisers to encourage a territorial 'Sunni' entity have met with marked resistance. The mediocre local response to this federalism propaganda drive has almost universally been explained (again, by outsiders) with reference to the absence of energy resources in this region and the supposed lack of incentives for pro-federal attitudes. But elsewhere in the world, areas that are far poorer than the Iraqi north-west have produced vibrant secessionist and pro-federal movements. There is much to suggest that one factor impeding the crystallisation of a 'Sunni' region is territorial attachment to smaller units—often towns rather than whole regions as such. (Lately, foreign Islamists have become another advocacy group for a 'Sunni' region, but they too have met with resistance by their native brethren.) As for Kurdistan, many analysts argue that what was formerly often described as 'internal regional tensions' between eastern and western parts of Kurdistan are now a thing of the past. Nevertheless, the process of establishing a Kurdistan region within a federated Iraq is in itself an act of regionalism: Kurdish leaders thereby seek a pragmatic role for themselves as Kurds within an Iraqi federation, separate from the much wider Kurdish world, and at least partially in opposition to pan-Kurdish nationalist sentiment that calls for Kurdish unification on a far larger scale.

This volume takes Iraqi regionalism seriously. Instead of dismissing regionalism as a residual category forever consigned to a secondary role in Iraqi history and subordinate to 'primordial' ethnic identities, we take a long view of Iraqi history and put Iraqi regionalism in focus. The great potential of the regions as building blocks for the future Iraq is that, in addition to being comparatively untainted ideologically, they have historical depth. They represent a historical *longue durée* that might serve as antidote to savage sectarian warfare (whose history in Iraq is far more episodic) and its perversions of traditional religious doctrine. Not least they could function as beacons for the wider region, dispelling fears of 'Shiite Crescents' and perpetual ethno-sectarian conflict in the Middle East. However, not all parts of Iraq are equally well endowed with strong regional legacies. Any realistic effort to capitalise on the regions as a resource in the democratic restructuring of Iraq must take into account this historical imbalance within Iraq. Clearly there are 'regions' (as defined by outsiders) which in reality have seen only scant tendencies of regionalism, and where competing concepts of identity dominate—often tribe, town or sect, but also well-developed large-scale nationalisms, whether 'Iraqi', 'pan-Arab', or 'pan-Kurdish'.

The realities of regionalism in Iraq in turn have consequences for constitutional questions and issues relating to the design of Iraq's political system. Those few foreign experts who have looked beyond the ethno-religious paradigm for a federal Iraq have tended to tout Spain as a model, with its combination of unitary and federal elements in the same system, and with popular initiatives 'from below' the mechanism for demarcating its administrative map. On the surface the Spanish model seems eminently suitable for Iraq—a polity whose regions differ strongly with regard to the strength of local patriotism, and where there are various degrees of competition from other forces such as sectarianism or tribalism. At the same time, however, it is clear that there are enormous discrepancies between Spain and Iraq. In Iraq, those regions that are identifiable today are not as well entrenched as their counterparts in Spain were in the late 1970s. Iraqi politicians disagree a lot more than the Spaniards did about exactly what are the historical regions of their country. In order to employ regions as a middle-of-the-road solution for a new decentralised Iraq, Iraqis must make sure that their mechanisms for forming new regions in a federal system are attuned to the highly complex legacies of their collective past. If Iraq is to successfully combine nationalist and regionalist legacies in a single polity, a minimum of checks and balances will be required.

The stolen regional legacy

To a considerable extent, the marginalisation of Iraq's regional identities is the work of twentieth-century historians. The most prevalent fallacy has been that of equating the old Ottoman provinces of Iraq with ethno-religious sub-communities and assigning sectarian colours to them. Already prior to the 2003 Iraq War, there was a widespread misperception in Western academic circles that the old Ottoman *vilayet* of Mosul was historically 'Kurdish', Baghdad 'Sunni Arab', and Basra 'Shiite Arab'. Frequently, the three provinces were portrayed as entirely disparate sub-units of the Ottoman Empire, with nothing more in common than a loose sense of Ottoman super-identity among their local elites. After 2003, this facile sketch has rapidly proliferated and has spread beyond academe: today it is the staple of many a crash course on Iraqi history.[1]

This erroneous ethnic stereotype of Ottoman Iraq is something far more serious than a mere pedagogic simplification of complex realities. As a portrayal of the Ottoman situation, it is simply plain wrong. In the early twentieth century, Basra had important Sunni elements, Baghdad was in fact the largest Shiite province in the region, and Mosul was inhabited by a mix of Arabs, Kurds, Turkmens and Christians. One reason for the perpetuation of the distorted 'ethnic' map (with its vast exaggeration of how ethno-religious and historical maps supposedly correlate) is simply that the old Ottoman provin-

---

1 For typical examples, see Peter Galbraith, *The End of Iraq: How American Incompetence Created a War Without End*, New York: Simon and Schuster, 2006, p. 7; Douglas Little, 'A Night to Remember: Walt LaFeber's Last Waltz', *Society for Historians of American Foreign Relations Newsletter*, August 2006; Edwin Black, 'Can We Succeed in Iraq', October 2004, at http://bankingonbaghdad. com/archive/AdrianLenawee20041021/LenaweeBlack.php; Michael Kelly, 'Stay Saddam's Death Sentence', *Jurist*, November 2006; remarks by the Earl of Onslow at House of Lords debate, 24 September 2002, as quoted in *Lords Hansard*, column 1002; Pat McDonnell Twair, 'Desert Queen: The Extraordinary Life of Gertrude Bell', *The Middle East*, March 1997; Jason Zych, 'Iraq', in *The 1995 Review and Extension of the Nuclear Non-Proliferation Treaty* (ACDIS Occasional Paper), December 1996; Robert Kaplan, 'Tales from the Bazaar', *The Atlantic Monthly*, August 1992.

cial borders are regularly misrepresented on sketch maps used in the West—by the media as well as by prestigious academic publishers. Contrary to what is commonly thought, the boundary line between Basra and Baghdad was in fact located very close to the Gulf. It ran from north of Amara to north of Nasiriyya and thus separated the Shiites of Basra from those of Najaf, Karbala and Baghdad. In late Ottoman times, the centre of Shiism in the region was firmly located in the province of Baghdad.[2]

Few examples better illustrate this problem than the widespread misuse of Hanna Batatu's magisterial *The Old Social Classes and the Revolutionary Movements of Iraq*. Batatu knew perfectly well where the Ottoman border was, and incorporated this knowledge in his writings. In a much-quoted passage, Batatu offered the following interpretation of regional relations:

> The ties of Mosul were with Syria and Turkey, and those of Baghdad and the Shiite holy cities with Persia and the western and south-western deserts. Basra looked mainly to the sea and to India. The different schemes of weights and measures in the different towns of Iraq, the wide variation in the prices of the same commodity by reason of the dissimilar marketing conditions, and the extensive use of different currencies attested to the latent economic disunity.[3]

But whilst this account clearly describes Baghdad as a Shiite centre of gravity with extensive Persian links, numerous writers have quoted this exact account to construe an image of an Iraq divided into three *vilayet*s, each with its own sectarian colouring (and Baghdad invariably as 'Sunni').[4] It is true that the theme of social subdivisions was

---

2 A description of the boundary at the time of World War I is given in WO/157/776, General Staff, summaries of intelligence, report dated 12 June 1915 (War Office records in the Public Record Office/UK National Archives, Kew, London).

3 Hanna Batatu, *The Old Social Classes and the Revolutionary Movements of Iraq*, Princeton: Princeton University Press, 1978, pp. 16–17.

4 Malik Mufti, *Sovereign Creations: Pan-Arabism and Political Order in Syria and Iraq*, Ithaca: Cornell University Press, 1996, p. 23.

central to Batatu, but it is plain that in this particular case he was describing regional and not sectarian divisions.

By 2007 and with the growing politicisation of Iraq's history following the US invasion in 2003, these kinds of fallacies were being reproduced for increasingly greater audiences, and with an ever greater likelihood of becoming directly inserted into policy-making decisions. 'Historians Offer Dismal Outlook for Iraq' shrieked an Associated Press headline in January 2007.[5] Historians of various backgrounds tended to agree that Iraq was about to break apart along sectarian lines.[6] David Fromkin was quoted as follows:

In his classic study of those times, *A Peace to End All Peace*, Boston University's Fromkin quoted an American missionary who warned the British in Baghdad against tying Arab and Kurdish provinces, Sunni and Shiite provinces together: 'You are flying in the face of four millenniums of history if you try to draw a line around Iraq and call it a political entity!'

Exactly what went wrong in this interview is difficult to establish. The journalist may well have misrepresented Fromkin. At any rate, the correct interpretation of the statement of the American missionary involved—John Van Ess—can be found in Fromkin's original book from 1989, where it becomes clear that Van Ess was talking about regional and not sectarian antagonisms—more specifically between Assyria and Babylonia (whose original ethnic characters had gradually given way as Akkadian and then Aramaic became *lingua francas*), several millennia before Shiism and Sunnism even existed.[7]

The problem of misrepresenting the past goes beyond the categorisation of individual provinces. It is also linked to the portrayal of the historical relationship between the various units that were formally joined together in the Arab kingdom of Iraq in 1921. It is cor-

---

5 AP article by Charles J. Henley, 21 January 2007.

6 Characteristically, the one Iraq historian in the sample, Phebe Marr, remained a lot more cautious than the rest.

7 David Fromkin, *A Peace to End All Peace*, pbk edn, Harmondsworth: Penguin, 1989, pp. 450–1. See also Dorothy F. Van Ess, *Pioneers in the Arab World*, Grand Rapids: Eerdmans, 1974, p. 113.

rect that by 1914 there was administrative separation between Basra, Baghdad and Mosul. But this separation was not more than 30 years old. Before that period, there had been long intervals of administrative unification with Baghdad as a paramount centre—as seen for instance from the 1860s to the 1880s, in almost a whole century from the 1760s to 1850, in the early eighteenth century and, again, in the 1670s. On top of this, the pre-eminent position of Baghdad had persisted even in times of formal administrative differentiation: for long periods the city had served as military headquarters also for Ottoman forces in the adjacent provinces, and it had often maintained supreme judicial authority over its 'independent' neighbours, as had been the case with regard to Basra in the late nineteenth century.[8]

No discussion of regionalism in Iraq can be complete without some mention of the identity concept that accompanied this administrative subordination of Basra and Mosul to Baghdad. To the extent that there existed nomenclature at a higher level than the individual provinces, there was in reality no competition: 'Iraq' was the one concept that dominated. Persian travellers in the eighteenth century referred to 'Iraq'.[9] Basra historians of the early nineteenth century employed expressions like 'Basra and all of Iraq'.[10] Ottoman administrators in Mosul of the 1890s referred to their city as 'part of the region of Iraq'.[11] The widespread contention in modern scholarship that 'Iraq' was an invented name, given to a population that was entirely ignorant about this geographical concept, simply does not stand up to scrutiny. Conspicuously, claims about Iraq's supposed 'artificiality'—popular as this interpretation is among contemporary

---

8 A good overview of Baghdad's leadership role for the greater Iraqi region is provided in Stephen Hemsley Longrigg, *Four Centuries of Modern Iraq*, Oxford: Clarendon Press, 1925.

9 Longrigg, *Four Centuries*, p. 333.

10 Ibrahim Ibn al-Ghamlas, *Wulat al-basra wa-mutasallimuha* [Basra's governors and sub-governors], Ali al-Basri (ed.), Baghdad: Dar al-Basri, 1962, p. 43.

11 Ottoman archives, BOA, Y/MTV/72/43, letter from the governor of Mosul dated 20 Rabi' al-thani 1310/10 November 1892.

commentators and generalist historians—is invariably presented without references to nineteenth-century sources, whether Ottoman or Western ones.

The marginalisation of regionalism

What, then, has prompted historians to embrace such a distorted view of Iraq's past? In particular, why have regional concepts—which clearly did exist—fared so badly in historiography? Western Orientalism must take its share of the responsibility. In the views of many authors with essentialist views of Islam, Muslims have historically been reluctant to think in terms of regions, or indeed in terms of any subdivisions within the vast and unified Dar al-Islam ('House of Islam'). Max Weber opined that the pervasiveness of Islam was such that the cities of past Islamic empires were unable to develop autonomous spheres and corporations (from which localist movements theoretically could have flowed).[12] Rather than seeing the Islamic world as a tapestry of regions, these authors tend to construe Islamic polities of the past as a collection of urban nodes that greedily sought to extract taxes from as much of the rural hinterland as possible, without ever seeking to consolidate their spheres of influence to an integrated region.[13] Some Westernised Arab writers like Albert Hourani also embraced elements of this approach, for instance by suggesting that the idea of showing affection for a given territory was largely a foreign and European idea imported to the Muslim world by a few Egyptian intellectuals in the nineteenth century.[14]

Other manifestations of this Orientalist bias include the widespread expectation among Western scholars that ethno-religious maps of

---

12 Max Weber, *Wirtschaft und Gesellschaft: Die Stadt*, student edn, Tübingen: J.C.B. Mohr, 2000, pp. 1–35.

13 R.W. Brauer, *Boundaries and Frontiers in Medieval Muslim Geography*, Philadelphia: The American Philosophical Society, 1995.

14 Albert Hourani, *Arabic Thought in the Liberal Age, 1798–1939*, Cambridge: Cambridge University Press, second edn, 1983, pp. 78–9.

the Middle East should necessarily translate into a corresponding political geography, with separation between different religions and sectarian denominations. Ever since the wars of religion in Europe in the sixteenth and seventeenth century and the emergence of state churches with their vernacular editions of the Bible, Europeans have shown a propensity for thinking of religion and language in territorial terms. There is a certain intellectual continuity from the states of the old German empires (where subjects followed the religion of their princes, as confirmed in the 1648 Westphalia peace agreement), to the breakdown of multi-ethnic Yugoslavia in the 1990s (where 'ethnic' differences based on miniscule dialect differences were augmented and fanned by ideas of sectarian distinctiveness). This pervasive European heritage has become the baggage of intellectuals worldwide schooled in the Western tradition, to the point where even United Nations experts almost by default tend to prefer separative (and mostly federal) 'solutions' whenever they encounter ethno-religious complexity.[15] Ignored is the Ottoman idea of *millet* (sect or nation) coexistence—a concept which in its original incarnation was deeply problematic in terms of the stratification between a Muslim *Staatsvolk* and non-Muslim 'protected subjects', but also a promising point of departure for defining citizenship without resort to ideas about sectarian exclusivity.

Even some of the most sophisticated attempts at using an essentialist framework to account for political behaviour in territorial issues in the Middle East run into problems. In *Imams and Emirs*, Fuad I. Khuri introduces a distinction between 'sects' and 'religious communities' in the Islamic empires, suggesting that the former category is made up of peoples who tried to escape the sovereignty of the state (Alawites, Druzes, Shiites, Christian Maronites) whereas the latter comprises those communities that were integrated into

---

15 On attempts by international experts to convince the Iraqi Sunni Arabs of the virtues of a federal system, see Jonathan Morrow, *Iraq's Constitutional Process II: An Opportunity Lost* (USIP Special report), Washington, DC: United States Institute of Peace, November 2005, p. 14.

the state structure (Sunnis, smaller Christian minorities and Jews).[16] Khuri claims that sects—who are in search of sanctuaries outside the realm of the state—have a greater propensity for seeking territorial exclusivity than religious communities. At the macro level, this shows interesting correlation with episodes of sect-based secessionism in the Middle East, notably with regard to the Maronites of Lebanon, as well as in the case of a people not discussed in detail by Khuri, the (Nestorian) Assyrians of Iraq. But there are limits to this kind of explanation. Khuri seems to admit that the Shiites—labelled by him as a 'sect'—do not quite live up to the theory's prediction of sectarian territorial devotion (which in the cases of other sectarian communities is expressed for instance through the building of shrines in their areas of demographic concentration). Similarly, if the theory were to be projected onto the Christians of Iraq, it would be difficult to explain why the Chaldean community has proved far more reluctant than the Nestorians to join in an ethnic 'Assyrian' umbrella identity for all the Iraqi Christians.[17] And Lebanon, the land of sects *par excellence* according to Khuri's definition, never collapsed into separate statelets despite the decades of civil war and much talk of partition, again especially in Western circles. Clearly, there is no automatic correlation between ethno-religious characteristics and political ambitions.

It is unsurprising that this sort of essentialist legacy should have fostered a school of Iraq historians blind to regions and obsessed instead with sects and ethnicities. A prominent example is Elie Kedourie, an Anglicised Iraqi who angrily criticised Iraqi Shiite authors of the monarchical period for 'under-stressing' and 'muffling' the Shiite dimension in Iraqi politics, thereby 'hiding' their 'real' identity under

16 Fuad I. Khuri, *Imams and Emirs: State, Religion and Sect in Islam*, London: Saqi, 1990, esp. pp. 61–76.

17 On diverging trends among Iraq's Christian communities, see John Joseph, *Muslim–Christian Relations and Inter-Christian Rivalries in the Middle East*, Albany: State University of New York Press, 1983.

a nationalist cloak.[18] After 2003, ad hoc experts on Iraqi history have elaborated this perspective—but sadly without the rich empiricism that makes Kedourie's oeuvres so worthy of reading. As a result, it is now difficult to find introductory texts on Iraqi history that do not posit the three largest ethno-religious communities of the country as principal units of analysis. Additionally, a more practical factor has augmented the ethno-religious stranglehold on Iraq's past. To experts in the social and political sciences who lack a background in Iraq's local languages and religions, it is immensely expedient to portray Iraq as an artificial entity—an accidental country without any regional legacies, where only sectarian communities exist. This kind of interpretation conveniently absolves analysts of the need to read hundreds of tomes on pre–twentieth century Iraqi history (mostly in Arabic), and provides an imaginary *tabula rasa* onto which they can let loose their theories and comparisons in the field of 'ethnopolitics'. It is no small coincidence that such experts and consultants from various international organisations have spearheaded the initiatives to transform Iraq into a federation based on ethnicities, not regions.[19]

The actual picture of 'Islamic imperatives' that would ostensibly act as barriers against regionalism is far more nuanced. In Sunnism, especially, regional sub-units are ideologically unproblematic and have a long tradition. Even though the theory of the all-embracing caliphate has formed a historical imperative towards Islamic unity, the institution of sultanates—semi-independent principalities whose rulers were acknowledged in coinage and during Friday prayers (along with symbolic mention of the caliph)—is almost as old as the caliphate itself. The list of autonomous polities that rose and fell within the theoretical jurisdiction of the caliphate is a long one, and comprises everything from city-states (as seen in East Africa) to

18 Elie Kedourie, 'The Iraqi Shi'is and Their Fate', in Martin Kramer (ed.), *Shi 'ism, Resistance, and Revolution*, Boulder: Westview Press, 1987, pp. 135-6. There is a parallel debate in studies of Syria, where scholars such as Volker Perthes have noted the existence of a 'confessional paradigm'.
19 The rebranding of Balkanists as 'Iraq experts' has been particularly conspicuous.

Bedouin chiefdoms (for instance in medieval Syria).[20] In Iraq, the semi-independent rule of the Georgian mamluks of Baghdad—their reign lasted from 1747 to 1831 and covered the vast area between Basra and Mosul—is a prominent example. And while it is true that secessionist movements within the Muslim world (i.e. those that aimed for complete independence from the caliphate) often materialised on an ethnic or religious basis or even created new sects as a pretext for secession, truly 'regional' separatist episodes can be found as well. In the period after the fall of the caliphate in 1924, this tendency became even stronger and many regional 'sultanates' of the past acquired new forms of political independence. There are more recent examples of such regionalisms without sectarian connotations as well: in the 1950s and 1960s a pro-colonial movement in Aden by a coalition of local merchants sought to keep that area separate from the wider Yemeni hinterland, and since the 1980s Arabs in parts of Sudan have been engaged in regionalist struggles against (Arab-dominated) Khartoum.[21]

The Shiite-majority areas of the Muslim world have been less prolific with regard to regional initiatives, and in this case one might perhaps speak of a less permissive intellectual climate. Shiism lacks the straightforward and utilitarian dualism of caliph and sultan found in the Sunni tradition; instead it has historically been divided between an apolitical core tradition (whose adherents scoffed at the idea of any close links between clergy and temporal power) and a more recent activist and strongly pan-Islamist trend that followed in the path of Ayatollah Khomeini and the Iranian revolution.[22] Nevertheless, regional initiatives were far from non-existent. Some

---

20 A particularly interesting collection of studies on city-states that emerged in an Islamic context is included in Mogens Herman Hansen (ed.), *A Comparative Study of Thirty City-State Cultures*, Copenhagen: C.A. Reitzel, 2000.

21 A theoretical introduction to the relationship between Islamic ideals and secular international politics is given in James P. Piscatori, *Islam in a World of Nation-States*, Cambridge: Cambridge University press, 1986.

22 Moojan Momen, *An Introduction to Shi'i Islam*, New Haven: Yale University Press, 1985, pp. 189–99.

of the Arab tribal principalities of the medieval period (such as the Mazyadids of Iraq) were for instance headed by Shiites and, in more recent history, Shiites in Pakistan's Northern Areas region (Gilgit and Baltistan) have been engaged in regionalist movements with a non-sectarian character.[23] The widespread use of distinctly regional toponyms in personal names long before the nineteenth century (al-Ahsa'i for al-Hasa in Eastern Arabia, al-Jaza'iri—literally 'the islander'—for the marshlands north of Basra) is another testament to regionalist sentiment in the Shiite world.[24]

Twentieth-century pan-Islamism, which inherited the role of Islamic unifier from the old caliphate, may have had a certain restraining role vis-à-vis regionalism in the Muslim world. But even here, the initial ethos of territorial unification was soon diluted by a more pragmatic approach to the realities of day-to-day politics. This has certainly been the case in Sunnism, where attacks on the hegemony of the learned elites have formed a central element of radical Islamist ideology, and where intellectual innovation has accelerated in turn, with scant respect for established axioms. One example is the recent tendency of radical Islamists—theoretically adherents of the caliphate theory—to work through the local or regional levels, as seen for instance in Algeria in the 1990s and more recently in Iraq, with the declaration of small-scale Islamic emirates (first formed at the level of towns but also seen more recently in a competing, more

---

23 For interesting examples of *de facto* Shiite state formation without the emergence of any ideological superstructure, see Ahmad al-Katib, *Tatawwur al-fikr al-siyasi al-shi'i min al-shura ila wilayat al-faqih* [The development of Shiite political thought from *shura* (consensus rule) to *wilayat al-faqih* (the rule of the jurisprudent)], Beirut, 1998, pp. 371-4. Similarly, for a historical example of how the Shiite periphery has contributed to the emergence of alternative practices—if not theories—in politics, see J.R.I. Cole, *Roots of North Indian Shi'ism in Iran and Iraq*, Berkeley: University of California Press, 1989.

24 There is also the Shiite usage of 'Bahrain' as a wider regional concept, embracing not only the island of Bahrain but also the coastal strip of present-day Saudi Arabia, see for instance Hamza al-Hasan, *Al-shi'a fi al-mamlaka al-'arabiyya al-sa'udiyya* [The Shiites of Saudi Arabia], Muassasat al-Baqi' li-Ihiya' al-Turath, 1993.

sectarian formula).[25] Similarly, within Shiite Islamism, regionalism has become acceptable as well. In the 1990s, Shiite Iraqi pro-federal politicians singled out the region (*iqlim*) as a legitimate and positive building block in a pan-Islamic quasi-federal system, and after 2003 many went on to condone 'geographically' or 'administratively' defined federal units (but not 'sectarian' ones) within the Iraqi state. It is noteworthy that Shiite clerics of a relatively high standing supported this turn to non-sectarian (or even anti-sectarian) regionalism; one example is Muhammad al-Yaqubi.[26] With the current drift in Shiite circles towards radical alternatives like Mahdism and neo-Akhbarism, the orthodox Shiite establishment is coming under ever greater pressure, and entirely new Shiite attitudes to questions concerning territorial identity could well be in the making.

Perhaps the more formidable factor in the internal marginalisation of regionalism in the Middle East has been Arab nationalism. In Arab nationalist discourse, 'regionalism' is not only a *faux pas*, it verges on taboo. Almost as old as Arab nationalism itself, the term regionalism (*iqlimiyya*) was used as early as the 1930s to denote divisive, particularistic practices that could derail the project of greater Arab unity.[27] By the 1960s and the heyday of Iraqi nationalism (and the time of a string of failed unification attempts) it had become part and parcel of a wider family of pejorative terms: localism, familism, sectarianism, and regionalism. Often, eruptions of regionalist or sectarian struggles were attributed to American or Israeli conspiracies to keep the Arabs divided and to thereby weaken Arab influence in

25 On the strategy of creating Islamic spaces, 'from below', see Olivier Roy, *The Failure of Political Islam*, London: I.B. Tauris, 1994, pp. 80–2.

26 On the historical development of Shiite attitudes to federalism, see Reidar Visser, 'Shi'i Perspectives on a Federal Iraq: Territory, Community and Ideology in Conceptions of a New Polity', in Daniel Heradstveit and Helge Hveem (eds), *Oil in the Gulf: Obstacles to Democracy and Development*, Aldershot: Ashgate, 2004.

27 Yehoshua Porath, *In Search of Arab Unity, 1930–1945*, London: Frank Cass, 1986, p. 14. The roots of the derogative use of *iqlimiyya* might even be in pan-Islamism (which in turn was opposed to Arab nationalism), see Hamid Enayat, *Modern Islamic Political Thought*, Basingstoke: Macmillan, 1982, p. 117.

the region. Still in the late 1970s, it was perfectly natural for an Iraqi author to refer to past regionalism in Basra derogatively, as a 'narrow regionalism' (*iqlimiyya dayyiqa*),[28] whereas in the late 1990s an Iraqi historian would detect 'Arab nationalism' in the nineteenth-century regional history of Mosul.[29] In Iraq and elsewhere, works on local history were published only after they had been embellished with references to the assumed role of local events in the greater national and pan-Arab struggles—however far-fetched and strenuous those links were. There was always a certain ambiguity to this Arab nationalist condemnation of regionalism, especially as time went by and it became clear that the Arab nationalists themselves remained hopelessly divided, in separate states. Indeed, one of the most fundamental divisions within the Arab nationalist camp—that between 'Syrians' and 'Iraqis'—had in fact been acknowledged without too much in the way of protests shortly after it crystallised in 1918, and rather than being a European plot designed to stem the rising force of Arab nationalism it happened to be the work of Arab officers involved in anti-Ottoman activities.[30] But whereas this kind of sub-division was sometimes acknowledged by the use of more positively laden terminology such as 'country' (*qutr*, derivative *qutri*), sub-divisions within these divisions remained a touchy subject.

The survival of regional sentiment in this kind of atmosphere, in Iraq and elsewhere in the Middle East, is all the more remarkable. But one consequence of the Western preoccupation with ethnicity (and to some extent the Iraqi focus on ideologies with transnational dimensions) has been a complete disregard for Iraqi regions in the existing literature on the country. Regions held no interest for West-

28 Hamid Ahmad Hamdan al-Tamimi, *Al-basra fi 'ahd al-ihtilal al-baritani, 1914–1921* [Basra during the British occupation, 1914–1921], Baghdad: Markaz Dirasat al-Khalij al-'Arabi, 1979.

29 Sayyar al-Jamil, *Zu'ama' wa-afandiyya* [Traditional notables and effendis], Amman: Al-Ahliyya, 1999, pp. 195–197.

30 WO/158/619, telegram from the commanding officer at Aqaba dated 16 December 1918 (War Office records in the Public Record Office/UK National Archives, Kew, London).

ern researchers bent on portraying Iraq as a country of quarrelsome ethno-religious groups, and were a mere distraction for Iraqi politicians who above all professed their interest in schemes of greater integration across state borders. True, recent years have seen a growing interest in the Ottoman history of some of the Iraqi regions, among Western and Iraqi academics alike.[31] But these analyses not only tend to use Ottoman administrative units as their frame of analysis, they also invariably limit themselves to the period before 1900, and often sidestep the question of identity in relation to specific territorial spaces. And what limited attention has been paid to 'regional' varieties of federalism after 2003 has been of a decidedly theoretical character—with proposals of mechanically converting the existing eighteen governorates in Iraq into federal states dominating over any attempt at investigating regional identities as such.[32]

Regionalism in the Iraqi constitution

However much foreign experts and advisors have sought to reject Iraq's regional legacy, Iraq's constitution of 2005 recognises it. Despite the dominance during the constitutional drafting process of three parties that advocated an ethno-religious structuring of the new Iraqi federation (Kurdistan Democratic Party or KDP, the Patriotic Union of Kurdistan or PUK, and the Supreme Council for the Islamic Revolution in Iraq, SCIRI), there was never any attempt to enshrine this kind of state model in the constitution except through recognition of Kurdistan as a separate region. Probably this

---

31 Mosul has been covered in two studies, Dina Rizk Khoury, *State and Provincial Society in the Ottoman Empire: Mosul, 1540–1834*, Cambridge: Cambridge University Press, 1997 and Sarah D. Shields, *Mosul before Iraq: Like Bees Making Five-Sided Cells*, Albany: State University of New York Press, 2000; for Basra as a region, see Hala Fattah, *The Politics of Regional Trade in Iraq, Arabia, and the Gulf, 1745–1900*, Albany: State University of New York Press, 1997.

32 This idea was in vogue in American circles in late 2003 but was soon vetoed by the Kurds.

was so simply because even these pro-federal parties were realistic enough to anticipate negative popular reactions in the other parts of the country. Instead, the new political system in Iraq south of Kurdistan is to be built 'from below', through referenda, with the existing governorates as building blocks. Essentially, each governorate can choose between two options: to remain in its current status, as a decentralised unit within a unitary state framework, or to become a region (*iqlim*)—either in its own right as a uni-governorate region, or through combining with other regions. There are no size limits on the formation of regions, but under no circumstances can Baghdad become part of a greater region.

The law for the formation of regions, adopted in October 2006, specifies this procedure in greater detail. The most ambivalent point in the constitution concerns the mechanisms for forming regions of more than one governorate in cases where several competing visions prevail: some in Basra may want to join with neighbouring Dhi Qar and Maysan; again others may be eyeing a larger federal unit. This is resolved in the detailed legislation, which stipulates that in the case of several competing initiatives (these can be made either by a tenth of the electorate or a third of the governorate council members), a pre-referendum poll will be held in each governorate to decide which regional vision will be put to the vote in a referendum. In order to succeed, a federal initiative must win this stage in every governorate concerned and then receive an absolute majority in the subsequent referendum—again in each of the governorates targeted in the regional initiative.[33]

In practice this means that forming big regions will be quite difficult, and that smaller regions will have a greater chance for success. True, there are certain factors that play into the hands of those with grand designs: failed federalisation attempts can be given another

---

33 For some of the problems related to this process, see Reidar Visser, 'Federalism from Below in Iraq: Some Historical and Comparative Reflections', paper presented to an Iraq workshop in Como, Italy, November 2006 available at http://historiae.org/federalism-from-below.asp.

chance once every year (in contrast to the comparable system of Spain where there is a five-year moratorium on this sort of exercise), and there is no demand for territorial contiguity (another contrast with Spain)—meaning that larger regions may repeatedly try to squeeze unyielding governorates into accepting a federal formula. But on the other hand, once formed a region may not combine with other regions (this amendment was introduced during the parliamentary debate of the law), and due to the requirement for unanimity in all governorates concerned by a federal initiative, it is highly likely that one or more permanent 'gaps' will be established in some of the large-scale regional visions that are tentatively being floated today. The constitution itself could become an incentive for regionalism: again there is the Spanish precedent, where the creation of the uni-provincial regions of La Rioja and Cantabria—deemed 'artificial' by those who take an orthodox approach to the idea of 'historical' regions—showed that regional identities may also be constructed under certain circumstances, if not entirely from scratch. Other legislative acts, such as a new petroleum law, may become another stimulant for small-scale regionalism in Iraq.

At the level of state structure, then, regionalism is bound to become ever more important in Iraq when the implementation of federalism starts in 2008. Of course, one possible outcome would be the conversion of one or more existing governorates into new uni-governorate regions. However, many of these governorates possess only a limited sense of historical identity. Indeed, many of the governorate names in use during the decades of Baathist rule are already being replaced, mostly with new references to the provincial capital cities as governorate names. (The limited enthusiasm for the US proposal launched in 2003 to build an Iraqi federation of the existing eighteen governorates may have had to do with this factor.) It is therefore quite likely that many governorates will look for partners to form medium-sized entities. By late 2006, even politicians sympathetic to the idea of grand sectarian federal units expressed the view that the successful formation of such large-scale entities was distinctly unrealistic given the legal complexities involved. Therefore, the question of meso-level regional identities will become ever more acute in Iraq. Which are the geographical formations of Iraq that can be expected to prove durable over time, as federal units? In which part of the country are such ideas about regional identity likely to trump Iraqi nationalism and the idea of staying within the unitary state structure as 'ordinary' governorates? And where can sectarianism or ethnic ideology be expected to prevail? These are questions that we try to shed light on in this book.

Structure of the book

The book starts with a chapter on the geographical area often referred to in international media as 'southern Iraq'. 'The Two Regions of Southern Iraq' shows that the idea of a single 'southern' and 'Shiite' region of Iraq is primarily a Western construct. Instead, two other trends have historically dominated in Shiite areas south of Baghdad. The first is the non-territorial universalism of the higher ranks of the Shiite clergy, who have tended to aspire to a leadership role for Sunnis and Shiites alike, and whose public pronouncements have by and large offered support for existing state structures. The second historical trend south of Baghdad is regionalism, a concept cultivated by tribal leaders, secularists and the lower-ranking Shiite clergy. Two distinctive regional currents have appeared: one concentrated in the far south and corresponding to the old Ottoman province of Basra; another appealing to the idea of a 'Euphrates' identity (rather than a 'southern' one) and with a focus on central Iraq around the Shiite holy cities of Najaf and Karbala. Both trends were visible during the British mandate—in Basra, as a scheme for the separation of the far south as a pro-British mercantile protectorate, and on the Euphrates as a campaign for local decentralised authority (*lamarkaziyya*)—and both resurged within a year after the US invasion of Iraq in 2003. The idea about sectarian contiguity in a single federal Shiite unit from Basra to Baghdad, on the other hand, is a far more

recent project. Since 2005, extraordinary developments in the Iraq
War have propelled this vision to a certain prominence—certainly
in the international media—but today it is still being challenged by
Shiites who prefer small-scale solutions more in tune with the strong
regionalist heritages of the areas south of Baghdad.

Chapter 3 turns to Baghdad and the 'capital region' of Iraq. Fanar
Haddad and Sajjad Rizvi investigate how inhabitants of Baghdad
relate to the mounting debate about federalism for the regions that
used to form their vast hinterland. In general, the authors find widespread scepticism towards federalism as a political model for Iraq—a
sentiment that exists in equal measure in Sunni and Shiite districts
of the capital. To most Baghdadis, despite the steep escalation of
sectarian violence during 2006, Iraqi nationalism remains the most
popular overall paradigm for political reform in Iraq. The territorial
shell of the state is not challenged as such; it is on the definition of
Iraqiness that sectarian sentiments clash. The place of Baghdad in all
of this is viewed accordingly. Baghdad is seen as a united capital city
rather than as a cake that can legitimately be partitioned—whether
by greedy 'regional' neighbours, or for transformation into one or
more decentralised metropolitan regions. The weak sense of Baghdad regionalism identified in this chapter may also be of relevance
to other parts of Iraq where competing visions of Iraqi nationalism
prevail (such as Diyala), or where Iraqi nationalism clashes with
Kurdish nationalism (for instance in Kirkuk). Even though battles
for sectarian hegemony within a single nationalist framework may be
just as bloody as those between two or more competing nationalisms,
it is of critical importance to questions concerning territory and state
structure that the distinction between these two phenomena is well
understood. Haddad and Rizvi's findings are a timely reminder that
it may be counterproductive to try to enforce an all-encompassing,
'symmetrical' federal model on the whole of Iraq. The Iraqi constitution actually allows for considerable flexibility in this regard (only
regions with a strong desire for autonomy will need to opt out of
the unitary state structure), but in the West this nuance is poorly

understood. Most Westerners with an interest in Iraq's federalism question run against the wind by their insistence on universal conversion to pro-federal attitudes among all Iraqis, instead of accepting the widespread scepticism to radical devolution that exists in many parts of Iraq, such as Baghdad.[34]

Chapter 4 moves on to the situation north of Baghdad. Ronen Zeidel shows how in Salah al-Din province, regional identity is in reality town identity. By the early twentieth century, a distinctive urban patriotism had crystallised in the small town of Tikrit on the Tigris, and formed the basis for a separate identity that distinguished Tikritis from their neighbours in Samarra and more distant river towns like Mosul. Symbolically, this Tikrit sense of identity was founded upon an ancient Christian heritage, common tribal ancestry, the notion of Tikrit as a sanctuary in a hostile environment and the Tigris as the artery of the local economy. Gradually, during the course of the twentieth century, people from Tikrit turned this local patriotism and solidarity into a means for meteoric advancement in the institutions of the modern state of Iraq, to the point where they became the true ruling elite under Saddam Hussein in the 1980s. In the course of this process they substituted pan-Arabism for regionalism as ideology; in terms of solidarity, ever more narrow patterns of tribalism replaced the original civic focus on the urban population as a whole. After 2003, however, Tikrit's legacy as Saddam Hussein's birthplace and recruitment ground for his regime has become a burden for the inhabitants of the region. Their Tikrit regionalism has been tainted due to its past connections with the Baathist regime, and so far few alternatives of a wider regional scope have emerged. Like many other Sunni-majority towns in Iraq, Tikrit is increasingly leaning towards a sectarian identity, but without translating this into a demand for a separate territorial space.

---

34 For an important exception to the trend towards 'symmetric federalism' in Western blueprints for a federal Iraq, see the International Crisis Group, *After Baker–Hamilton: What To Do in Iraq?* (Middle East Report no. 60), December 2006, available at www.crisisgroup.org/home/index.cfm?id=4580andl=1.

Quite similar patterns prevail further to the west, in the border-lands towards Syria that are covered in James Denselow's chapter. Denselow focuses on the arbitrary character of the Anglo-French twentieth-century border demarcation in this historical region—often referred to as al-Jazira or 'the island'—which effectively bisected what had formerly been a contiguous economic zone linking the upper Euphrates towns and Mosul in Iraq with Dayr al-Zur, Raqqa and Aleppo in Syria. In many ways, transnational sentiment cutting across the border has survived until modern times, with close links between 'Syrian' and 'Iraqi' branches of the same family or tribe still remaining strong. Nevertheless, as in the case of Tikrit, this is a regional sentiment that does not seek expression primarily in a quest for a special homeland or autonomous region. Rather, it is the resumption of normal ties within an ancient socio-economic region that has been the main demand historically. Today, the contentious issue of normalising Syrian–Iraqi relations remains convoluted due to problems of border smuggling and persisting disagreement between Syria and US military authorities in Iraq about the role of the border region as a transit zone for Islamic militants en route to western Iraq. Hanna Batatu explained political radicalism in Mosul with reference to the suppression of latent regional feelings; perhaps today's unsatisfactory conditions along the Syrian–Iraqi border may account for much of the pan-Arab and anti-Iraq government attitudes found in the north-western part of the country and in the Anbar governorate.

Chapter 6 heads further north, beyond the plains and into the mountainous Kurdistan region. Gareth Stansfield and Hashem Ahmadzadeh trace an interesting project by Kurdish elites to define Kurdistan in Iraq in non-ethnic terms, as a homeland not only for the Kurds, but for all the peoples inhabiting the area—including minorities of Assyrians, Yazidis, and Turkmens. Both leading Kurdish parties, the KDP and the PUK, have made determined efforts to define versions of a civic form of nationalism in which Kurds would focus on their region inside Iraq rather than on their ethnic links with the wider Kurdish world in the neighbouring countries. Stansfield and Ahmadzadeh argue that this regionalist approach is increasingly coming under pressure, especially from the grassroots level in Kurdish politics, where support for Kurdish nationalism, often in a pan-Kurdish variant, is fast becoming the dominant trend. In Kurdistan today, regionalism and ethnic nationalism largely overlap; the key question for the future will be to what extent the balance tips towards an ethnic definition of Kurdistan, with possible consequences for the Kurds' relations with neighbours like Syria, Turkey and Iran, and with implications for areas claimed as Kurdish irredenta within Iraq, such as Mosul and Kirkuk.

The subject of Iraq itself as one of the most persistent 'regions' of Iraq is discussed by Alastair Northedge in Chapter 7. No understanding of the remarkable endurance of Iraqi nationalism after 2003 is possible without an appreciation of the antiquity of 'Iraq' as a geographical concept. Tracing its roots from ancient Mesopotamian civilisations, Northedge shows how Iraq as a geographical term became firmly established in the classical Islamic age, and tended to connote the area from Basra in the south to Samarra in the north—beyond which lay the Jazira region. Punctuated as its history may have been by regionalist episodes on a smaller scale, 'Iraq' remained a meaningful category to travellers and cartographers—occidental and oriental—right up until modern times. To a considerable extent, this historicity and heritage may help account for the staying power of Iraqi nationalism in Iraqi regions that have seen little in the way of resurgent regionalisms: the central Tigris areas around Kut, Baquba and Kirkuk to the north-east of Baghdad, as well as the capital region itself and much of western Iraq.

To what extent is this tentative system of 'nationalist' and 'regionalist' zones in Iraq locked in place? Where is the external fence strong and where is it weak? These are questions addressed by Richard Schofield in Chapter 8. Schofield traces the historical evolution of the external boundaries of Iraq, and shows how Britain had a dominant role in designating the exact outer lining of the Iraqi regional core. Iraq inherited boundaries with Iran and Kuwait from agreements that date back to Ottoman days, whereas Iraq's borders with Saudi Arabia, Jordan and Turkey were negotiated on its behalf by Britain in the 1920s and 1930s. The period after 2003 has witnessed increased militarisation and securitisation of the borders with Turkey and Saudi Arabia in particular, and with gradually stronger attempts to seal the Syrian border. Conversely, less has been done to control the Iranian border to the east. As a consequence of the situation described by Schofield, trans-border regionalism—particularly strong in the Jazira region towards Syria—is not allowed to express itself freely in the west of the country. In the south, small-scale regionalism faces at least two possible scenarios: it could become subjected to the growing threat of heavy-handed manipulation by Iran and its partners in some of the Iraqi Shiite political parties, but there is also the possibility of a more positive way forward, with a defusing of tensions and full restoration of the borderland component in the historical southern region—which always had close links to the heterogeneous, mostly Arab population of south-western Iran.

In Chapter 9, Liam Anderson bridges the regional map of Iraq with political science theory in the field of federalism. The chapter provides an overview of different approaches to the issue of territorial demarcation of federal units, and charts a continuum that ranges from purely ethnic models (as for instance in Ethiopia since the 1990s) to aggressively anti-ethnic formulas (as attempted in the demarcation of some of Nigeria's federal states). Anderson posits 'regional federalism' as a compromise alternative, whose chief virtue is that it 'ignores ethnicity'. Regional federalism—exemplified by cases like Spain, Italy and South Africa—neither encourages nor combats ethnic identity. In theory it should be well suited to the kind of political configuration described in this volume for today's Iraq: an Iraq of two non-ethnic regions south of Baghdad; a largely nationalist zone from Baghdad to the West (preferring the unitary state model and hoping for a normalisation of border relations with Syria to allow for a 'softer', non-territorial expression of Jazira regionalism); and with another area of strong regionalism in Kurdistan, where regionalism coexists with powerful Kurdish nationalist sentiment. The gradual implementation of federalism in Iraq from 2008 onwards will show how theory fits Iraqi realities.

In the concluding Chapter 10, Gareth Stansfield charts possible future scenarios that could become relevant if the current Iraqi constitutional process should derail completely. This danger is very real. Especially among critics of the Bush administration in the United States, there is only limited respect for the Iraqi constitutional process as such, and a growing conviction that a more crudely designed federation of three ethnic communities is the best method for extricating US forces from Iraq. Stansfield shows how in a worst-case scenario the city of Kirkuk (possibly followed by Mosul) might turn into the orifice through which 'Balkans logics'—hitherto an import article as far as Iraq is concerned—could become entrenched in Iraqi politics. Much will probably depend on how Kurdish elites choose to navigate in the near future. It is possible that they will discover how maximalism over Kirkuk and Mosul will almost automatically push them towards a pan-Kurdish logic which ultimately could threaten their own small-scale fiefdom(s) of Kurdistan in Iraq. On the other hand, if they persevere—and Stansfield and Ahmadzadeh's analysis clearly points to pressures in this direction from the Kurdish grassroots level—this sort of scenario could lead to a situation entirely antithetical to the vision of an Iraq based on geographical regions.

2

THE TWO REGIONS OF
SOUTHERN IRAQ

Reidar Visser

On 11 August 2005, international media was ablaze with news about alleged Shiite plans to establish 'a separate state' in Iraq south of Baghdad. 'Iraq Shiites hammer home autonomy demands' was Reuters' headline.[1] According to the *New York Times*, 'One of Iraq's most powerful Shiite politicians on Thursday strongly backed demands for the formation of a semi-independent region in the oil-rich south'.[2] The *Washington Post* published the following account: 'Waving posters of Iran's late Ayatollah Ruhollah Khomeini, thousands of chanting Shiite Muslims signalled approval for a call Thursday by their leaders for a separate Shiite federal state in central and southern Iraq... "We must not miss this chance", said the party's leader, Abdul Aziz Hakim, dressed in robes and turban.'[3]

True, the ingredients were there. A sizeable crowd, chants, and turbans. And at one point the word 'federalism' was indeed uttered. But the audiotape of the public meeting in Najaf that formed the basis for these reports reveals an altogether different picture of how the various elements in the press reports actually fitted together.[4]

---

1 Reuters, 11 August 2005.

2 'Top Shiite Politician Joins Call for Autonomous South Iraq', *New York Times*, 12 August 2005.

3 'Shiites Call for Own State in South', *Washington Post*, 11 August 2005.

4 Real Audio recording (file titled assayed.rm) of Hakim's speech on 11 August 2005.

The recording of Abd al-Aziz al-Hakim's Najaf speech runs to thirty-four minutes. The address was given on the occasion of the commemoration of the death of his late brother, Muhammad Baqir, and much of the text concerns generalities rather than nitty-gritty specifics related to the intense constitutional debate that was going on at the time. In the introduction, the rhetoric is decidedly universalistic—Hakim salutes the 'martyrs of Halabja [in Kurdistan]' alongside those of 'the marshes [in the far south of Iraq]', and goes on to speak about his late brother as the defender of the rights of 'all Iraqis', before he dwells on the ongoing suffering of the Shiites at the hands of terrorists. Hakim then proceeds to deal with current political issues, such as the constitution (including points on the role of Islam and how to deal with ex-Baathists), security and reconstruction. Before, throughout and after the speech, Hakim is interrupted by enthusiastic chants from the crowds—'Yes, yes to Islam', 'Yes, yes to Hakim'.

After twenty-seven minutes, Hakim briefly—for some forty seconds—focuses on Shiite federalism. 'We believe it is necessary to erect a single region of the centre and the south of Iraq due to the existence of commonalities...' He stops. Once more the chants from the crowd grow louder. More 'No, no to the occupation' and 'Yes, yes to Hakim'. Was this a moment of ecstatic joy over the new federalism proposal? Expressions of a unison popular desire to carve out a separate sectarian homeland for the Shiites?

It rather appears to have been another crowd interruption. Whilst the constant choruses by the audience make it clear that Hakim is enormously popular among the party faithful, there is also a sense of complete disconnect—competition for space even—between a speaker with pioneering ideas, and well-rehearsed old slogans whose crescendos and diminuendos seem to have no particular correlation to the message that is being delivered from the stage. In fact, Hakim is cut off in the middle of what was supposed to be the first-time public announcement of the idea of a single Shiite federal region. He starts all over again. 'We believe it is necessary to erect a single region of the centre and the south of Iraq due to the existence of commonalities between the inhabitants of these areas, as well as the singularly oppressive policy with which the former regime confronted them. This opportunity of realising such a holy project must not be let go of, and the necessary steps of implementing it must be taken.' This time, Hakim's voice is trembling: *iqamat iqlim'in wahid!* ('the creation of a single region.') But there is no audible reaction from the crowd. Hakim quickly moves on and concludes his speech with remarks about the upcoming referendum on the constitution.

The discrepancies between the international media accounts of the August 2005 Najaf meeting and the taped record of the event aptly reflect the more general problem of grasping the concept of 'southern Iraqi regionalism'. In Western mainstream media, the existence of a 'Shiite' stroke 'southern' yearning for a separate homeland has been taken for granted since the 1990s. Today, this goes hand in hand with a widespread belief that the Shiites of Iraq form a monolithic entity whose 'core' is represented by those who make the loudest sectarian shouts. Among Iraqi Shiites themselves, on the other hand, the idea of territorial Shiite concentration is completely novel, to the point where several leading Shiite politicians admitted to having reacted with shock and horror when they learnt about Hakim's speech.

This tension is the subject of the present chapter. The main argument is that in Iraq south of Baghdad, two non-sectarian ideological currents have historically been far more important than the idea of Shiite consolidation in a territorial bloc. The first is the universalism of the leading Shiite ulama—in theory pan-Islamist and cutting across sectarian divides between Shiites and Sunnis; in practice defending the integrity of the modern Iraqi state within its present borders. The second is the regionalism of the urban centres and the tribes. This trend focuses not on a single Shiite homeland but on distinct regions: firstly, 'the south' (*al-janub*), which among Iraqis tends to connote what Westerners will describe as the 'far south' or the triangle of Basra, Nasiriyya and Amara, and, secondly, 'the Middle Euphrates' (*al-furat al-awsat*).

Only as a distant third in this ideological race comes the project of establishing a separate Shiite entity. In modern history this had been contemplated only once before 2005—in 1927, when it was quickly abandoned. Today, powerful forces, many of them actually outside the Iraqi Shiite community, are oiling the wheels of this project to give it momentum on a scale never seen before. A growing number of Western analysts unquestioningly accept it as the 'dominant trend' among Iraqi Shiites. In Iraqi regional history, though, it remains highly parenthetical. This intellectual marginality and lack of historical depth needs to be taken seriously by proponents of the scheme and the outside world alike—for the sake of a more realistic understanding of the prospects of a single Shiite region in Iraqi politics, as well as the possible complications that may arise from its implementation at the expense of competing visions that are more firmly entrenched in history.

The universalism of the Shiite ulama

Political theory enjoys a rather marginal position in Shiite intellectual history before the twentieth century. The main reason is the doctrine of the *ghayba* or 'absence': the Twelfth Imam of the Shiites went into hiding in the late ninth century, but he remains the ultimate source of political authority for the community. Hence, Shiite ulama have traditionally been reluctant to become closely integrated in modern state structures. On the basis of the same logic, Shiite religious leaders have also tended to refrain from modifying the 'established order'; as a consequence, Shiite writers on 'the state' have either chosen to overlook this category completely (and instead relate to an abstract and imaginary Islamic ideal state), or they have quietly accepted the existing state system.[5]

---

5 Reidar Visser, 'Shiʻi Perspectives on a Federal Iraq: Territory, Community and Ideology in Conceptions of a New Polity', in Daniel Heradstveit and Helge Hveem (eds), *Oil in the Gulf: Obstacles to Democracy and Development*, Aldershot: Ashgate, 2004.

Historically, in the case of the lands that became the modern state of Iraq, this has meant that the clergy has tended to acquiesce in the existing system, despite its mostly Sunni-dominated character. Occasionally, there would be mild expressions of support for the Shiite-dominated regimes of Persia (where some ulama did co-operate with the government), but on the whole there has been negligible support for ideas like carving out a Shiite polity in the Shiite-inhabited areas under Ottoman and later British and Iraqi control. Accordingly, the political–geographical nomenclature of the leading clergy has followed that of the population in the region, with 'Iraq' constituting the clearly most persistent identity category in Shiite cultural production based in the zone between Basra and Samarra. Shiite writers have used the name 'Iraq' in their book titles since medieval times, and Shiite pride in this geographical concept has been such that several luminaries of earlier centuries included it as part of their names or honorifics, for instance as *shaykh al-'iraqayn* or 'shaykh of the two Iraqs [i.e. the Persian and the Arab one]'.[6]

After the formal establishment of the modern state of Iraq in 1920, these patterns of universalism and acceptance of the existing—now explicitly 'Iraqi'—order have persisted, even despite a growing tendency of politicisation of the clergy. Those ulama who became involved in anti-British activities in the 1920s instinctively used 'Iraq' as the natural frame of reference for their activities. Others strove towards greater inter-sectarian unity between Shiites and Sunnis on a more pan-Islamic basis. A leading Basra cleric of the 1920s scorned secular local politicians who tried to establish a Shiite-only sectarian movement: he compared this to the sectarian excesses of the Wahhabis of the Arabian interior who at that time were busy desecrating the holy tombs of Mecca. In general, the top ulama offered no support for lay politicians and lower-ranking clerics and preachers who

---

6 Werner Ende, 'Iraq in World War I: The Turks, The Germans and the Shiite Mujtahids' Call for Jihad', in Rudolph Peters (ed.), *Proceedings of the Ninth Congress of the Union Européenne des Arabisants et Islamisants*, Leiden: Brill, 1981.

31

often, not least for pecuniary reasons, were eager to take the Shiites into a more sectarian direction.[7]

During the second half of the twentieth century, this Iraq template was projected onto Shiite discourse even as new ideas about Shiite activism gradually came to the fore. Several Islamist groups came to focus on Iraq—all of Iraq—as their sphere of operation; this included such core entities as the Daawa movement which became prominent in the 1970s. To the extent that any territorial alternative existed, this was internationalist and pan-Islamist and not sectarian—as could be seen in the stance of some of the Daawa factions, and in Shiite participation in organisations with an ecumenical or even Sunni orientation such as the Hizb al-Tahrir. Even aggressively sectarian Shiite parties like the Jund al-Imam movement refrained from launching any projects that would establish any intimate connection between the Shiites and the territory that formed their homeland south of Baghdad.[8]

To grasp the degree of scepticism towards a Shiite federal entity among Iraq's top Shiite clergy after 2003—and even after the provocative attack on the Shiite shrine of Samarra on 22 February 2006—one needs only take a look at their public announcements. In September 2006, at a time when many Shiite lay leaders had drifted towards pro-militia attitudes, the Grand Ayatollah Ali al-Sistani still called for the building of a single Iraqi national army, and warned about paramilitary forces as a grave danger (*fi ghayyat al-khutura*).[9] In October, Muhammad al-Yaqubi of the Sadrist trend was more specific as regards federalism and the idea of sectarian territorialisation: 'It is true that Kurdistan has its distinctive geographical, national and cultural borders, but the rest of the governorates of Iraq are in-

---

7 Reidar Visser, *Basra, the Failed Gulf State: Separatism and Nationalism in Southern Iraq*, New Brunswick, NJ: Transaction Publishers, 2006, p. 125.

8 On the lack of a territorial component in Shiite activism in southern Iraq from the 1970s to the 1990s, see Reidar Visser, 'Basra, the Reluctant Seat of Shiastan', *Middle East Report*, no. 242, spring 2007.

9 *Bayan* dated 8 Sha'ban 1427/2 September 2006.

terwoven, intermarried and mixed (*mutadakhila wa-mutazawija wa-mutamazija*) in a way that does not permit the erection of barriers (*hawajiz*).'[10] It is not always clear what the exact religious justification for these *de facto* nationalist attitudes is, but they tend to go hand in hand with anti-sectarianism and ideas of a minimum of Islamic unity—unity which may remain imperfect in a system of nation states, but which stands in danger of disintegrating further should federal subdivisions be introduced in the existing system (and more so if the subdivisions were based on sectarian geography). Whatever the exact justification, the insistence by the leading ulama on preserving Iraqi national unity has been so constant after 2003 that its reversal (or its conversion into support for a separate Shiite statelet) would require an intellectual earthquake of considerable magnitude in Najaf, probably on the scale of Khomeini's revolutionary turn to clerical activism in the 1960s. Any regionalist acrobatics in the Shiite areas of Iraq should be viewed against the backdrop of this formidable, if often misty massif of nationalist sentiment.

The regionalism of the urban centres and the tribes

Historically, to the extent that the inhabitants of the alluvial plains south of Baghdad have engaged in state-building attempts of their own, they have done so in regional rather than sectarian frameworks.

Perhaps the best examples of this are a string of regionalist initiatives in the city of Basra and its immediate hinterland. In the seventeenth century, local strongmen of the Afrasiyab dynasty sought to challenge the Ottomans by establishing a separate emirate at the head of the Gulf, supported by European powers, and with policies that emphasised multi-religious tolerance between Shiites, Sunnis, Christians and Mandaeans. In a chronicle by a Shiite author from this period there is no mention of Iraq—this is actually unusual for the period—but also there is no mention of Shiite areas north of Basra's immediate hinterland. Instead, the narrative contains place-

---

10 Press release from the Fadila party dated 3 October 2006.

names that signify ideas of local and regional attachment: the Jaza'ir
marshlands, 'the lands of Bani Asad', and the 'Batina' (all slightly
north of Basra); Huwayza, Duraq and Qubban (technically in Persia); and al-Hasa (in modern-day Saudi Arabia).[11]

Later, in the early twentieth century, another inter-sectarian regionalist coalition materialised in Basra under the leadership of the
(Sunni) notable Sayyid Talib al-Naqib, who advocated decentralisation for the province of Basra within the Ottoman Empire. Contrary
to what is commonly thought, the *vilayet* of Basra did not extend
further north than Nasiriyya on the Euphrates and Amara on the
Tigris—meaning that this was yet another attempt at launching a regionalist project with the Shatt al-Arab delta as its core, rather than a
scheme aimed at control of the 'Shiite heartland' closer to Baghdad.
And in the 1920s, regionalist sentiment in Basra reached its zenith
as local merchants—mainly Sunnis, Christians, Jews and Persians
but also a few Shiite Arab tribal leaders—embarked on a venture to
make Basra a commercial hub of the British Empire, again with its
northernmost borders drawn to the immediate north of the Gulf city,
at Qurna. Its leaders even tried to promote the view that this coastal
enclave was a separate country, distinct from its northern neighbour,
Iraq. Basra, they maintained, had been deeply influenced by its interaction with foreign merchants, and its cosmopolitan character meant
that it would have other aspirations than those prevalent in Iraq.[12]

It should be added that all these regionalist episodes faded away
rapidly. Most did so after one or more factions in the Basra area
reacted with hostility to the separation bids, advocating instead the
re-establishment of ties with Baghdad. In this way, extensive contact
between Baghdad and Basra was maintained even in the periods
when there was formal administrative separation (chiefly, between
the 1720s and 1740s, 1850–1863 and finally 1884–1914). With it

---

11 Fath Allah al-Ka'bi, *Zad al-musafir* [Provisions of the traveller], Baghdad,
1924, pp. 17–18, 20, 37.

12 On the various regionalist and separatist initiatives of Basra in the twentieth
century, see Visser, *Basra, the Failed Gulf State*.

came proliferation of the dominant identity concept current in the Ottoman provincial capital of Baghdad: 'Iraq'. Thus it was perfectly normal for an early nineteenth-century Shiite writer from Basra— Abd al-Jalil al-Tabataba'i—to employ 'Iraq' as a basic regional point of reference, in expressions such as 'the goodness of Iraq and its people'.[13] Similarly, the 1920s saw a perfectly peaceful renunciation of Basra separatism. Interaction with Baghdad remained an enduring feature of Basra's history even if loud and muscular regionalisms would occasionally emerge.

With these forces in operation, Basra particularism gradually faded away during the period of the monarchy. Basrawis complain that during the war with Iran, those Basrawis forced to seek refuge in other Iraqi cities were met with disdain: '[We would rather have] a thousand Egyptians and not a single Basrawi' (*alf misri wa-la basri*) was reportedly the message they would get from some of their fellow Iraqis.[14] But even if Basra would sometimes highlight its local grievances by establishing separate factions within the opposition, the platforms on which they mobilised remained Iraqi nationalist. As late as in 2001, key Basra figures in the exiled Iraqi opposition wrote extensively on Iraqi society, history and politics without divulging the slightest interest in local regionalism.[15]

After the US-led invasion of Iraq in 2003, regionalism in the Basra area has again asserted itself, now perhaps more forcefully than in the past. Basra was the first of the mainly Shiite areas in Iraq to respond to the new ideas of federalism introduced when the old regime fell. But once more, the framework chosen was regionalist not sectarian.

---

13 'Abd al-Jalil al-Tabataba'i, *Diwan*, Cairo, 1966, pp. 70–1 and 264–5.

14 Riyad al-'Ali, 'Laysa jumhuriyat al-basra bal iqlim al-basra' [Not the republic of Basra; rather, the region of Basra!] 31 December 2005, www.kitabat. com/i11745.htm.

15 Baqir Yasin, *Qawl ma la yuqal 'an al-mu'arada al-'iraqiyya* [Saying that which cannot be said about the Iraqi opposition], Beirut: Dar al-Kunuz, 2002; idem, *Ta'rikh al-'unf al-damawi fi al-'iraq* [The history of bloody violence in Iraq], Beirut: Dar al-Kunuz, 1999. After 2003, Yasin would go on to become a prominent Basra regionalist.

Some incarnations of the new regionalist trend simply foresaw the conversion of the Basra governorate to a regional entity; this would leave Basra as a Dubai-like, self-contained maritime trading enclave roughly within the borders proposed by the separatist Basra notables of the 1920s, with the additional advantage of control of Iraq's most important oil installations. Other variants aimed for a greater region: the 'Region of the South' (*iqlim al-janub*). By this term was meant what many Iraqis consider 'the south', the comparatively small triangle of Basra, Nasiriyya in Dhi Qar governorate, and Amara in Maysan governorate, distinct from the Western idea of a grandiose 'southern Iraq' from the Gulf to Baghdad.[16]

Interestingly, whilst a few secular protagonists of this regional vision toyed with references to the old (non-Arab) Sumerian civilisation that had its core in this area,[17] the principal rationale for the new scheme was modern and utilitarian: a perception of local under-development—not only in comparison with Baghdad, but also when measured against Shiite areas further north. The war with Iran had left the south far more exposed than the other Shiite areas and,

16   Whereas journalists writing for Western audiences may employ terms like 'deep in the south of the country' when referring to Diwaniyya just to the south of Baghdad, Iraqis often use the term 'the south' to distinguish between the Basra area and the Shiite core area around Baghdad. See for instance Sabah Jerges, 'Police Station South of Baghdad Destroyed', AFP, 26 September 2006, and, for typical examples of standard Iraqi usage, "Asha'ir al-wasat wa-al-janub: taf'il dawr al-'asha'ir li-injah wa-dam al-masalih al-wataniyya' [Tribes of the centre and the south: activating the role of the tribes to support the national interest], *al-'Adala*, 27 June 2006 (the first sentence of this article reads, *akkada ru'sa' al-'asha'ir fi al-manatiq al-janubiyya wa-al-furat al-awsat...*or, 'tribal chiefs of the southern areas and from the Middle Euphrates confirm that...') and Najib al-Salihi, *Al-zilzal* [The earthquake], London, 1998, where the 1991 anti-Baathist uprising is discussed as a project spearheaded by 'the south' rather than by the Shiites as an ethno-sectarian community. Due to the widespread practice in the post-2003 Iraqi press of verbatim translating Western wire reports, these distinctions are however becoming increasingly blurred.

17   As could perhaps be expected, this aspect is the sole element of southern regionalism that has received a certain coverage in Western media. It is also frequently being mixed up with the project of a much larger Shiite region, whose Islamists protagonists have never shown any interest in this ancient civilisation.

after 2004, southern regionalists frequently invoked the old regime's destruction of the lush marshlands north of Basra and the thick belt of date-gardens along the Shatt al-Arab as examples of a legacy of suffering. This in turn was used as an argument for local control of the oil industry (or at least a solid share of the proceeds), as Muhammad Sa'dun al-Abbadi, a leader of a pro-regionalist faction of the Daawa party, made clear when he stated that no longer would the south act as 'the camel' for the rest of Iraq—a reference to the often overlooked fact that almost all of Iraq's oil south of Baghdad is in fact concentrated in the far south around Basra and is not evenly distributed across the Shiite territories.[18] Yet another shade of the regional grievances of the south had a cultural edge to it. People from the south, and in particular those of Amara, have often found themselves denigrated by other Iraqis for being *sharqawis*—a term whose etymological roots are disputed, but by chauvinist Iraqis has been employed to signify Marsh Arab, non-Arab or Persian racial connections. Southerners migrating to Baghdad (where they account for a huge proportion of the inhabitants of Sadr City) have been targeted in particular. After 2003, some southerners have tackled this legacy of discrimination in a pro-active way, by expressing pride in southern distinctiveness and *sharqawi* control of Iraq's energy resources.[19]

As on earlier occasions, southern opinion has been split as to the wisdom of proceeding along a regionalist path. The first federal initiatives from Basra in early 2004 were headed by a Shiite secularist—Wail Abd al-Latif—but others in the secular camp (notably Sunnis and Christians) have increasingly become sceptical about such projects, especially as Islamists gained a stronger position in the south during the course of 2005. In that period, the Fadila party, a Sadrist splinter group associated with the Najaf cleric Muham-

18 See Fadila press release, 5 October 2006, and *al-Manara*, 28 November 2006.

19 For historical background on the migration from Amara to Baghdad, see Batatu, *The Old Social Classes and the Revolutionary Movements of Iraq*, Princeton: Princeton University Press, 1978, pp. 134–7.

mad al-Yaqubi and in control of the provincial assembly in Basra, emerged as a vocal proponent of the regionalist scheme. Support from tribal forces in Dhi Qar and Maysan also continued. And whereas many citizens of the south became exasperated with their local politicians after the breakdown of security in Basra in 2006 and the entanglement of most local Islamist factions in turf wars involving oil smuggling and other mafia-style activities, still in November 2006 the regionalist winds were strong enough to prompt a coalition of local secular parties to include a reference to Basra's oil wealth and its 'claims to a share of it' in an otherwise strictly nationalist political programme.[20] However, to become a truly cross-cutting regionalist vanguard, leading Shiite forces such as the Fadila will need to offer vulnerable groups like secularists, Sunnis and Christians effective protection against political violence; otherwise Iraqi nationalism, severely bruised as it may be, will probably once more present itself to the Basrawis as the preferable option. Unless Basra regionalism reconnects with its cosmopolitan roots, its prospects as a constructive force in Iraqi politics may be limited.

Further to the north, yet more regional impulses have made their mark through history. Here, the Middle Euphrates (*al-furat al-awsat*) is the area that stands out. With the advent of steamship traffic in the mid-nineteenth century, the more easily navigable Tigris became the highway of the state, and, despite Ottoman counter-measures, several pockets of *de facto* tribal self-rule materialised along the comparatively neglected Euphrates. The region was among the last areas of Iraq to fall to effective British control, and shortly afterwards it became the focal point of a violent uprising against the British in 1920. Hagiographic accounts of this uprising have construed it as an 'Iraqi nationalist revolution', but many acts by the rebels—such as the tearing up of railway tracks—strongly suggest a desire to keep any government, whether British or Arab, at arm's length.[21] At the

---

20   Programme of the 'Nationalist Current of the Basra Governorate', as published in *al-Manara*, 10 November 2006.

21   For a useful summary of interpretations of the uprising, see Amal

same time, a regionalist dimension came to the fore. Whereas the Euphrates tribes were up in arms against the British, those of the Tigris and the Gharraf (a major branch of the Tigris south of Kut) remained passive. Soon they were targeted by their counterparts on the Euphrates in the war cry *shatt nar, shattayn kasasa*'—literally 'one river is fire, two rivers are cunts', a rather barefaced revolt against any idea of larger sectarian unity.[22]

This regionalist tendency in the Middle Euphrates area asserted itself on numerous occasions during the British mandate. Protests over taxation were particularly strong in the Hilla–Diwaniyya area, and one influential shaykh, Muhsin Abu Tabikh, in 1926 headed a project that sought to create some kind of 'Shiite state' in the region, as a counter-measure to increased interference by the central government. Importantly, this was not a project that aimed beyond the Euphrates: Shamiyya, Mishkab and Hindiyya (all in the Hilla–Diwaniyya area) were specifically targeted, and the principal allies were from other local tribes, like Bani Hasan and Fatlah.[23] In 1930 the project surfaced again, this time in the shape of a 'Tribal Party' whose basic demand was a 'decentralised form of government' (*lamarkaziyya*).[24] And in 1933, upon rumours about a revival of the separatist movement in Basra, more agitation followed in the Euphrates area: if Basra and Kurdistan pressed for separation or autonomy, why

---

Vinogradov, 'The 1920 Revolt in Iraq Reconsidered', *International Journal of Middle East Studies*, vol. 3, 1972.

22 Interview with Iraqi exile, November 2006. See also Batatu, *The Old Social Classes*, p. 16.

23 AIR 23/312, Special Service Officer Diwaniyya to Air Head Quarters, 21 April 1926 (Royal Air Force records in the Public Record Office/UK National Archives, Kew, London). See also Batatu, *The Old Social Classes*, pp. 194–5. The activities of Muhsin Abu Tabikh were later construed as acts of Iraqi nationalism, see *Mudhakkirat al-sayyid muhsin abu tabikh* [The memoirs of Sayyid Muhsin Abu Tabikh], Beirut: Al-Mu'assasa al-'Arabiyya li-al-Dirasat wa-al-Nashr, 2001.

24 AIR 23/267, Special Service Officer Baghdad to Air Head Quarters, 14 August 1930.

should the Euphrates not do the same thing?[25] Ideologically, pride in Arab heritage and tribal values was central to these regionalist initiatives, not least a belief in 'complete independence'—*al-istiqlal al-tamm*—whether from Ottomans, the British or from corrupt Baghdad officials.[26] Shiism was secondary to the regional idea but not unimportant; on several occasions the Euphrates ringleaders held their meetings in the holy cities of Karbala and Najaf, and they gave their oaths on the tomb of Abbas, the classical Shiite hero.

After 2003, Middle Euphrates regionalism has again been discernible, if perhaps more sporadically than its Basra counterpart. In December 2004 and January 2005, meetings were held in Najaf and Samawa to achieve 'solidarity between Middle Euphrates governorates', primarily by focusing on security co-operation. By June 2005, this had translated into plans for a regular federal entity limited to Shiite governorates of central Iraq. Importantly, a degree of regional particularism on the Euphrates survived also after August 2005, at which point the text of the draft constitution made it clear that there would be no ceiling on the number of governorates allowed to amalgamate into federal regions, prompting some Shiite leaders to call for federal entities on a far larger scale. In late October 2005, leaders of Babel and Karbala visited Najaf to co-ordinate 'Middle Euphrates' demands vis-à-vis the central authorities, including railway links between their three provincial capitals, the establishment of an oil refinery in the Euphrates region, and improved security for the Baghdad–Hilla highway.[27] One month later, the same three regions joined in common criticism of the central government (and the ministry of municipalities in particular), whereas statements by the Najaf governor in July 2006 indicated that further variations of

---

25 AIR 23/589, Iraq Police, Abstract of Intelligence no. 16, report dated 22 April 1933.

26 Fariq al-Mazhar al-Fir'awn, *Al-haqa'iq al-nasi'a fi al-thawra al-'iraqiyya sannat 1920 wa-nata'ijiha* [The plain truth about the 1920 Iraqi revolution and its results], Baghdad, 1952, pp. 21–2.

27 *Al-Manara*, 30 October 2005.

the Euphrates regionalism theme were possible as well: complaining over 'centralist problems' in the Iraqi government, he emphasised how Najaf, as a single governorate, would stand to gain from de-centralisation—by gaining greater control of the booming tourism sector and thus achieving a more financially independent position.[28] Indeed, reconciling these various themes could prove a tricky challenge to modern-day Euphrates regionalists. Historically, their local patriotism has been strongly focused on the values of Arabism (and sometimes disdain for what was seen as the cultural corruption of the cities); today, however, promotion of pilgrim tourism from Iran is a central driver in the quest for local autonomy in some areas, notably in Najaf.

Arguably a third regional trend—'pattern' may be a more accurate description—is detectable in the history of the areas south of Baghdad. But this regionalism is more reactive than self-assertive. It centres on the tendency of relative political aloofness among the tribes of the central Tigris districts around Kut—who refused to join the 'nationalist' revolt of the Euphrates shaykhs in 1920, but also refrained from regionalist adventures of the kind their counterparts further south around Amara at times were involved in.[29] Despite accusations of 'docility' (and, sometimes, Persian 'connections'), after 2003, the people of Wasit governorate have reportedly remained strong in their support of Iraqi nationalism, and express opposition against schemes for greater Shiite territorial unity has been reported.[30] In contrast to the south and the Middle Euphrates, there is less pre-history to fan the flames of regionalism, and the existence of hydrocarbon wealth of some significance—outside the southern triangle Wasit is the Shiite governorate with most oil—has not translated into any modern, pragmatic autonomy movement so far.

---

28 *Al-Manara*, 12 November 2005 and 11 July 2006.

29 Batatu, *The Old Social Classes*, p. 116.

30 Peter Harling and Hamid Yasin, 'Unité de façade des chiites irakiens', *Le Monde diplomatique*, September 2006.

A Shiite region?

In modern times, no serious attempt has been made at unifying the Shiite core areas between Baghdad and the Gulf in a single territorial bloc. And even if the history of the region is traced back to medieval times, there is scant evidence of Shiism as a motor for substantial state-building projects. In the eleventh and twelfth century a tribal emirate dominated by the Shiite Mazyadid dynasty did briefly extend from Hilla south to Basra, but this episode of temporal Shiite power did not yield any revolution in political theory that could ruffle the generally apolitical attitude of the Shiite clergy.

Even with growing interest in politics on the part of the Shiite ulama after the Persian constitutional movement in the first decade of the twentieth century, the Arab Shiites of the region refrained from advocating a specifically Shiite state to rival the emerging Iraqi state entity. The only noteworthy exception dates from 1927. After a slow start, the new (Sunni-dominated) Iraqi monarchy established in 1921 was beginning to make its presence felt outside the capital, and in particular it appeared to be more interested in enforcing military conscription than its Ottoman predecessors had been. This provoked angry reactions among rural Shiites who worried that their sons would come under Sunni domination in the new Iraqi army, and in this context some secular Shiite leaders introduced the idea of a separate, British-protected Shiite state as a potential way out of the crisis. Agitation along these lines proliferated rapidly after an ugly confrontation between Iraqi soldiers and Shiite worshippers at the holy city of Kazimayn in the summer of 1927; during the subsequent autumn even some lower-ranking clerics (but symptomatically none of the senior ulama) began attending meetings where 'separation' was discussed.[31]

Perhaps the most notable feature of the 1927 Shiite separation plan was its limited and ephemeral character. The lay leadership fervently courted the leading clerics of Najaf to obtain their assent

---

31 This movement is covered in Visser, *Basra, the Failed Gulf State*, pp. 121–5.

for the project, but this never materialised. No powerful symbolic superstructure specific to the idea of a separate Shiite state evolved, and no justification rooted in Shiite political theory was offered. The British intelligence community became completely engrossed in the project due to the potentially dramatic consequences of its implementation, but outside the caucus of separation-minded elites, the scheme seems to have had only limited impact. By early 1928 the movement had disintegrated completely; its 'powerful' leader Amin al-Charchafchi—at one point seen as the leading Shiite politician by British commentators—had extreme difficulty in securing a parliamentary seat for himself in Baghdad. A high-ranking British official summarised the situation thus:

Amin al-Charchafchi, chief of the Nahda, who became quite formidable last summer, has been to see me several times. The Nahda now cuts very little ice owing to internal dissension, and Amin himself is looked upon as a hot-headed mountebank. He has failed to secure election in quarter after quarter as a secondary elector and was probably becoming a laughing stock. Yesterday however he secured election in two quarters—one an Armenian! The leader of the Shiites. It is rather rich...[32]

Another important aspect of the aborted bid for separation was its dualism and ambiguity. True, the basic idea was sectarian: to unify all the Shiite communities from Basra to Baghdad in a single territorial entity. 'Autonomy' south of Baghdad, 'Shiite rule in Shiite districts', and 'partition' were among the demands that came to the surface. But in terms of actual support, the movement appeared more restricted. It never really gained ground among the Shiites of the south around Basra; rather its core area of support consisted of those Euphrates districts of Hilla and Diwaniyya that had previously been involved in regionalist movements limited to the Middle Euphrates. Indeed, regionalism seems to have competed with the all-Shiite rhetoric favoured by the Baghdad leadership and some of the lower-ranking clerics: the idea of decentralisation (*lamarkaziyya*) featured

---

32 Private papers of C.J. Edmonds in the archive of the Middle East Centre, St. Antony's College, University of Oxford, diary entry dated 4 May 1928.

prominently, and the vision of a 'Shiite government for the Euphrates area' coexisted with the more clear-cut sectarian demands.[33] Adding to the unease was the fact that whereas the central leadership tried to flirt with the British, the tribal support base in many areas remained critical of any alliance with the mandate power. Even one of the few Iraqi intellectuals who made an effort to compose literature supportive of the separatist project—Ali al-Sharqi—ended up writing articles on separate sub-regions, such as the marshlands in the Basra area.[34] And in general, there was a feeling in British circles that their zealous young intelligence officers had rather overblown the significance of the movement. A few years later, one of them, a Royal Air Force 'special service officer' was accused of writing his reports 'in great hurry, from an exalted altitude, and with no particular regard to facts.'[35]

To this group of tentative sectarian ventures belongs also the vision of a nine-governorate Shiite federal entity launched in August 2005 by Abd al-Aziz al-Hakim of the Supreme Council for the Islamic Revolution in Iraq (SCIRI). Received by foreign media and diplomats with fanfare resembling that prevalent in British intelligence circles in 1927, it also echoes the Shiite separation bid of the 1920s in that it has been slow to acquire widespread popular support beyond a core of party faithful (and an interested international audience). For a long time, its main proponents were a tightly-knit group of SCIRI cadres—including such figures as Ammar al-Hakim (the son of Abd al-Aziz), Hadi al-Amiri (leader of the Badr militia), Sadr al-Din al-Qubbanji, and Jalal al-Din al-Saghir (both the latter are preachers, neither is reckoned as a senior cleric). Geographically, the most enthusiastic response came from Najaf (where the governor is pro-

33 Indeed, in 1928, British observers retrospectively viewed the 1927 movement as a Euphrates-based project. AIR 8/94, note by Edward Ellington dated 19 January 1929.

34 See articles in *Lughat al-'Arab* for 1926–7 (pp. 526–30 and 575–9), 1927–8 (pp. 535–9), and 1928–9 (275–9).

35 AIR 23/102, office note dated 27 March 1931.

SCIRI) whereas the south apparently remained unimpressed—some favouring the small-scale regionalist vision launched already in 2004, others protesting against the basic idea of decentralisation. Ideologically, as well, the new project has remained circumscribed. SCIRI has employed pragmatic ideas to defend the project (mainly arguing that territorial consolidation can protect the Shiites from Sunni terror attacks), but has not attempted to put forward justifications of the scheme that are distinctly Shiite or Islamic (save perhaps a rather strenuous assertion that the classical Islamic empires were divided into provinces on 'federal' lines—this overlooks the fact that never were those lines drawn up on a sectarian basis). Endorsement on the part of the leading clergy has remained as elusive as it was in 1927,[36] but the Western press consistently eschewed what would have been the most plausible headline:

HAKIM IS TURNED DOWN AGAIN AS HE PETITIONS SISTANI FOR SUPPORT OVER SHIITE FEDERALISM

Certain changes in the prospects for the single Shiite region took place after the upsurge of sectarian violence in the wake of the bombing of a major Shiite shrine in Samarra in February 2006. With Sunni terrorists—many of them of non-Iraqi origin—systematically targeting Shiite victims, SCIRI's argument for sectarian division gained some ground. For the first time, some politicians outside SCIRI also voiced support for the idea of Shiite federalism—among the most prominent converts were members of the 'Iraq branch' (*Tanzim al-Iraq*) of the Daawa movement. More SCIRI governors came out in support of the project, for instance in Hilla. The adoption in October 2006 of a law on implementing federalism marked a victory of sorts for SCIRI (whilst the law does not determine any particular configuration of new federal units, it also does not impose any size

---

36 The Shiite clergy reluctantly voiced support for the Iraqi constitution—including its provisions from federalism—ahead of the October 2005 referendum, but this is very different from a specific approval of the scheme to create a sectarian entity, which would be antithetical to the ideas of national unity so systematically defended by the leading ulama after 2003.

limits), and the composition of the committee charged with revising the Iraqi constitution was perhaps even more of a triumph (SCIRI dominance among the Shiites on this committee meant that any reversal of federalism south of Kurdistan, as had been hoped for by many Sunnis, grew increasingly unlikely).[37]

Still, even in this sectarian climate, resistance from within Shiite ranks to the project of a single federal Shiite entity remained remarkably strong. The limits to SCIRI's influence within the grand Shiite coalition known as the United Iraqi Alliance (UIA) were clearly exposed in April 2006 during their defeat in the internal contest over who should be the UIA prime ministerial nominee. Those fault lines again came to the fore during the debate over the law for implementing federalism, when significant blocs within the UIA such as the Sadrists and the Fadila party boycotted the vote and almost prevented the Iraqi parliament from reaching quorum on voting day.[38] And in late 2006, the campaign in favour of the sectarian federal scheme remained surprisingly stale, defensive even, despite an appreciable build-up in the amount of propaganda during the preceding summer. Even after the adoption of the new law on federalism, vocal SCIRI members like Rida Jawad Taqi would announce that SCIRI in fact 'had never intended a federal but rather a "decentralised" (*lamarkazi*) system of government'; it was Sunni concessions to Kurdish federalism that had prompted

37 On the modest growth of support for the sectarian federal project during 2006, see Reidar Visser, 'Basra Crude: The Great Game of Iraq's "Southern" Oil', *NUPI Paper*, March 2007, available from http://historiae.org/oil.asp.

38 This opposition was more anti-federal than regional, especially so with respect to the Sadrists who reject the idea of federalisation 'in the context of occupation'. The position of the Fadila party is more ambiguous; some of its criticism of the law pertained to its timing and its potential negative impact on reconciliation efforts vis-à-vis the Sunnis, but they also sought to limit the size of prospective federal entities to one governorate only—which would be more consonant with the stance of the party's local branch in Basra and its small-scale regionalism in the range of one to three governorates. Secular advocates of the Basra regionalist project such as Wail Abd al-Latif and Khayrallah al-Basri voted in favour of the law; debate programme on Iraqi television 13 October 2006 chaired by Samar Jabir.

them to make similar demands for the Shiite areas. And in a speech on the occasion of the end of the holy month of Ramadan, SCIRI leader Abd al-Aziz al-Hakim resorted to rather tenuous arguments in an attempt at garnering support for his federal ideas: in his opinion, the history of federalism worldwide demonstrated that 'none of the world's federal countries has any separatist problems'.[39]

Perhaps the most glaring weakness of the movement in favour of a single Shiite region is the lack of a proper name. Awkwardly labelled 'The Region of the Centre and the South' (*iqlim al-wasat wa-al-janub*), the project does not seem to correspond to any particular pre-existing regional identity. In fact, the name of the project implicitly recognises the existence of competing regional ties—those of the 'south' (the Basra core area), as well as those of the 'centre' (above all the Middle Euphrates—the Baghdad area is excepted from the scheme as the capital is constitutionally barred from joining any region). Typically, in the West the project is sometimes referred to by the completely artificial term 'Shiistan', and, characteristically, is also sometimes mixed up with references to 'Sumer' that have more to do with the secular project of a small-sized southern region. Even the most radically anti-Iraqi Shiites—they are not very numerous and mostly long-time exiles who have yet to return to Iraq—cannot quite seem to liberate themselves from the Iraq concept and replace it with something more congenial to their ideas about an independent Shiite homeland: so far, their most innovative suggestion has been to rename the territory from Samarra down to the Gulf as 'the historical Iraq' (*al-'iraq al-ta'rikhi*)—which may well make sense historically, except that millions of Sunnis also live in this country, and have a long tradition of mixing with their Shiite compatriots.[40]

39 SCIRI press release of Hakim's speech at Eid al-Fitr, 24 October 2006.

40 On these more radical trends, see Reidar Visser, 'Shiite Separatism in Southern Iraq: Internet Reverie or Real Constitutional Challenge?' *NUPI Paper* no. 686, August 2005, available at http://historiae.org/shiseparatism.asp.

Conclusion

The territories of Iraq south of Baghdad may well be headed towards a single Shiite federal entity, but this is not a project that is sustained by any longstanding regional legacies.

Quite the contrary, an historical approach to the federalisation question in Iraq emphasises the tension—sometimes incompatibility—between the idea of a unified Shiite statelet and regional identities on a smaller scale. To the historian, the recurrent and most powerful notions of regional identity in this area are those focused on Basra, the Middle Euphrates, and indeed Iraq itself. These forces still stand a chance of succeeding through democratic means. The pro-sectarian forces among Iraqi elites never dared to enshrine sectarianism directly in the constitution or in the law on implementing federalism, and so any federalisation of Iraq—the process is scheduled to start in April 2008 at the earliest—is to be decided on a governorate level. Governorates may choose to retain their current status within the unitary state, or may opt for a federal solution, either as a uni-governorate region or as a larger region with other governorates. In the case of competing federal visions—as is likely in places like Basra and Najaf—a pre-referendum poll will decide which particular federal scheme is to be put before the electorate in the decisive vote. Barring the influence of external forces, referenda on uni-governorate regions like Basra and Najaf, or small-scale regions like 'the south' and 'the Middle Euphrates' should be just as probable as a vote on a nine-province Shiite mega-region.

However, a host of other factors mean that history may play only a limited role in the reconfiguration of the Iraqi polity which is currently underway. By mid-2007, Iraq found itself in an unprecedented sectarian frenzy, and political projects daring to challenge the now dominant sectarian discourse were facing an uphill struggle. It would be reductionistic to place the blame for the situation in any particular corner, but there is little doubt that several key forces have played their part in the vicious circle that has led towards sectarian polarisation. Before the war, Iraqi exiles were responsible for cultivating a

48

sectarian spoils logic in their efforts to organise the opposition; the United States accepted and nurtured such attitudes. After the occupation, in the second half of 2003, radical Sunni Islamists—most of them foreigners sympathetic to al-Qaida—launched a vicious anti-Shiite terror campaign; in 2004 they intensified it. 2004 saw important steps towards increased ethnification of the Iraq situation in the northern parts of the country, especially in the recognition in the Transitional Administrative Law of 'disputed' areas and cities—key among them Kirkuk—instead of a decision to deal with the problem of displacement during the former regime at the individual level. In August 2005, SCIRI introduced the divisive Shiite federalism idea; this came in the wake of visits by their leader Abd al-Aziz al-Hakim to Tehran, the party's steadfast sponsor. One month later, al-Qaida reciprocated and escalated: they declared holy war on the Shiites, and 'moderate' Sunni Arab statesmen outside Iraq did not help matters by their scaremongering about the imminent establishment of a 'Shiite Crescent'. Then, in early 2006 the United States blatantly interfered in the internal Shiite prime ministerial selection process to the detriment of the anti-federal Ibrahim al-Jaafari. During the prolonged stalemate over who should be prime ministerial nominee came the Samarra bombing; this in turn prompted another defection from the Iraqi nationalist camp of Shiites, as Shiite militia forces theoretically loyal to Muqtada al-Sadr began to ignore their leader's lofty nationalist rhetoric and instead engaged in sectarian violence just as horrific as that perpetrated by al-Qaida.

Factors of this kind were absent in 1927, when the scheme for a single Shiite territorial entity foundered so miserably. After 2003, on the other hand, the bedrock of regionalist and nationalist sentiment—widespread as it may have been at the popular level—became increasingly irrelevant in politics as party elites introduced artificial 'sectarian' categories and succeeded in convincing Iraqi militants that these were somehow the fundamental building blocks of Iraqi society. Importantly, they also persuaded the outside world to think in such ways. Throughout, the international media has insisted on reading the Iraq conflict in facile sectarian terms. In the summer of 2006, foreign journalists were quick to add another notch by introducing terms like 'Shiite East Baghdad' and 'Sunni West Baghdad' and speaking of 'mixed areas' as if they constituted an anomaly.[41] By the time of the US mid-term elections in November 2006, the international community's conviction about the primacy of sectarianism in Iraqi politics was such that many leading US politicians apparently thought the Iraqi law on implementing federalism automatically implied a three-way division of the country. Whereas Iraqi political partics of different sectarian colours continued their efforts to provide an alternative political platform of anti-federalism and a demand for a timetabled US withdrawal, the signals from Washington—from Republicans and Democrats alike—only served to stoke sectarianism and added further pressure on the Iraqis to think as sectarians: the Bush administration chose to invite SCIRI's leader Abd al-Aziz al-Hakim to the White House as a supposed gesture to the 'moderate centre' in Iraq (in reality, few projects have done as much to unsettle any idea of a moderate centre in Iraqi politics as SCIRI's scheme for a single Shiite federal entity), whereas the Democratic Party, clearly driven by a desire to hammer out an 'alternative' Iraq policy, embraced the most far-fetched accounts of Iraqi history in order to make the case for territorial separation between its three ethno-religious communities, supposedly to bring an end to their alleged 'centuries-long' conflict.[42]

History would have suggested that the nine-province Shiite region ended up as a parenthesis just like the abortive Shiite separation attempt of 1927. But the exceptional conditions of post-2003 Iraq may lead to a different outcome: the emergence of a Shiite region whose name no one had even heard about before 2005.

---

41 See Burhan al-Mufti, 'Mixed Areas: A Dangerous Term', *Middle East Report*, no. 239, summer 2006, p. 28.

42 On the false premises of this position, see Reidar Visser, book review of Peter Galbraith's *The End of Iraq*, History News Network, August 2006, at hnn. us/roundup/entries/29297.html.

3
FITTING BAGHDAD IN

Fanar Haddad and *Sajjad Rizvi*

This is a plan that they [The United States and Iran] had for Iraq. They planted it and succeeded. The aim of this plan is to destroy the Iraqi people... Iraqis killing each other... These people who came with the Americans were having fun in the West for twenty years and then they came for power without understanding what the Iraqi people were and what we wanted.[1]

The sectarian violence that has enveloped Iraq has been held up as proof that the only political solution for Iraq is federalism. Conventional wisdom dictates that Iraq, an artificial creation and the product of early twentieth-century European geo-strategic concerns, was doomed to failure.[2] Such an artificial state, therefore, requires a strong centre and an extensive security and intelligence apparatus to ensure the cohesion and perpetuation of the state. Consequently, the present absence of an Iraqi state, or at the very least, the absence of a functioning executive with the powers and properties of a 'state', means that Iraq is disintegrating and will eventually dissolve. This argument brushes Iraqi nationalism aside by considering it to be an equally artificial concept forcefully imposed from above, denies that Iraq is a 'nation-state' and refutes the existence of an Iraqi na-

<hr>

1 Telephone interview with Baghdad resident, Zayyuna district, November 2006.

2 For an extreme version of this account, see Peter W. Galbraith, *The End of Iraq*, London: Simon and Schuster, 2006. For a more detailed analysis of the question of Iraqi artificiality see Hala Fattah, 'The Question of the "Artificiality" of Iraq as a Nation-State', in Shams Inati (ed.), *Iraq: Its History, People and Politics*, New York: Humanity Books, 2003.

tion. The countless rebellions and insurgencies against the state in twentieth-century Iraq would also be used to illustrate the idea that the people inhabiting Iraq have no desire to be Iraqis. However, if we were to accept the 'artificiality debate', then the same logic of dismemberment would apply to the rest of the Middle East and, indeed, to most of the states in the world. Furthermore, to negate the existence of an Iraqi national identity or of Iraqi nationalism is to deny the historical experiences of over eight decades of Iraqi statehood. It is through this unitary state that the concept of an 'Iraqi nation' has survived throughout the twentieth century. However, this has not equated to unity and social harmony: Iraqi statehood and the historical experience of different interest groups (social, religious or political) coexisting and competing for power within a common state have led to a series of competing narratives of the 'Iraqi nation'.

This chapter addresses two main issues. Firstly, it deals with the problems associated with any proposed federal structure in today's Iraq. Secondly, it discusses popular reaction to federalism from a Baghdad viewpoint. One of the fundamental obstacles to implementing any federal system in Iraq is that it is an external imposition on a people who do not understand and are deeply suspicious of the very concept of federalism. In some parts of the country—such as Baghdad—federalism does not resonate with any pre-existing sense of regional (as opposed to national) identity that could support it. Whilst the pre-2003 model of over-centralisation is neither a viable nor desirable option for Iraq, popular ignorance of such central features of the proposed 'new Iraq' can act as a hindrance to the successful implementation of federalism.

The analysis that follows is based on twenty in-depth telephone interviews with ordinary Baghdadis. Certain areas of the capital were targeted by dialling specific area codes within Baghdad followed by random numbers.[3] Interviewees were then presented with a list of

---

3 The areas targeted were A'dhamiyya, Sadr City, Zayyuna, Karrada, Sha'ab, Haifa, Baya'a and Jadiriyya.

pre-set questions regarding federalism, the constitution and the general post-war situation.

Federalism from above

In the run-up to the invasion of Iraq in 2003, visions for a postwar Iraq revolved around a federal entity that would embrace democracy and human rights. Spokespersons for the coalition forces and members of the Iraqi opposition spoke of a federal Iraq as if it were a foregone conclusion. However, in 2003, the idea of a federal Iraq was a novel one for the majority of the Iraqi opposition, and a completely alien one to the majority of the Iraqi people. Whilst opposition to the central government has been a common feature of twentieth-century Iraq, calls for regional autonomy have not. If the overly simplistic three-way division of Iraqi society is employed, it becomes clear that only the Kurds have been consistent in their calls for decentralisation and/or autonomy. As far as Iraqi opposition movements are concerned, the major actors have been members of the Kurdish and/or Shiite communities. Shiite opposition groups and figures have, throughout the twentieth century, been overwhelmingly in favour of a unitary state—as would be expected by virtue of Shiite numerical dominance. Their opposition revolved around the role they felt they deserved within that state. Unlike the Kurdish opposition, mainstream Shiite opposition groups did not aspire to a redrawing of Iraqi borders, nor to a separate Shiite state. From the tribal revolts of the 1930s to the 1991 *intifada*, Shiite opposition focused on a greater share of power, commensurate with their numbers, within the Iraqi state. In fact, as late as January 2003, members of the Daawa Party were referring to federalism as an 'American plot'.[4]

With the exception of the Kurds, those Iraqi opponents of the Baathist regime who did embrace federalism were lending support to what was an abstract idea as far as they were concerned. In the

---

4 Visser, Reidar, 'Shi'i Perspectives on a Federal Iraq', in Daniel Heradstveit and Helge Hveem (eds), *Oil in The Gulf: Obstacles to Democracy and Development*, Aldershot: Ashgate, 2004, p. 131.

1990s and during the years preceding the war, there was no Iraqi debate on what federalism entailed, and no effort to agree on a detailed definition of federalism. Whilst viewing decentralisation as a safeguard against a repetition of the monopolistic concentration of power which has been such a constant feature of Iraqi politics, non-Kurdish support for federalism was largely a response to on-the-ground realities. By 2003, the Kurdish north had enjoyed over twelve years of autonomous self-rule; for the Kurds a unitary state with a hegemonic capital was simply not an option. From the outset, therefore, the federal project has been spurred on by the Kurds and the political realities of the Kurdish north.

As it stands, the new Iraqi constitution actually sets the ground for federal entities to be formed 'from below', with the initiative for forming regions lying with the electorate and regional politicians rather than with Baghdad. Spanish federalism has been held up as a model for Iraq, as it is seen as the most similar system to the hybrid form of federalism that is being instituted in Iraq. Article 115 (later renumbered 117) of the Iraqi constitution and article 143 of the Spanish constitution both stress the importance of local initiatives in drawing regional borders rather than following the more common practice in other countries of simply converting existing administrative units into federal regions.[5] However, as will be explained shortly, the likelihood of a push for federalism from below in today's Iraq is quite unlikely, especially if evidence from the capital region is anything to go by. As for the Kurdish areas, popular sentiments on the issue of state structure are in fact more pro-independence than pro-federal, as was shown by the informal Kurdish referendum of January 2005.[6] Additionally, the historical record suggests that such a framework of grassroots federalism can descend into federal chaos with repetitive

5 Reidar Visser, 'Building Federal Subunits by Way of Referenda: Special Challenges for Iraq', 9 June 2006, available at www.historiae.org.

6 See 'Harakat al-istifta' fi kurdistan tahsi aswat akrad al-'iraqiyyin al-raghibin fi al-infisal' [Kurdish referendum movement counts pro-secession vote amongst Iraqi Kurds], *Al-Sharq al-Awsat*, 1 February 2005.

calls for referenda based on never-ending federal initiatives. This is especially valid in the Iraqi case, because the constitution stipulates that a mere one-year moratorium shall follow any failed attempt at creating a region (whereas the Spanish constitution, for example, sets a five-year moratorium).

Federalism 'from above' is almost equally problematic in the Iraqi context. The Spanish experience owed its success largely to two factors: the force of history and elite agreement.[7] In Iraq today there is no historical precedent for the division of the country into sub-units, especially with regard to 'super-regions' such as the southern region as envisioned by SCIRI—which is based on an intra-Shiite struggle for dominance rather than on ideological conviction. This of course does not make it impossible that a viable region can be established without a historical precedent; however, the benefits of historical experience around which legitimacy and popular support can be built will be lacking. In southern Iraq, for example, some of the arguments used to justify calls for a southern region(s) appeal to security concerns and the need to ensure that the provinces do not suffer the neglect that characterised their relations with the central government throughout the twentieth century.

On paper, Spanish federalism begins at the grassroots level, relying on a popular mandate to form a region. However, the reality is that in order to avoid federal chaos, Spanish legislators assumed a leading role and in effect dictated many aspects of the new federal Spain. Initially, as with Iraq, it was assumed that there would only be two or three regions formed in Spain. However, after the unexpected proliferation of proposed regions and after the military coup attempt of 1981, Spanish politicians decided that greater control from above was needed and this effectively directed the formation of a federal Spain. The whole exercise required a considerable degree of co-operation amongst the Spanish political elite. Bearing in mind the marked ambivalence of Arab Iraqi opposition figures towards federalism in the years preceding the war, it is not surprising that the

---

7   Visser, 'Building Federal Subunits'.

post-2003 federalist project in Iraq has been characterised by confusion and disagreement. This is especially inauspicious considering that it took Spanish legislators five years to draw Spain's federal map despite a considerable degree of consensus on what the new map should look like.

Another federal experiment of relevance to Iraq is Nigeria. The thirty-six states that make up modern Nigeria are amongst the most powerful sub-national bodies in Africa.[8] This power has come at the expense of the central government's ability to maintain its effective control and authority over all the regions. There is the danger, especially when bearing in mind what are at times the Kurds' maximal demands, that what has been referred to as Nigerian 'hyper-federalism' will be repeated in Iraq. Many of the flaws of the Nigerian system are being recreated in Iraq today. For example, the autonomy of the Nigerian regions has been (in some cases at least) particularly problematic economically and legally. Some regions have seen officially sanctioned vigilantism instituted to improve law enforcement. In some cases, regional laws are coming into effect despite contradicting federal statutes; a number of states have introduced Sharia law. Most worryingly, some regions in Nigeria have withheld from the centre profits accruing from natural resources despite the constitution clearly outlining the economic relation between the centre and the periphery.[9] There is no guarantee that the same will not happen in Iraq. In fact, with the weakness of the central government, such a scenario seems likely. One can even interpret the violence in Iraq today as a grab for power and resources by various actors in a bid to establish on-the-ground realities—realities which, they hope, will have to be considered in any final settlement that is agreed upon. Iraq today has seen the rise of kangaroo courts run by various militias and parties that have stepped into the vacuum which the post-2003 governments have been unable to fill. In many areas of the country,

---

8   Adam M. Smith, 'Fractured Federalism: Nigeria's Lessons for Today's Nation Builders in Iraq', *The Round Table*, vol. 94, no. 1, January 2005, p. 129.
9   Ibid., p. 135.

services and law and order (such as they are) are provided not by the state but by individual parties and their militias. These same actors have been accused of extensive oil smuggling.[10] With vigilantism, local extra-legal courts and militia control rampant in Iraq, and with the Kurdish north having many of their own legal and administrative structures (some since the 1990s) one wonders how all this will be reconciled with whatever central system is agreed upon.

These are but some of the problems that the Iraqi federal project might encounter. The fact that the constitution has yet to be finalised and that the exact form of a federal Iraq has yet to be agreed upon means that the success or failure of Iraqi federalism is still in the balance. With the increasing divisions within Iraqi politics and society and with the increasing ferocity of the civil strife that has been a feature of Iraq since February 2006 there is little room for optimism. One of the major unresolved points of contention within the federal debate is the split of natural resources. Article 110 (later renumbered as article 112) of the Iraqi constitution outlines the administration of oil and gas from current fields and leaves the question of oil reserves that have yet to be discovered open to interpretation. The second part of the article is written vaguely: whilst promising that federal and regional governments will work together, 'to develop the oil and gas wealth in a way that achieves the highest benefit to the Iraqi people ...', it fails to define what such noble terms mean.[11] Many opponents of federalism fear that Baghdad and the surrounding areas will be economically starved and will in effect be dependent on the regions. It is to be hoped that such fears are merely unfounded exaggerations; nevertheless, the fact remains that as has happened in places like Nigeria, the periphery may withhold that which it is constitutionally

10 Bilal A. Wahab, 'How Iraqi Oil Smuggling Greases Violence', *The Middle East Quarterly*, vol. 13, no. 4, 2006. Lionel Beehner, 'The Challenge in Iraq's Other Cities: Basra', Council on Foreign Relations (Washington, DC), available at http://www.cfr.org/publication/11001.

11 Text of the Iraqi constitution, http://www.washingtonpost.com/wp-dyn/content/article/2005/10/12/AR2005101201450.html.

obliged to hand over to the centre. In such a situation, federalism, instead of abating conflict and tension, will in fact increase it.

Imported politics

As can be discerned by any follower of events in Iraq, the issue of federalism has thus far clearly been animated from above. One can say that it is a concern of the elite that holds little bearing for ordinary Iraqis' everyday lives. To speak of 'Shiite aspirations' for a region of this kind or another is highly misleading, as this would only be a reflection of what certain Shiite parties have been advocating rather than a reflection of the aspirations of a meaningful percentage of the Iraqi population. In the 2005 elections, many parties were elected despite their political programmes—or even in the absence of programmes. Unfortunately, in light of the ever-deteriorating security situation, accurately gauging Iraqi public opinion has been very difficult. What can be said without fear of exaggeration is that the major post-2003 political parties of Iraq are not truly popular and representative of the Iraqi populace and have only limited constituencies—despite the number of votes they gained. With few exceptions (such as the Fadila Party and the various Sadrist movements), the most significant parties have been those that arrived in Iraq after the downfall of Saddam Hussein's regime, and whilst the Iraqi people may not have been overly fond of Saddam, there was no reason for them to pledge loyalty to the new political elite who had been living in exile for decades. What exacerbated this problem was that alongside the issue of returning exiles who did not enjoy constituencies of note within Iraq, there was the fact that the nature of the Iraqi state under Saddam Hussein had left no room for any political personalities or movements to grow within Iraq itself. These and other issues are partly why politics in post-war Iraq quickly deteriorated into a sectarian affair as was demonstrated by the earliest elections: people overwhelmingly voted for their sect or ethnicity rather than for a political programme or even a political personality.

The gulf between ordinary Iraqis and the newly arrived Iraqi op-
positionists-turned-politicians was made glaringly clear from the
earliest post-Saddam days. A telling example of things to come was
the announcement in July 2003 by the Iraqi governing council of 9
April as the national holiday to celebrate the birth of a new Iraq.[12]
Whilst the former opposition in exile saw this as a day of liberation
worthy of commemoration, many Iraqis, especially in the streets of
the capital, saw it as the day Baghdad fell and thus could not possibly be celebrated no matter what other connotations positive or
otherwise 9 April held.[13] Even within the new political elite, those
that have been in Iraq and have endured the hardships of the past few
decades make a distinction between themselves and those who came
back to Iraq in 2003.[14] Disbanding the Iraqi army, de-Baathification
and federalism are but a few issues that left many ordinary Iraqis
perplexed.[15] Such policies are a reflection of the mindset of those
Iraqis living abroad who had dedicated a significant part of their lives
opposing what they saw as an abhorrent regime. Their prolonged
exile meant that they had completely lost touch with Iraqi society as
it has been shaped and evolved by the events of the last three decades.[16] Their insular social life meant that they seldom encountered
Iraqis who were not like-minded in their political views. This may lie

---

12 See, 'Iraq Moves Towards Self-Rule', BBC, 13 July 2003, available at
http://news.bbc.co.uk/1/hi/world/middle_east/3062037.stm.

13 See entries for 19 and 24 July 2003 at Juan Cole's blog *Informed Comment*,
at www.juancole.com.

14 For an Iraqi politician's views on the opposition in exile and an interesting
analysis of the Middle East's prospects for democracy see 'Iraqi MP Iyad Jamal
Al-Din: Democracy in the Middle East Can Only Be Established by Force', 28
December 2006, clip no. 1351 at the MEMRI (The Middle East Media Research
Institute) website, available at http://memritv.org/Transcript.asp?P1=1351.

15 See for example, L. Paul Bremer III, *My Year in Iraq*, New York: Simon
and Schuster, 2006, pp. 58–9 for a glimpse of how news of the dissolution of the
Iraqi army was received by prominent members of the new political elite.

16 For example, the farcical attempt to revive the monarchy under Sharif Ali
bin al-Hussein's Constitutional Monarchy Movement which was part of the
Iraqi National Congress.

behind Iraqi assurances to Western policymakers that Iraq is 'highly secular', or that foreign troops will be welcomed into Iraq with, in the words of Kanaan Makiya, 'flowers and sweets'.[17] Federalism in Iraq is a product of the new Iraqi political elite that has collided with the Iraqi people's vision(s) for themselves and for the future of their country. The fact is that, as with the Iraqi political elite that came into existence in the 1920s, today's Iraq is nominally presided over by politicians who have no significant roots within the country and who carry a political worldview—forged in exile—that is largely alien to the Iraqi people. A social, political and intellectual gulf separates politicians from the people they claim to represent. This was perhaps the most apparent conclusion reached through the telephone interviews conducted in preparation for this chapter.

Federalism from below in Baghdad?

Federalism in Iraq is first and foremost an issue animated from above. Many have used the various political developments in the country as reflections of public opinion. These include the elections of January and December 2005 and the October 2005 constitutional referendum. However, such a reading of the situation overlooks the fact that today's climate of violence and fear has negated the possibility of real popular political debate emerging, especially in Baghdad and other restless areas such as the western provinces. It would be difficult to claim that ordinary Iraqis are involved in a political process that engages them. One retired army officer in Baghdad thus complained:

All these politicians... they have no contact with the people, they are not in touch with any of us. They do not interact with us and have no idea what we go through... I have no form of contact with these politicians, such as my minister or my parliamentary representative...[18]

---

17 For full transcript see, 'Transcript of Iraq Seminar with Richard Perle and Kanaan Makiya Sponsored by Benador Associates', available at http://www.benadorassociates.com/article/664.

18 Telephone interview with Baghdad resident, Jamila district, November 2006.

Whilst one can say that these are the criticisms that the people of any country would direct at their political elites, the fact remains that in Iraq a deeper barrier between the political elite and the people exists: a physical barrier in the form of the Green Zone, and a political barrier in terms of ideas and ambitions. The federal issue that has generated such interest in the West is barely understood by ordinary Iraqis and, in Baghdad at least, it seems that people are deeply suspicious of the whole concept.

The interviews in this survey began with a question about what the term 'federalism' meant to the respondent. Almost all the respondents demonstrated a complete ignorance of what federalism entailed. The most common response was that federalism is the first step towards the division of Iraq. This, so the theory goes, will be the fulfilment of a plot designed by the United States, Iran and Israel with the aim of destroying Iraq and its people. Such sentiments are far from unique to our research; they proliferate in internet Arabic chat-rooms, and can be found in readers' comments (Iraqi or otherwise) on Arab news websites such as Al-Jazeera and Al-Arabiyya. These alarmist and conspiracy-laden views—and the fact that the majority of Iraqis do not accurately comprehend what federalism involves—can be attributed to the political cocoon that Iraq turned into under the Baath regime. However, this also reveals a failure, deliberate or otherwise, on the part of the coalition authorities and the new Iraqi political elite to educate the Iraqi people about new political concepts such as federalism. This shortcoming is something that many Iraqis are acutely aware of, as was shown by the respondents' comments. It was repeatedly stated by many interviewees that there had been no public awareness campaigns that explained what such new political concepts meant. One respondent complained that the only source of information on federalism and the constitution had been the satellite channels, which had been woefully inadequate as the electricity supply was unreliable.[19] From talking to Iraqis, one

19 Telephone interview with Baghdad residents, Jamila and Karrada districts, November 2006.

gets the impression that they view federalism as merely one of the many ideas that came with the war and its disastrous aftermath. One man from A'dhamiyya summarised his views on federalism and the new Iraq:

All these ideas that they brought with them... we don't know what they are; they are alien to us. When they [the coalition authorities and their supporters] leave we will fix our own problems because *we* are the sons of Iraq not those that came with the Americans and it is the sons of Iraq [as opposed to the recently returned exiles] that will fix Iraq's problems.[20]

Similarly, a man from Haifa Street aired his pessimism and lack of faith in the political developments of Iraq in general and federalism in particular:

It [federalism] is a new phrase for us and it doesn't sound good to me... it is a rotten idea. We all know who is behind it and who is insisting upon it but ultimately it all goes back to the Americans.[21]

Shiite respondents tended to be guardedly optimistic about federalism but still maintained that, ideally, Iraq would be centrally ruled. Furthermore, whether for or against federalism, they displayed the same ignorance and confusion that almost all respondents did, as shown by this extract from an interview with a resident of Sadr City:

I would prefer rule from the centre as long as everyone is taken care of. I don't know much about this federalism; it sounds like a good idea but it is a completely new and foreign notion to us. Overall, I am optimistic because for thirty years we have suffered, but Baghdad will be a problem if this federalism was to happen. What will Baghdad do for resources? I believe Baghdad should have a superior role whatever system we have, but who knows what will happen? We just don't know; they [the government] didn't tell us what federalism is... now we're hearing that you will need a visa to go to the provinces.[22]

---

20 Telephone interview with Baghdad resident, A'dhamiyya district, November 2006.

21 Telephone interview with Baghdad resident, Haifa Street district, November 2006.

22 Telephone interview with Baghdad resident, Sadr City district, November

Of the Baghdadis interviewed, a few were willing to show some faith in the federal idea. They used examples such as the United Arab Emirates to illustrate that federalism can work. However, two points should be made with regards to the Baghdadi optimists in the sample: firstly, they were a minority (only one respondent expressed total and unreserved support for federalism); secondly, what limited faith they had in federalism was completely detached from any sectarian, ethnic or regional identity. Rather than using regions to foster their identities, their concern was with functional matters such as the division of resources and abuse of power. A teacher from Sadr City showed support (albeit limited) for the formation of regions in the south. He mentioned the city of Amara—from where many residents of Sadr City originate—and pointed to past hardships to justify the formation of regions:

I would prefer centralised rule provided all regions of the country are looked after...look at Amara and Basra... they are sitting on a sea of oil but they have always been poor because of government neglect. The people of Amara are our people; they have a right to a share of their oil.[23]

The point to be made is that this limited support was not due to the respondent's southern ancestry or for any desire to stress his Shiite identity; rather, he saw federalism as a way to avoid repeating the mistakes and injustices of the past. Of the respondents that showed some enthusiasm for federalism, all based their support on a desire to see a more equitable relationship between Baghdad and the provinces. This echoes feelings also noted in other studies, where it has been suggested that support for SCIRI's proposed nine-province southern super-region has been limited and that regionalism on a sectarian basis is opposed by a significant proportion of Iraqis.[24] The

2006.

23 Telephone interview with Baghdad resident, Sadr City district, November 2006.

24 International Crisis Group, *After Baker-Hamilton: What to do in Iraq* (Middle East Report no. 60), 19 December 2006, p. 4. In fact, SCIRI has limited support outside the shrine cities; see Reidar Visser, 'Beyond SCIRI and Abd al-Aziz

interviewees saw the Kurdish north as a special case, and few opposed the formation of a Kurdish region unless it would also encompass the disputed city of Kirkuk. Such views strengthen the case for forming a diarchy in Iraq, as even some Sunni Arab politicians have come to realise that one way or another, some kind of special status will inevitably have to be accorded to the Kurdish north.

Arguably, the federal project in Iraq was initiated to accommodate the on-the-ground realities of the Kurdish north. However, Kurdish aspirations conflict with popular Arab expectations of a federal Iraq—that is, to the extent that such expectations actually exist. For example, the Baghdadis in the sample who supported federalism, however guardedly, qualified their support by saying that any federal framework would have to subordinate the regions to Baghdad, and that oil must be distributed by the capital. Such sentiments fly in the face of Kurdish demands and political realities. A similar detachment from political reality was seen when questions regarding the constitution were asked. The respondents were asked how a person can be for the constitution yet against federalism (as was often the case). One woman from Baya'a was adamant that the constitution did not advocate federalism:

Q: 'Were you for or against the constitution?'

A: 'Most people did not know what the constitution entailed; we did not know what the clauses were. They mentioned that they will provide services and so forth but we haven't seen any progress. Basically it's a set of nice ideas that have not been implemented.'

Q: 'Bearing in mind that the constitution strongly advocates a federal Iraq, how can you be for the constitution but against federalism?'

A: 'I don't know about that; I don't think that's true. Anyway, none of it is implemented.'[25]

al-Hakim: The Silent Forces of the United Iraqi Alliance', 20 January 2006, available at www.historiae.org.

25 Telephone interview with Baghdad resident, Baya'a district, November 2006.

Questions regarding the constitution revealed that even those who were for it as a 'set of nice ideas' would insist that changes needed to be made to it, especially concerning the issue of federalism. Out of a sample of twenty, half of the respondents were for the constitution in principle but against federalism. Accordingly, they stated that their continued support for the constitution was contingent upon changes being made to it. Nine interviewees were against both the constitution and federalism, having no faith in either. Only one respondent, a resident of Sha'ab of Kurdish descent, was in favour of both the constitution and federalism. Those who were against the constitution based their opposition on one of two things: either they linked the constitution with the security situation and the level of services (thereby considering the constitution a failure as neither has improved since the referendum); alternatively, opposition was based on a complete lack of trust in all post-2003 political developments, as expressed by this resident of A'dhamiyya:

The whole idea [constitution and federalism] does not sit right with me. I don't go near any of it; it's all lies and it's not in Iraq's benefit. I didn't vote for the constitution and wouldn't vote: let's say my father is responsible for a family; whether he is good or bad is not the point. The family is his responsibility and his alone. So you can't take someone out of their house and form a government in the shadow of an occupation... that cannot be right.[26]

The fact that many respondents associated the government's poor performance with what they believed to be the constitution's failure is telling of a lack of understanding as to what the primary purpose of the constitution is. Again, as with federalism, much blame must be placed on the coalition authorities and the new political elite. From the sample, those that supported the constitution did so only because they believed that a constitution, in principle, will protect their rights; however, with only one exception, they were largely against federalism in any shape or form for the Arab regions of Iraq.

---

26 Telephone interview with Baghdad resident, A'dhamiyya district, November 2006.

Rulers, ruled and Iraqi nationalism

One of the major hurdles facing the new Iraq is the gulf separating the people from the political elite. As far as the issue of federalism is concerned, there are politicians working endlessly to reach consensus on a project that is not understood by a deeply suspicious Iraqi people. This is merely one manifestation of how Iraqis view their new leaders more generally. The majority of Iraqis consider the exiles that went back to Iraq in 2003 not as prodigal sons of the nation but as outsiders. Their impressions of the exiles have not been bettered by the widespread corruption and the dismal performance of Iraqi governments. The political process as a whole is associated with the exiles even if it contains many local figures. However, in many cases, even home-grown politicians and political parties such as the Sadr movement are viewed by their opponents as stooges for various foreign powers (the Sadr movement, despite its somewhat anti-Iranian stance, is accused by its detractors of subservience to Iran). This all serves to reinforce the view that Iraq has been inundated by outsiders of every sort who have devastated the country: Americans, British, Iranians, Arabs, Israelis/Zionists and the exiles are some of those held responsible for the post-2003 situation.

In the final section of the questionnaire respondents were asked about the general situation after the fall of the old regime. They tended to blame the new Iraqi political elite rather than the coalition authorities for the problems of post-2003 Iraq. Unprompted, some interviewees vented their frustration about the returned Iraqi exiles who were variously referred to as 'those that came on the backs of American tanks,' 'those that eat pork,' 'those that have been having fun,' 'stooges' and 'traitors'. The logic that is followed is that since there was no sectarian strife prior to 2003 it must be the coalition authorities and their supporters who spread sectarianism in Iraq after 2003. This is largely a manifestation of nostalgic sentimentality for times of stability in the face of chaos and, even allowing for the likelihood that the respondents' answers were coloured by the interviewers being outsiders, the answers revealed that no one claimed a monopoly on morality or victimhood for their side/sect. In the ideal world that the respondents were trying to portray, Iraqis do not discriminate on the basis of ethnicity or sect; rather, they are struggling against outsiders:

There is a civil war ongoing in Iraq today. The militias are killing Iraqis everywhere... Shiites and Sunnis are interrelated...we never had these problems before. By God those that came on the backs of the American tanks are responsible for spreading this... those that ran away from Iraq all those years ago to escape justice for their crimes. The sectarianism you are seeing today is imported but unfortunately it is spreading. Here in A'dhamiyya, we don't have a sectarian streak... we have a lot of Shiites and we will protect them.[27]

Similarly, a resident of the mostly Shiite Karrada district denied that sectarianism was ever an issue for Iraqis before 2003:

There are people who are trying to push Iraq into a civil war and in some areas they are succeeding. Sectarian tension was created by the occupation and by terrorists who came from abroad and who do not want Iraq to succeed... we are one people but sadly the terrorists have infiltrated certain areas but not our area. I challenge anyone to name me one man who was driven out of Karrada. It doesn't matter whether he is a Shiite or a Sunni, in our area we protect each other.[28]

Even something as harrowing as having a son tortured to death is blamed on outsiders. The following is an interview with an elderly woman from Haifa Street who recounts the circumstances of her son's death. The video is posted on the internet under the title 'Safavid Crimes against the People of the Sunna' (*jara'im al-safawiyya fi ahl al-sunna*) in what is clearly a propaganda video aimed at highlighting the oppression of Sunnis by the Shiite-dominated government:

... the national guard took my son... they assured me that it was just a routine interrogation and that after the weekend they would release him...

---

27 Telephone interview with Baghdad resident, A'dhamiyya district, November 2006.

28 Telephone interview with Baghdad resident, Karrada district, November 2006.

After the weekend I heard from the people of Rahmaniyya that my son had been killed... I found him there [in Yarmuk Hospital] wrapped up. I saw what God Almighty wouldn't allow... They tortured him in unimaginable ways. They had left nothing—electricity and drills—I don't know what they had done to his back, it might have been acid. I just want to call on all righteous people... did the Jew in Palestine do this? The people of Iraq have done it; not the righteous Iraqis but those that came from abroad. They're the ones that did it; Jaafari's mob and Abd al-Aziz al-Hakim's mob and the Badr brigade, they are the ones that did it... If we fight the occupation the state fights us. Why does the state fight us? They [the state] divided us and lit the fires between us.[29]

There is no way of telling whether this interview is authentic. Even if it is, it has clearly been filmed and distributed for a very obvious agenda. However, what is remarkable is that the blame was assigned to outsiders. The term 'Safavid' is almost a synonym for Shiite foreigners (namely, Iranians), used by those who are against the Iraqi government. Nevertheless, if the interview is staged, the perpetrators easily could have told the woman to use the general word 'Shiite' rather than lay the blame on a small group of Shiite outsiders. Judging from how the woman phrased her words, it is clear that the problem, for her or her scriptwriters, is an external one.

Whilst fitting into the pervasive Middle Eastern belief in con-spiracy theories, the readiness with which Iraqis blame outsiders shows an unwillingness to lay the blame on local forces. Some may say that this is a stubborn refusal to admit to many of the internal problems of Iraq, and therefore that it is a direct contradiction of reality. However, at the same time it does show a belief in Iraq and in Iraqi national identity. Whether such sentiments have a grain of logical rationality within them is beside the point. What is clear from this survey is that Iraqi nationalism, in the capital at least, is very much a force still to be reckoned with, and it is a force that is largely against federalism.

---

29 Available at http://www.youtube.com/watch?v=dZ1h9_hQ_pwandmode=relatedandsearch=.

It should be pointed out here that the existence of a national identity does not necessarily mean social harmony. What it does mean, however, is that it a civil war will not automatically revolve around boundaries and questions of territorial integrity. Today's civil war in Iraq is not based on any secessionist drive. The only secessionist tendencies that are clearly visible are those of the Kurds and they are not involved in the fighting. This Iraqi civil war is firstly about power and resources, but it is underlined and animated by a nationalist undercurrent. What we are seeing is a conflict between various groups each claiming to represent the true Iraq by being the Iraqi *Staatsvolk*. Such dynamics are far more reminiscent of Lebanon than of Chechnya, and they negate the idea that there is no Iraqi nationalism. Even though the Iraqi state with its modern borders may be an artificial creation, today it carries eighty years of shared experiences that have turned its artificiality into something quite real. It is competing visions of that reality that are fighting each other today. The issue is not whether or not Iraqi nationalism exists; rather, it is a question of which of the multiple nations as imagined by various Iraqi socioeconomic and religious groups will triumph. The protagonists of this civil war have not called for a redrawing of the borders, nor have any of them called for a separate state. The various sects that make up the Arab Iraqi population may not trust each other and may even view each other with disdain, but the goal of extremists on all sides seems to be to gain a position of ascendancy within the Iraqi state vis-à-vis the other, rather than to separate from them.

Sectarian identity, then, is a vehicle for national identity rather than its substitute. The final question in the survey was what the solution to Iraq's post-2003 troubles in general—and the civil war in particular—was. Ominously, over half the sample said that the problem was the new Iraqi political elite, with no less than a quarter of the sample saying that Iraq what Iraq needs is a *hakim 'adil* and/or *hakim qawi*: a just leader and/or a strong leader. The remainder, just under half of the sample, mentioned 'unity' as the solution, or as a part of the solution.[30] Despite most of the respondents having ties to the provinces, none displayed any regionalist and/or sectarian feelings that would require a separate state or federal region to satisfy. Nor did they differentiate their Baghdad identity from their Iraqi national identity in a way that would merit a label such as 'regionalism'. Even those committing the most heinous of atrocities on a daily basis are doing so for power within Iraq, rather than in the name of a 'Shiastan' or a 'Sunnistan', to use some of the farcical new terms that have emerged in the international media. However, it is clear that in light of recent and continuing events in Iraq, it is questionable how long such nationalist tendencies will survive. In the future, perhaps all the talk of sectarian regionalism among Westerners and Iraqi exiles will be viewed as a self-fulfilling prophecy. At the moment, however, the whole concept of federalism is not only poorly understood by the majority of Iraqis but is also something of an irrelevancy—with security, the economy and services being their main priorities. As one man who declined to participate said, 'My friend… I am speaking to you from a dark room with no electricity. We have bigger things on our mind.'

History repeating itself?

That the current Iraqi political system is imported from abroad and that it is dominated by people who have spent significant parts of their lives in exile is not in doubt. After hearing respondents complain about the occupation and the new Iraqi political elite who had been 'having fun' in the West whilst Iraqis languished under the sanctions regime one cannot help drawing parallels with previous attempts at Iraqi state building. In August 1921, Faysal bin al-Hussein (son of Sharif Hussein of Mecca) was enthroned as Faysal I, King of Iraq. He was later to prove himself a skilful politician. However, no amount of political skill could overcome the fact that Faysal was

---

30 One woman from Zayyuna sarcastically said that the solution is, 'nothing short of a miracle from the Almighty.'

an outsider and had no roots or popular base in Iraq. Consequently, he was forced to rely on a narrow base of support consisting of the Sharifians (Ottoman officers who had joined the Arab Revolt led by Sharif Hussein of Mecca and his sons in mid-1916) and ex-Ottoman officers. The majority of these, in turn, also lacked a popular base and so politics became a highly incestuous affair. To illustrate, the monarchy saw a total of 23 men hold the office of prime minister (in a total of 58 terms); 14 of the 23 men were of a military background and they alone held the premier office 42 out of the total 58 terms.[31] In addition to that, not only were politics the preserve of an insular elite but these men were also detached from the common people's aspirations and desires—as evidenced by reactions to unpopular policies and initiatives after 1945, such as the 1948 Portsmouth Treaty with Britain, efforts to establish the Baghdad Pact in the 1950s, and the agrarian policy.[32] The nature of Iraqi politics in the pre-1958 era facilitated the entry of the army into politics. Politicians (many of whom had military backgrounds themselves) lacked popular support and tried to gain leverage over each other by appealing to the army; this was to have disastrous consequences for Iraqi political development. The monarchy was brought down in 1958 and even though the 'revolution' was the exclusive affair of the so-called Free Officers who constituted no more than five per cent of the entire Iraqi officer corps,[33] it quickly gained popular support

---

31 'Aqil al-Nasiri, *Al-jaysh wa-al-sulta fi al-'iraq al-maliki* [The army and the state in monarchical Iraq], Damascus: Al-Hassad, 2000, p. 209.

32 The relationship between the landed elite and the political elite changed from an antagonistic one where the landed sheikhs were a threat to the central government to an inflexible one after an informal 'alliance' between the two was developed. Of the inflexibilities that this 'alliance' carried were that it ruled out the possibility of effective land reform and meant that the central government was unable to present the landed elite with realistic tax demands. See David Pool, 'From Elite to Class: The Transformation of Iraqi Leadership, 1920–1939', *International Journal of Middle East Studies* (Cambridge), vol. 12, November 1980.

33 Robert A. Fernea, and Wm. Roger Louis (eds), *The Iraqi Revolution of 1958: The Old Social Classes Revisited*, London: I.B. Tauris, 1991, p. 48.

once news of its occurrence had become public knowledge. Central to popular and military opposition to the monarchy was the fact that the pre-1958 regime was seen as dependent on and subservient to the British.

The parallels with today's situation are obvious. The entire Iraqi post-war political order loses popularity daily in the capital as a result of the never-ending deterioration of security, and because of the government's inability to provide services. Regardless of whether there is much that the government can actually do to alleviate the situation, residents of the capital associate the post-war political system with chaos, and view politicians and their policies with suspicion. One cannot help but wonder whether today's politicians are destined to fail regardless of how sage their policies and initiatives might be or might become. For, like the monarchy, they may forever be tainted with the accusation of collaboration with a foreign and hegemonic force. Perhaps federalism will never be wilfully accepted by the people of a capital who will always associate it with the war and its disastrous aftermath.

Conclusion

Suspicions regarding federalism among Baghdadis seem to be grounded in a fear that this model of government will lead to the disintegration and dismemberment of Iraq. Perhaps a two-region solution may allay such fears. On a popular level, such a design would enjoy a considerable degree of support as it is already widely recognised amongst Arab Iraqis that the Kurdish north will inevitably have a special arrangement with the centre. There remain problems concerning overlapping jurisdictions in a two-region model;[34] however, these will be contingent upon how the Arab region of a two-region Iraq is formed.

---

34 See Liam Anderson and Gareth Stansfield, 'The Implications of Elections for Federalism in Iraq: Towards a Five-Region Model', *Publius: The Journal of Federalism*, vol. 35, no. 3, 2005, p. 15.

Today, there is no push for federalism from below in Iraq, and it is unlikely that such a thing will materialise in the future—above all because there is little understanding of the concept and there is no ongoing debate. What was discernable from the telephone interviews conducted with Baghdadis for this survey (and from various other indicators of popular sentiment in post-2003 Iraq) is that ordinary Iraqis, certainly in the capital, are largely suspicious of—if not entirely against— federalism. The underestimated force of Iraqi nationalism still runs through Arab Iraq; however, this is a sentiment that is expressed and envisaged differently by various segments of Iraqi society. Most of the Baghdadis interviewed were adamant that Iraqis are one people and that they harboured no sectarian-based antagonisms towards one another. This may have been a skewed answer given to outsiders but it nonetheless reflects what Iraqis consider to be the ideal. This is why, despite the reality of sectarian war, no Iraqi politician or group has openly called for the wholesale annihilation of Sunnis or of Shiites: this simply would be unacceptable to prevailing ideals. Instead, groups within the Sunni community (for example, Salafis/Wahhabis) and groups within the Shiite community (for example, those accused of links to Iran) have been openly declared as enemies by various militants.[35]

What the Baghdad interviewees did not delve into were the questions of who they considered to be an Iraqi and who is included in the Iraqi nation. Undeniably, Iraqi nationalism is a potent force; however, reaching a consensus on a definition of the 'Iraqi nation' has proved elusive. An 'Iraqi' will mean different things to different people. For example, since 2003, the previously banned (Shiite) Ashura ceremonies have seen strong pro-Iraqi sentiments on display in the processions, with Iraqi flags and banners calling for unity be-

---

35 Even militant groups within the Sunni insurgency have tried to disassociate themselves from attacks that target Shiite civilians, in order to bolster their nationalist credentials. See International Crisis Group *In Their Own Words: Reading the Iraqi Insurgency* (Middle East Report no. 50), 15 February 2006, pp. 19–20.

ing amongst the most noticeable symbolic displays.[36] This linking of Iraqi Shiite identity with Iraqi nationalism will undoubtedly be at odds with many Sunni Iraqi nationalists who have a different conception of the Iraqi nation and who view the 'Iraqiness' of many (though not all) Shiites with suspicion.[37] The various expressions of Iraqi nationalism are colliding in the chaotic post-2003 Iraq. However, there remains a popular belief in the existence of an Iraqi nation, and in the need to defend and preserve it (to this could be added the need to define it). Federalism is seen as inimical to the interests of a united Iraq, and despite the bloody rivalry between Arab Iraqis the overwhelming majority still desire a united Iraq. In the words of one sociologist, '[t]he nation is imagined in terms of the rival discourses and contests between its fragments.'[38] In other words, today's sectarian war is being fought within the parameters of the Iraqi nation-state and, whilst the ongoing tension is testing the limits of Iraqi nationalism, it has yet to lead to separatist or regionalist movements demanding a redrawing of the Iraqi map.

---

36   Sami Jumaili, 'Shi'ite Pilgrims Call for End to Violence in Iraq', Reuters, 29 January 2007. Available at http://today.reuters.com/news/articlenews.aspx?t ype=topnewsandstoryid=2007-01-29t145042z_01_col940617_rtrukot_0_text0. xmlandsrc=012907_1608_topstory_iran_warned_on_iraq.

37   For a summary of the variances between Shiite and Sunni conceptions of Iraqi nationalism see Yitzhak Nakash, *Reaching for Power: The Shiites in the Modern Arab World*, Princeton: Princeton University Press, 2006, pp. 82–94.

38   Sami Zubaida, 'The Fragments Imagine the Nation: The Case of Iraq', *International Journal of Middle East Studies* (Cambridge), vol. 34, May 2002, p. 212.

4

THE DECLINE OF SMALL-SCALE REGIONALISM IN TIKRIT

Ronen Zeidel

The small provincial town of Tikrit, 180 kilometres to the north of Baghdad, and its inhabitants, the Tikritis, went a long way from humble beginnings in the early twentieth century to a supreme position of control of Iraqi political life toward the end of the century. The Tikrit case exhibits a remarkably successful usage of regional solidarities in politics. This success was as much a result of the preservation and use of their regional identity as it was the outcome of the integration of Tikritis in the process of state building. It was also done within the framework of Sunni supremacy in the modern state of Iraq established in 1921. This chapter will describe the interaction between regional identity and the rise of Tikrit, emphasising the process of overall state formation. Eventually, the great dependence on Sunni supremacy and state formation brought about the demise of the Tikritis with the dramatic change after the fall of the Baathist regime in April 2003.[1]

'Regionalism' has no exact parallel term in Arabic. The corresponding terms, *iqlimiyya*, *mahalliyya* and *manatiqiyya*, equally refer to an affiliation to a small town or to a large geographical region. In the case of Tikrit, regional identity is not limited to the municipal borders of Tikrit, but rather encompasses smaller towns and villages

---

1 For more on Tikrit see Ronen Zeidel, 'Tikrit and the Tikritis: A Provincial Town, Regional Community and the State in 20th Century Iraq', unpublished Ph.D. thesis, University of Haifa, August 2003.

in the vicinity of the town as well as the people of Bayji—in addition to Tikritis who have emigrated to Baghdad. Yet, the concept of Tikrit regionalism certainly does not contain the whole of the Salah al-Din province, of which Tikrit is the centre. This province is of recent formation: it was severed from the Baghdad governorate as late as 1976, mainly in order to promote Tikrit in administrative terms. Lacking geographical distinctiveness and long administrative history, this area has long been a collection of disparate medium-sized and small towns along the Tigris river. Predominantly Sunni, the province has some Shiite towns in the south (Balad, Dujayl), a Sunni town with a Shiite minority (Samarra), as well as Kurdish and Turkmen presences in the north-east (Tuz). All these factors prevented the formation of regional identity beyond the very small scale of the town and its surrounding areas.

A brief history of Tikrit before the twentieth century

Though the exact date of its foundation is not known,[2] Tikrit is an old town, rich in history. History is a vital ingredient in Tikrit regional identity. Between the second and seventh centuries AD, the tribes of Tikrit adopted Christianity, and in the fifth century Tikrit became an important centre of the Jacobite branch. In 637, Tikrit was occupied by the Muslims, and many, though not all, of its inhabitants accepted Islam. Only from around the twelfth century did the Christians lose their majority in the population. The last mention of Christians in Tikrit is from 1652.[3]

Apparently, Tikrit reached the peak of its prosperity between the tenth and thirteenth centuries. Tikritis are proud to mention that their town was the birthplace in 1138 of Salah al-Din al-Ayyubi, the

---

2 Compare Tariq 'Abd al-Wahhab Mathlum, 'Tikrit wa-makanha fi hadarat wadi al-rafidayn' in *Mawsu'at madinat tikrit*, Baghdad: Wizarat al-Thaqafa wa-al-I'lam, 1995, vol. 1, p. 119, with 'Abd al-Razzaq 'Abbas Husayn, *Nash'at mudun al-'iraq wa-tatawurruha*, Baghdad: al-Matba'a al-Fanniyya al-Haditha, 1973, pp. 19–23.

3 Yusuf Jirjis al-Tuni, 'Al-masihiyyun fi tikrit', in *Mawsu'at madinat tikrit*, Baghdad: Wizarat al-Thaqafa wa-al-I'lam, 1997, vol. 3, pp. 117–20.

son of the Kurdish commander of the local fortress. However, Salah al-Din lived in Tikrit only until the age of three, and the town had no actual importance during his subsequent career.[4]

From the tenth century to the Ottoman occupation in 1516, domination of Tikrit changed hands between the rulers of Mosul and Baghdad. Consequently, connections between Tikrit and those two major urban centres developed. Yet, Tikrit still maintained its relative autonomy and managed to prosper in an unstable period. Baghdad and especially Mosul had a significant impact on Tikrit's local culture. The Tigris river is only navigable downstream from the north. Thus, goods and products from Mosul were brought to Tikrit, and with the commercial influence came cultural influence. The Mosul dialect had a key influence on the Arabic of the Tikritis, and many local folkloric tales originate in Mosul. Tikritis migrated to Mosul long before they 'discovered' Baghdad.[5]

A significant demographic change occurred in Tikrit in the seventeenth and eighteenth centuries, under Ottoman rule. In 1743, the Persians laid siege to Tikrit and eventually destroyed the town. The governor of Tikrit, Omar Bey from the Albu Nasir tribe, recruited an army among the 'original Tikritis' (called Takarta) as well as among other local tribes, thereby succeeding in driving the Persians away. In appreciation, the Ottomans gave those tribes parcels of land in and around Tikrit. Their settlement alongside the original Tikritis created the modern demographic make-up of Tikrit society.[6]

The nineteenth century was generally a period of deterioration for Tikrit. The general decline of the *vilayet* of Baghdad—of which

4 Ofra Bengio, *Iraq shel saddam*, Tel Aviv: Hakibutz Hameuhad, 1996, pp. 104–8 (in Hebrew).

5 Muhyi Hilal al-Farhan, 'Muhafazat tikrit min al-ihtilal al-islami wa-hatta nihayat al-'ahd al-'abbasi', *Mawsu'at madinat tikrit*, Baghdad: Wizarat al-Thaqafa wa-al-I'lam, 1996, vol. 2, pp. 25–44; Sayar Kawkab al-Jamil, 'Al-jughrafiyya al-tarikhiyya li-madinat tikrit fi al-'asr al-hadith', *Mawsu'at madinat tikrit*, Baghdad: Wizarat al-Thaqafa wa-al-I'lam, 1998, vol. 4, pp. 21–3.

6 Al-Jamil, 'Al-jughrafiyya', p. 24; Fadil Mahdi Bayat, 'Tikrit fi al-'ahd al-'uthmani', *Mawsu'at madinat tikrit*, vol. 4, pp. 57–8.

Tikrit was now a part—was certainly felt in its poorest quarters. The Ottoman administration, with its corruption, taxation and forced conscription, was a major threat to the Tikritis. Another significant threat were the marauding tribes living in the vicinity of Tikrit: the Azza, Shammar and Ubayd.[7] Despite these trends, however, the nineteenth century witnessed the strengthening of social cohesion among Tikritis. The recently settled population, which by that time formed the majority, became integrated with the native Tikritis. No historical sources mention any rivalry between these groups, and it seems likely that the threats felt by the Tikritis from external sources may have contributed to a sense of common solidarity among them. A sense of local identity was also a response to the ceaseless external threat posed by the tribes. In a manifestation of mutual responsibility and solidarity, all the local groups took part in necessary defensive activities, such as the maintenance of the walls of the town.[8]

Though Tikrit remained largely isolated, there was a slow and gradual development of its connection to Baghdad. Administratively, Tikrit remained firmly in the *vilayet* of Baghdad.[9] Following the Baghdad flood in 1832, Tikritis, like other people from provincial Sunni towns, started migrating to parts on the western bank of the Tigris river, establishing their own quarters. In these quarters, the migrants preserved regional identity away from their hometown and ensured its survival in the big city environment.[10]

---

7   Zeidel, 'Tikrit and the Tikritis', pp. 34–45; James Felix Jones, *Memoirs of Commander James Felix Jones*, Bombay: Bombay National Education Press, 1857, p. 22; John F. Williamson, 'A Political history of the Shammar Jarba Tribe of Al Jazira', unpublished Ph.D. thesis, Indiana University, 1975, pp. 46, 62 and 99–101.

8   Zeidel, 'Tikrit and the Tikritis', p. 34.

9   Fadil Mahdi Bayat, Tikrit, p. 61.

10   Anwar al-Nasiri, *Suq al-jadid*, Baghdad: Dar al-Shu'un al-Thaqafiyya, 1997, vol. 1, p. 18; Jamal Haydar, Baghdad: *Malamih madina fi dhakirat al-sittinat*, Beirut: Al-Markaz al-Thaqafi al-'Arabi, 2002, p. 30; Muzahim al-'Ani, 'Tarikh al-hijra al-kharijiyya fi madinat tikrit', *Mawsu'at madinat tikrit*, vol. 4, p. 248.

The beginning of the twentieth century was a period of unrest throughout the Ottoman Empire. In Tikrit, this unrest reached its pinnacle with the revolt of the Begat branch of the Albu Nasir tribe in 1908–1909. Its violent repression by the authorities had a profound impact on the local population, regardless of tribal affiliation.[11] This was partly why Tikrit, unlike neighbouring Samarra, would abstain from rebellious political activities at later junctures.

During World War I, Tikrit in 1918 became the arena of a battle between the advancing British army and the withdrawing Ottomans. The British laid siege to the town, causing starvation and famine. Both sides used artillery to bombard Tikrit. To the local population, the consequences were severe. Not only was the commercial town of Tikrit cut off from its food supply in the rural areas, but many of its men were forcefully recruited to the Ottoman army to serve in far-away places, where they would suffer from the abuse of Turkish officers. Many died in distant lands. It is unsurprising that the Tikritis should remember the war as a period of famine, destruction and forced recruitment. In general, the Tikritis maintained a neutral attitude to the confrontation surrounding them, but in the end the situation became so desperate that they petitioned the British to occupy their town. The British takeover took place on 12 July 1918.[12]

Tikrit regional identity

Every person's identity is layered. Only the circumstances of life dictate which layer of identity will be emphasised. The Tikriti—a man or a woman born in or originating from Tikrit and its environs—is simultaneously a member of a family, a tribe, a regional community, a sect (Sunni), a state (Iraq), a linguistic community (Arabic-speak-

---

11 Zeidel, 'Tikrit and the Tikritis', pp. 42–5; 'Abd al-'Aziz al-Qassab, *Min dhikrayati*, Beirut: 'Awaydat, 1962, pp. 57–60.

12 Zeidel, 'Tikrit and the Tikritis', pp. 49–53; Hashim Salih al-Tikriti, 'Al-ihtilal al-baritani li-al-tikrit', *Mawsu'at madinat tikrit*, vol. 4, p. 90; E.J. Thompson, *Beyond Baghdad with the Leicestershire*, London: Epworth, 1919, pp. 124–44.

ers) and a religion (Muslim). Frequently, it is others who determine a person's identity: one may prefer to be an Arab or a Muslim, but to others one would be, first and foremost, a Tikriti. Individuals may react differently to this sort of ascription: some may take offence at a 'parochial' label; others may develop pride in their regional identity, including its 'controversial' content.

In Middle Eastern societies, as in other traditional societies, there is a strong connection between individual and collective identities. Moreover, the identities of the collective may have a strong influence over the individual. Regional identity is shaped by primary elements such as local nature, as well as the unique ecology, geography, culture and history of the region involved. Additionally, other factors such as local administration or the attitude of other collectives may play an important role in the formation of regional identity.

In Iraq, regional identity is characteristic of small and medium-sized towns (such as Tikrit, Samarra, Haditha and Ana), whose populations are not made up of a single dominant tribe. Generally, regional identity is stronger in old towns. In villages and tribal or ethnically distinct towns, regional identity is generally subdued by other and stronger identities. Equally, in the big cities (primarily Baghdad, Basra and Mosul) large and diversified populations prevent the intimacy of the small town and create strong social and residential subdivisions like the *mahalla* (urban quarter, especially in the old city, and usually characterised by close neighbourly relations).

Tikrit regional identity, not unlike that of other provincial towns in Iraq, was born out of several factors. Firstly, there was the feebleness of the local tribes, socially detached from the surrounding tribal populations. The second factor was the isolation and remoteness of Tikrit. And thirdly, the ever-lurking threat of an attack by outsiders—whether the tribes, the Ottomans or a foreign invader—played a role. All these factors helped cement regional identity in Tikrit from the eighteenth century and onwards.

Originally, Tikrit regional identity revolved around three key themes: the unique history of Tikrit, including its Christian past;

the town's role as a safe place for weak and small tribes surrounded by a dangerous environment; and, finally, the Tigris river. All of these themes were expressed in local myths and folkloric tales, which helped mould Tikrit regional identity. Through its *diwans* (private social gatherings) and coffee shops, the town inspired a sense of historical pride in its people. One of the most outstanding Tikrit intellectuals in the twentieth century, Jamal al-Din al-Alusi (who moved to Baghdad at the age of fourteen), expressed this feeling:

I knew that Tikrit's uniqueness was the factor which influenced the ancestors and their descendants to form the authentic identity (*hawiyya*) of the land.

Yet, Alusi's Tikritiness is also tinged with Arab identity:

Arabic was taught in the *katatib* (Koranic elementary schools), the *takaya* (places of Sufi gathering) and in the homes. We learned that the Koran is Arab, that our history is Arab … We learned that from Tikrit because the town was created by Arab destiny.[13]

The Christianity of Tikrit in its early history is sometimes used against the Tikritis.[14] Whereas contemporary writers from Tikrit either claim that Christianity was not deeply rooted in town, or stress the common Arab origins of the Christian Tikritis with the Muslim conquerors, oral culture actually shows pride in this era. On the whole, both oral and written accounts by Tikritis consider the Christian past favourably—a clear manifestation of how attachment to Tikrit and its local heroes could trump what others would see as more politically correct.[15]

The main tribal groups in Tikrit are the 'original' Tikritis (Takarta), the Albu Nasir and the Hadithiyin. The latter are the descendants of

13 Hamid al-Matbaʿi, *Jamal al-din al-alusi*, Baghdad: Wizarat al-Thaqafa, 1987, p. 17.

14 Khalida ʿAbd al-Qahhar, *Sikritirat saddam tatakallam*, Cairo: al-Zahra, 1990, pp. 21–2.

15 Ronen Zeidel, 'Tikriti Regional Identity as Reflected in Two Regional Myths and a Folkloric Tale', *Middle Eastern Studies*, vol. 41, no. 6, November 2005, p. 903.

a merchant from Haditha, a town in western Iraq. In general, these tribes live only in the town of Tikrit proper— quite apart from other tribes in the countryside. Like other populations of small and medium-sized towns in Iraq, they were too weak to defend themselves against the powerful tribes in the area, and therefore were forged into an urban solidarity group by centuries of living within the walls of the same town. External danger helped minimise internal divisions: a 'united we stand, divided we fall' attitude prevails in Tikrit regional myths and in the regional identity derived from them.[16]

Finally, the Tigris river was the main artery connecting Tikrit and the outside world. For a long time, the river was the only relatively safe outlet from Tikrit. Built on a high embankment, Tikrit hardly ever suffered the onslaught of floods. On the contrary, much of the town's agriculture depended on seasonal inundations—which were always celebrated by the Tikritis. Additionally, for centuries Tikritis enjoyed almost a monopoly on the navigation of traditional rafts (*kalaks*), which were manufactured in Tikrit.[17]

However, during the twentieth century all of these factors lost much of their importance or even became totally irrelevant. The Christian population had disappeared. No longer isolated, Tikrit became connected by good roads to all the major urban centres of Iraq. Very few remains of the old town with its wall and citadel survived. The river lost its commercial importance; *kalak*s vanished altogether around the mid-1940s.[18] Thus, these components of Tikrit regional identity were in danger of becoming a matter of the past, urging some Tikritis to preserve them by publishing books and, in 1992, even building a museum dedicated to local traditions.[19] Such meas-

---

16   Ibid., pp. 902–6.

17   Salim Taha al-Tikriti, 'Al-kalak: kayfa yusna' wa-yustakhdam li-al-naql', *al-Turath al-Sha'bi*, no. 11, July–August 1971, pp. 83–7. 'Ata Taha al-Tikriti, 'Al-shatati', *al-Turath al-Sha'bi*, no. 11, 1975, pp. 79–86.

18   Zeidel, 'Tikriti Regional Identity', p. 902.

19   On official Iraqi historiography and Tikrit, including the publication of the five volumes of *Mawsu'at madinat tikrit*, see Zeidel, 'Tikrit and the Tikritis', pp. 5–8 and 'Awni Kamil Sha'ban, 'Al-mufradat al-mi'mariyya li-al-bayt al-turathi

ures were deemed necessary in order to protect the uniqueness of Tikrit, which was seen to be rapidly converting into an 'ordinary' Iraqi town. What actually remained of Tikrit regional identity was its social component: the affinity felt by Tikritis to their town and its people. This solidarity, extending beyond the confines of Tikrit, was to be maintained throughout the twentieth century and would serve the Tikritis in their quest for political supremacy. Whereas preserving the past characteristics of Tikrit identity served a romantic purpose, the social component of Tikrit identity had far more practical aspects: ultimately it solved the problems of an unemployment-stricken town. A lot of secrecy was to envelope the Tikrit regional connection. Prominent Tikritis, including Saddam Hussein, would try to hush insinuations about their regional origins.[20] Apparently, to some, like former Baathist president Ahmad Hasan al-Bakr, this was unimportant; others, however, felt ideological uneasiness in relation to this sort of parochialism because Baathist ideology repeatedly condemned regionalism (*iqlimiyya*).[21] A more important reason for discretion was the practical need to defy non-Tikriti opposition and therefore to nominate Tikritis to positions of power. Thus, regional identity was an element of major importance behind Tikrit dominance, but this would only seldom be publicly acknowledged.

The rise of the Tikritis during the twentieth century

Like most other Sunni areas, Tikrit was peaceful during the 1920 rebellion—but in the case of Tikrit, the reason was not the collaboration with the British of a powerful local tribal sheikh. Rather, this was a result of the Tikritis' traditional reticence from involvement in

---

fi tikrit', *Mawsu'at madinat tikrit*, vol. 5, 1998, p. 183.

20 Fu'ad Matar, *Saddam husayn: al-rajul, al-qadiyya, al-mustaqbal*, Beirut: Dar al-Qadaya, 1980, p. 94.

21 See the constitution of the Baath party in Sylvia Haim (ed.), *Arab Nationalism: An Anthology*, second edition, Berkeley: University of California Press, 1976, p. 236.

belligerent acts, in combination with a genuine fascination by them for the efficiency of the new administration. The Tikritis, reportedly, 'saw the difference between [the British political officer in Tikrit] and the Turks'. Shortly after taking Tikrit, the British cleaned the town from rubble and established a municipality, headed by a local man. British military bases in the area supplied much-needed employment opportunities. In their attempt to protect transportation, the British attacked the nomadic tribes, driving them away from Tikrit and thereby bringing an end to the tribal stranglehold. The British also developed the railway and the road system and thus helped end Tikrit's isolation.[22]

In general, the townspeople reacted favourably to these new signs of modernisation introduced by the British and the newly formed Iraqi state. In September 1918, only two months after the occupation, the British opened the first public primary school in the history of Tikrit. Despite the relatively high entry-level requirements and the intense competition with the local Koranic schools, enrolment was high and some locals even demanded that it be further developed to include more advanced levels of teaching. During the course of time the school did expand, enabling its teachers to send the best students to Baghdad where they could continue their education. In the biographies of Tikritis who rose to prominence, this primary school is usually mentioned as the first stage of their careers. To the children, local teachers were sources of imitation and even admiration.[23]

The increasing accessibility and growing importance of Baghdad brought many job-seeking Tikritis to the Iraqi capital. To these educated Tikritis, two venues for promotion existed: the ministry of education and the army. Fortunately for them, in those two state

---

22 Zeidel, 'Tikrit and the Tikritis', pp. 53–65; Salim Taha al-Tikriti , 'Safahat majhula min thawrat al-'ashrin', *Afaq 'Arabiyya*, June 1982, p. 19; 'Usama 'Abd al-Rahman al-Duri, 'Al-idara al-baritaniyya fi tikrit 1918–1920', *Mawsu'at madinat tikrit*, vol. 3, p. 112.

23 'Abd al-Majid Kamil al-Tikriti, 'Tikrit khilal fatrat al-intidab al-baritani 'ala al-'iraq', *Mawsu'at madinat tikrit*, vol. 4, p. 124; 'Usama 'Abd al-Rahman al-Duri, 'Al-idara al-barritaniyya…', pp. 117–18.

institutions there were already influential Tikritis in leading positions, who, inspired by regional solidarity, strove to promote their townsmen. One of them, Yusuf Izz al-Din al-Nasiri, was in the 1920s inspector of the ministry of education in Baghdad and later the director of the capital's teachers' seminar and of the main high school there. As such, he was in a position to attract young Tikritis into the ranks of the ministry and was able to make sure that they were given proper teaching jobs either in Baghdad or in Tikrit.[24]

Mawlud Mukhlis Pasha is the name often mentioned in association with the promotion of Tikritis through the ranks of the army. Mukhlis was born in Mosul to a family of Tikrit origins. Interestingly, for most of his youth his regional identity was connected to Mosul, fitting well with his vocation as a military officer (Mosul was known as a city of military officers). Mukhlis started World War I as an Ottoman officer, but, after being taken prisoner by the British, became a loyal officer in the Sharifian army and took an active part in the Arab rebellion of 1916. In 1922, one year after the coronation of Faysal as king of Iraq, he returned to his homeland and received a hero's reception in Tikrit. Later, he was given agricultural lands near Tikrit and, like other Sharifian officers, embarked upon a political career—at the apex of which he became president of the Iraqi senate. Mukhlis, who was at odds with most of his military colleagues, was very close to the royal family. His political career started to wane after the May 1941 coup d'état—in which he did not take part. In the second half of his life Mukhlis, the Mosuli, was behaving like the perfect Tikriti. Presumably, his self-importance grew more easily in Tikrit than in Mosul, where some of his rivals also had connections. Mukhlis attained the status of local dignitary, helping the people of his town by mediating with the government. Though he was not the only military officer from Tikrit during the 1920s and the 1930s, he

---

24 Zeidel, 'Tikrit and the Tikritis', pp. 210–12; Shakir 'Ali al-Tikriti, *Mudhakkirati wa-dhikrayati*, Baghdad: Wizarat al-Thaqafa, 1997, vol. 1, p. 25; *The Iraq Directory 1936*, Baghdad: Dangoor, 1936, p. 607.

certainly was more active than others in motivating young Tikritis to join the military academy.[25]

In the 1930s and 1940s, these young Tikritis were teachers or junior officers. During the second half of the 1930s, with the increasing prestige of the military, some teachers from Tikrit joined the military academy to become high-ranking officers; among them were some who would later rise to political prominence through the military ranks including Tahir Yahya (prime minister in the 1960s) and Ahmad Hasan al-Bakr (president 1968–1979).[26] Though the Tikritis were still far from positions of power, and their hometown remained distant from the centre (despite its administrative promotion to a provincial sub-division or *qada* in 1951),[27] something basic changed in the attitude of the Tikritis toward the Iraqi state and its government between the 1930s and the 1950s. Basically, a feeling that the state could be beneficial was beginning to take root. Throughout that period the town was gradually developing and its periphery became safer than ever before. There came more employment opportunities, both in the surrounding area as well as in Baghdad. People like Mawlud Mukhlis and Yusuf al-Nasiri maintained connections with the central government. Consequently, a positive dialogue was beginning to take shape between the Tikritis and the state. Importantly, the two venues through which the Tikritis made their way forward—the ministry of education and the army—were also the foremost standard bearers of Iraqi and Arab nationalism in the new state. By integrating into those institutions, the young gen-

25 Zeidel, 'Tikrit and the Tikritis', pp. 203–10; Salim Taha al-Tikriti, *Mawlud mukhlis*, Baghdad: Al-Dar al-'Arabiyya, 1990, pp. 10–13; Muhammad Husayn al-Zubaydi, *Mawlud mukhlis basha wa-dawruhu fi al-thawra al-'arabiyya al-kubra wa-fi tarikh al-'iraq al-mu'asir*, Baghdad: al-Huriyya, 1989, pp. 11, 48 and 199–201.

26 A table of Tikriti graduates of the military academy is provided in Zeidel, 'Tikrit and the Tikritis', pp. 209–10.

27 'Amir al-Kubaysi, 'Safahat min al-tarikh al-idari al-mu'asir li-madinat tikrit', *Mawsu'at madinat tikrit*, vol. 5, p. 38.

eration of Tikritis was imbued with nationalist values and came to identify wholeheartedly with the new state.

To the commissioned Tikritis in the Iraqi army—the most senior of whom were still only middle-ranking officers—the revolution of 14 July 1958 marked a great jump forward. In post-revolutionary politics, these officers supported Abd al-Karim Qasim's rival, Abd al-Salam Arif, and began courting the underground Baath party. Turbulent national politics penetrated the otherwise peaceful Tikrit: street riots between communists and Baathists became a common event.[28] However, from that time on, events in Tikrit itself would be of less importance to the Tikritis' ascendancy.

With the Baathist coup d'état of February 1963, officers from Tikrit came closer than ever to positions of power. Ahmad Hasan al-Bakr, an officer and a Tikriti of the Albu Nasir tribe became the first Tikriti to serve as prime minister of Iraq. In a party conference on 11 November 1963, only days before the downfall of the first Baathist regime, military officers conducted a putsch leading to the election of a new party leadership. Three out of its sixteen members were Tikrit army officers.[29] Thus, the Tikritis were beginning to control the Baath party. The ensuing downfall of the regime did not deter the Tikritis. Indeed, some of them were among the instigators of the November coup.

Nevertheless, in January 1964 there was a schism among the Tikritis collaborating with Abd al-Salam Arif: whereas two of them (Tahir Yahya and Rashid Muslih) remained in his government where they held the positions of prime minister and minister of interior, the other two (Ahmad Hasan al-Bakr and Hardan al-Tikriti) resumed

---

28 Ja'far 'Abbas Humaydi, Ghazi Faysal al-Rawi and Khudayr Hasan Salman, 'Dawr tikrit fi al-tatawwurat al-siyasiyya fi al-'iraq, 1958–1963', *Mawsu'at madinat tikrit*, vol. 4, pp. 167–9; Ibrahim al-Zubaydi, *Dawlat al-idha'a*, London: Al-Hikma, 2003, pp. 68–70.

29 Zeidel, 'Tikrit and the Tikritis', pp. 249–50. 'Ali Karim Sa'id, *'Iraq 8 shubat 1963*, Beirut: Al-Kunuz, 1999, pp. 328 and 330; Hani al-Fukayki, *Awkar al-hazima: tajribati fi hizb al-ba'th al-'iraqi*, London: Al-Rayyes, 1993, pp. 347–52.

their Baathist activities. At this point, regional cohesion could have suffered a fatal blow. Yet, the Tikritis in the underground had exploited regional solidarity in a masterful way. Bakr and, to an even greater extent, the young Saddam Hussein used their regional connections to the other two Tikritis in power in order to gain privileges: getting hold of information, obtaining shelter when they needed it, or improving conditions in prison and sometimes even securing release from jail. In this way, they were able to reorganise the Baath party for a second takeover on 17 July 1968. Regional solidarities, however, did not save Muslih, Yahya and Hardan al-Tikriti from their premature death under the second Baathist regime.[30]

The Tikritis were not the first ones to exploit regional ties in order to dominate the Iraqi regime. Under Abd al-Salam Arif (president from 1963 to 1966) and his brother Abd al-Rahman Arif (1966–1968), military officers from western Iraq filled most of the sensitive positions in the military and in government. There were other regional blocs in the army (such as the Mosulis), but these were wiped out following abortive coups. After the disastrous results of a failed coup attempt in January 1964, officers from Tikrit avoided participation in premature coups, concentrating instead on the preparation of their own putsch—which finally took place in July 1968. Needless to say, once in power, the Tikritis disbanded all the other regional groups in the army and elsewhere, starting with their fellow Sunni officers from western Iraq.

Between 1968 and 1974 the Iraqi leadership was torn by infighting between the military and the civilian wings of the Baath party. Tikritis participated on both sides of the confrontation line, but more were in the military wing. The elimination of prominent military officers from Tikrit at the instigation of another Tikriti, Saddam Hussein (who headed the civilian wing of the Baath), was the first serious blow

---

30 Zeidel, 'Tikrit and the Tikritis', pp. 251–4; 'Abd al-Karim Farhan, *Hisad thawra: mudhakkirat tajribat al-sulta fi al-'iraq*, second edition, Damascus: Al-Buraq, 1996, pp. 164 and 167; Jalil al-'Atiyya, *Funduq al-sa'ada: hikayat min 'iraq saddam husayn*, London: Al-Hikma, 1993, p. 225.

to Tikrit regional solidarity. Eventually, with the final victory of the civilian wing, Iraq came under the rule of two Tikritis from the Albu Nasir tribe, Ahmad Hasan al-Bakr and his powerful deputy, Saddam Hussein. This confrontation also signalled the rise of another generation of Tikritis: younger civilians, mainly from the Albu Nasir tribe, rising from the ranks of the expanding security services.

When Saddam Hussein became president in July 1979, the old guard of Tikrit officers was completely replaced by the younger generation represented by Saddam and his relatives. Though never a numerical majority in any of the governmental institutions, Tikritis controlled all the most sensitive positions in the state, thereby assuring the stability of the regime. Tikritis originating in the security apparatus took control of the army, the party and key cabinet ministries. Tikrit's dominance at the national level was now also beginning to make an impact in Tikrit itself: in 1976, the town was made the centre of a vast governorate—Salah al-Din— whose territories were mainly annexed from the Baghdad governorate. For the population in Tikrit, this meant more jobs. In the 1980s and even more so in the 1990s, the town became the centre of a personality cult around the figure of Saddam Hussein.[31]

After the Gulf War and the repression of the subsequent Shiite-dominated *intifada* uprising in 1991, Tikritis from the Albu Nasir tribe attained the peak of their influence. They exploited the growing fragility and weakness of the regime to increase their influence not only in the political field, but also in other associated activities, like commerce. Having saved the regime from an imminent collapse, they were quick to seek the dividends. Despite decadence, corruption and chronic infighting (reaching its peak with the escape and later the elimination of Saddam Hussein's in-laws in February 1996), no new 'Tikrit-led' change of government occurred, even if the United States at one point were actively encouraging precisely that kind of

---

31 Zeidel, 'Tikrit and the Tikritis', pp. 101–6; Kubaysi, 'Safahat', p. 42.

scenario.[32] Therefore, there was almost no change in the pattern of Albu Nasir dominance until the downfall of the regime in 2003.

Paradoxically, post-1968 dominance by Tikritis was a bad omen for Tikrit regional solidarity. When Mawlud Mukhlis and Yusuf Izz al-Din al-Nasiri promoted Tikritis, they had been doing so regardless of tribal affiliations. On the other hand, Saddam Hussein, who from the time of his childhood had resented the townsmen, always preferred his tribesmen, and acted accordingly. Regional solidarity may have helped the Tikritis attain political dominance, but now it was gradually being replaced by tribal solidarity. Throughout their thirty-five years in power the Albu Nasir managed to alienate all other tribal groups who once formed the Tikrit regional community: First, the Takarta (with the assassination of Hardan al-Tikriti in 1970); later the Hadithiyin, following the killing of some prominent members of that group in the 1990s. Internal feuds even alienated some other branches of the Albu Nasir, further narrowing the support base of the regime.

Despite all these developments, there was growing alignment between the Tikrit regional community and the Iraqi regime in the 1990s. This was partly due to the external identification of the regime as 'Tikriti'. In response, the regional community aligned itself with the regime. Tikritiness may have been a nuisance in the eyes of some, but regardless of attitudes toward the government, the local community in Tikrit would reassert its pride in its regional identity. Another reason for this alignment was the growing dependence of Tikritis on the state for employment: under the Baath, according to official figures, administration accounted for over 50 per cent of the workforce in Tikrit. The Albu Nasir may have controlled the state, but state benefits affected the lives of many in Tikrit.

---

32 A good account of this failed US attempt is given in Andrew Cockburn and Patrick Cockburn, *Out of the Ashes: The Resurrection of Saddam Hussein*, New York: Harper Collins, 1999.

The special circumstances behind the ascendancy of the Tikritis

There was nothing unique in Tikrit regional identity as such. One can find the same regional identity, with its social and cultural aspects, in other similar Iraqi towns. Also, regional solidarity does not withstand every challenge, and was seriously undermined by the underlying tribal solidarity of the Albu Nasir.

Tikrit regional identity and solidarity, then, are historical phenomena, created and changed over time. In order to understand the rise, and eventually the demise, of the Tikritis in the twentieth century, it is essential to analyse these trends in correlation with other processes, mainly Sunni supremacy in the Iraqi state and state formation. Whereas these processes affected the Iraqi population as a whole, it was the effective use of regional solidarity that helped the Tikritis where others failed.

Sunni supremacy long predated the establishment of the Iraqi state. The alignment between the Sunni Arab population and government apparatus under the Ottomans had alienated others (the Shiites) from that apparatus and prepared the Sunnis to fill governmental positions under the British. The tradition of serving in the Ottoman army—particularly strong in Mosul—paved the way to Sunni control of Iraqi army and from there to national politics. The newly formed state-dependent Sunni intelligentsia defined a pan-Arab ideology which was palatable mainly to Sunnis. All this helped the Sunni Arabs compensate for their status as a numerical minority in the new state. Moreover, the preferential attitude accorded to the Sunni minority sometimes limited competition to Sunnis alone, thereby facilitating Sunni chances of getting a job. In short, it was much easier for a Sunni to find employment in the administration than it was for a Shiite or a Kurd.

However, being a Sunni was not enough for social ascendancy through state service. There were other key requirements related to the process of state formation. Education became a precondition for jobs in the civil service. Under the British mandate, schools were built across the country, and their graduates were generally employed by the civil service. In many provincial areas, governmental jobs became a lucrative source of income after the collapse of commerce and agriculture, the two mainstays of the traditional economy.

Urbanisation was another major factor. The Iraqi state was almost exclusively centred on Baghdad. Due to the improvement of transportation, Baghdad was more accessible, even for people from outlying Tikrit. A vibrant hub for migrants, Baghdad received the first wave of Tikritis after the great flood of 1832. Subsequent waves in the twentieth century were accommodated by their long-settled relatives, who greatly facilitated their absorption in Baghdad. Therefore, unlike the rapid migration of rural populations to Baghdad seen during the twentieth century, migration by Tikritis was more gradual. Tikritis moved to Baghdad to continue their education, or to find a better job. Moving to Baghdad had become a crucial precondition to social and political ascendancy: all those who eventually made a successful career moved to the capital at an early age.

In the twentieth century, Iraqi Sunni Arab society underwent a continuous process by which people from small provincial towns settled in Baghdad and started filtering into government institutions. Under the monarchy, one could find many people from western Iraq in the ministry of interior and its subsidiaries: the police, the secret police and the administration of jails. These jobs required minimal education. In populating these institutions, migrants exploited the passivity of the Baghdad elite, who were more interested in the accumulation of material wealth. Tikritis were also part of this process: whereas the few educated Tikritis were now teachers or military officers, many other ordinary Tikritis could be found in the police or the jail administration.

The phenomenon of Tikrit ascendancy was a process of ever narrowing circles. It began with the narrowing of the Ottoman Empire into the confines of the state of Iraq, and continued with the narrowing of political participation in that state to the Sunni Arab minority and the emergence of people from provincial Sunni towns within that minority—eventually narrowing to one particular regional group: the Tikritis. Seen from the Tikrit point of view, however, this was a process of ever widening circles. An isolated and remote town suddenly opened to the wide world around it. Poor and illiterate people were getting access to public education in Tikrit and later in Baghdad. Urban migrants in Baghdad were finding their way to governmental service. After the 1958 revolution, officers and officials from the lower and middle class found their way to the centre stage of Iraqi politics.

The July 1958 revolution brought many people from provincial— mainly Sunni— origins to the forefront. In fact, people from western Iraq preceded the Tikritis in establishing regional recruitment patterns in government—a model which the Tikritis would later imitate and improve. Thus, until the late 1960s , the Tikritis and the people of western Iraq shared the same story, being part of the process of the emergence of Sunnis from provincial areas, within the general framework of Sunni supremacy. However, the story started to bifurcate in the mid-1960s, when the Tikritis, making good use of their caution and regional solidarity, survived purges that affected other regional groups. The cohesion of the political actors of Tikrit stood in stark contrast to the widening schism among the governing group from western Iraq. Possibly, political power weakened and corrupted the people of western Iraq. It is also plausible to assume that the cohesion of a group from a vast province might not be as solid as that of a group from a single town.

In the discussion of the Tikritis under the Baath it is imperative to mention two factors which helped them maintain influence and consolidate their control over the state. The immense oil wealth flowing to the national budget following the 1972 nationalisation of Iraqi oil allowed an expansion of the governmental apparatus, now firmly under the control of Tikritis. As this was not accompanied by any development of alternative sources of financing (and in the absence of a private sector) the government was taking the role of a distributor of goods, thus strengthening the dependency of many groups in Iraqi society on the state. Since the regime gave priority to maintaining its stability, oil wealth was channelled to the expansion of the security services. The process of expanding the security services, using state finances and Tikriti manpower, went on throughout the Baath period. This reinforced the alignment between the regime and the Tikritis who were required to protect other Tikritis in power.

The contribution of a strong personality like Saddam Hussein is more ambiguous. One of the reasons for the diminishing power of the people of the western towns of Iraq was certainly the weak personality of Iraq's president Abd al-Rahman Arif (1966–1968) who hailed from that region. Whereas Saddam's predecessor, Ahmad Hasan al-Bakr, was not interested in running the country on regional lines, Saddam was very much inclined to exploit this model. He consciously built a power base of fellow Tikritis. Undoubtedly, he was a leading figure behind the unprecedented development of Tikrit from the 1970s onwards. Without Saddam Hussein, Tikrit's ascendancy and dominance might just have been a passing episode. Yet, by favouring his tribal group, Saddam also sowed the seeds of dissension, undermining thereby Tikrit regional solidarity. Arguably, Saddam Hussein was more of a nemesis than a benefactor to Tikrit.

Tikrit in the 'New Iraq'

Tikrit regional solidarity did not withstand the US invasion of Iraq in 2003. In general, the Tikritis, including the Albu Nasir tribesmen, opted not to wage a chanceless battle to save Saddam Hussein. Few betrayed their leader; some joined the resistance. The runaway president was hidden by fellow Tikritis from his tribe until his capture. They did not betray him. Yet, another Tikriti from the Albu Nasir betrayed his relatives (Qusay and Uday, the two sons of Saddam Hussein who had taken refuge in this man's house in Mosul), actually causing their death. This was a blatant infringement on tribal norms, hence the tribe declared revenge on this tribesman's extended family.

When the Americans were at the gates of Tikrit in April 2003, the townsmen and local dignitaries resumed their traditional cautiousness and negotiated a surrender with the Americans.[33] The US military established the headquarters of their fourth infantry division in Saddam Hussein's palace in the town's centre, and went on to make their presence there felt day and night. In comparison with other Sunni towns, most noticeably neighbouring Samarra, Tikrit has been relatively peaceful since. This is probably due to the reinforced American presence. Yet, in other places this presence actually encouraged the resistance, so the comparatively placid attitude among the Tikritis may have roots of its own. Tikrit lacks the rebellious tradition of Samarra, the Islamic radicalism of Falluja or the tribal homogeneity of Ramadi. Throughout its history it tried to avoid wars. Apparently, this time is not an exception. At least this facet of regional identity seems timeless.

Somehow, the Tikritis, unlike other Sunnis, must have realised that their time is past. They have completely disappeared from government and not a single Tikriti is now found in the middle ranks of the administration or in its higher echelons. The local administration in Tikrit is staffed by administrators from the Jabbur tribe, which is external to Tikrit. The Tikritis are furious about that. Tikrit remains the official administrative centre of the Salah al-Din governorate which the Baathists had created during their heyday. Possibly, the new government was unwilling to further infuriate the Sunnis by changing the status quo. Or, the government may lack the finances required to move the centre of the province, or it simply feels comfortable with the situation in and around Tikrit. At any rate, this pre-eminent status as an administrative centre is all that remains to Tikrit from the former period.

In their effort to restart normal life in post-Saddam Iraq, the Tikritis face the de-Baathification committees. These committees have the capacity to blacklist people who worked and served the former regime. Those on the blacklists are barred from finding work in government. Naturally, Tikrit is more affected than any other place in Iraq; official figures claim that 50 per cent of the workforce was on

---

33 Al-Jazeera television, 13 and 14 April 2003.

the former regime's payroll whereas unofficial claims put the figure as high as 70 per cent.[34] Apparently, regional identity in Tikrit has now given way to a non-territorial, confessional Sunni identity. Like most other Sunnis, the Tikritis boycotted the January 2005 elections, voted 'no' in the plebiscite on the constitution in October 2005, and voted for Sunni parties in the December 2005 elections. Though not taking an active part in the resistance, many Tikritis support it.

It is interesting to compare the previous ascendancy and predominance of the Tikritis with another regional bloc that seems to be dominating Sunni politics at present: the Fallujis. Unlike the Tikritis whose rise to power was the result of state formation processes within the framework of Sunni supremacy, the current ascendancy of Fallujis has a different background. Prominent Falluja politicians (members of parliament, leaders of political parties and clerics) progressed from the ranks of the religious world and the resistance, in addition to those who had ties to the former regime. Some have their origins in the tribal world, particularly the Zawbaa tribe. Their rise is associated with the special status of Falluja, 'the cradle of the resistance', and not with the development and reform of the Iraqi state. The whole process occurs in the context of renegotiation of political power-sharing, rather than in the context of state formation. Most important of all, Sunni supremacy has now vanished. Falluja politicians act within the precinct of Sunni politics: politics based on overt confessional identity, striving to amplify and empower the Sunni community. As such, they may not attach great importance to their own regional origin. With Sunni supremacy gone and national politics moving on confessional lines, the chances that they will ever repeat Tikrit's success seem rather slim.

Conclusions

As a project of exploiting regional solidarity ties, the case of Tikrit may have been the most successful example so far in Iraqi history.

---

34 *Al-Sharq al-Awsat*, 2 August 2005.

However, from every perspective, this was a truly unique interaction unlikely to ever be repeated in precisely the same manner. The two main prerequisites for its success are now gone. Sunni supremacy no longer exists. Today, recruitment to government positions takes place on the basis of membership in political parties that are often defined in confessional or ethnic terms.

In times like these, Tikritis may prefer to emphasise different layers in their identity, mainly the Sunni, Iraqi and Muslim ones. Their regional identity still persists though. It is expressed when they want to be left alone, cautiously avoiding confrontation with the Americans and the government. At other times it is expressed when they demonstrate, supporting Saddam Hussein. These demonstrations—which are often covered in the international media and which take place almost exclusively in Tikrit—are probably more about reasserting regional pride than genuine expressions of love or even yearning for the deposed president. The problem is that they serve to further alienate the Tikritis from other Iraqis.

Tikrit's ascendancy and later domination in the second half of the twentieth century was accompanied by cruel repression of other groups, the elimination of any sign of pluralism in society and politics, and the imposition of a tyrannical hierarchy – headed by the president and his security services. It all ended with tribal oligarchy, torn by incessant feuds. There is no reason to believe that any non-Tikriti Iraqi should wish to see the restoration of anything remotely resembling that.

Tainted as it may be by its association with the former regime, Tikrit regional identity should not necessarily be dismissed as a harmful force. It was only its transfer to the realm of political domination that paved the way for Saddam Hussein's dictatorship. Its cultural contents—such as history and folklore—may well come to serve a more constructive purpose in the future, for instance as a basis for regional development projects and tourism that can provide employment and much-needed finances to the region. Such a project should also be sustainable, saving the town from an imminent decay in the foreseeable future. The European model of decentralised regional development of tourism may be a useful one. Unfortunately, in the harsh circumstances of contemporary Iraq, this seems like a distant dream.

5

MOSUL, THE JAZIRA REGION AND THE SYRIAN–IRAQI BORDERLANDS

James Denselow

This chapter will examine the region in Iraq arguably most influenced by transnational trends that have created a sense of cross-border identity inextricably linked to the international and regional politics of both Syria and Turkey. It examines the region of Jazira and the city of Mosul in a historical perspective from the birth of the modern state system in the Middle East and the impact of the creation of state boundaries that were unable to match the nascent emerging 'nations' of the early twentieth century. It is this mismatch that has led to the development of a certain degree of autonomy, both in terms of politics and identity, in this little studied corner of Iraq.

The chapter argues that a hugely ambitious but strategically flawed US policy towards Iraq has led to a deeply fragmented political entity with a plethora of local factors shaping regional dynamics following the 2003 invasion. The autonomy of identity should not be confused with ideas of separatism or willing difference: instead the balance of politics, identity and security have created a distinct milieu that varies between urban Mosul, Iraq's third city, the surrounding urban settlements, the rural periphery and along the border with Syria. Indeed this chapter argues that the inhabitants of this area of Iraq represent an identity that historically has been denied through the initial history of colonial boundary delimitation which split common bonds. Subsequently, this regional identity was challenged by a growth of Iraqi and Syrian nationalisms, only to be put into a limelight of security concerns following the 2003 invasion and the subsequent Iraqi insurgency.

Al-Jazira ('the island') in modern geographic terms describes the area that from west to east covers eastern Syria between the Euphrates and Tigris rivers, carrying across into Iraq where the Jazira eventually ends north of the Baghdad area. Overlying the traditional geographic description of an area that was so dependent on the irrigation flows of its rivers are the internal administrative boundaries of Syria and Iraq now separated by an international boundary: In Syria the Jazira is cut into three (Raqqa, Hasaka and Dayr al-Zur governorates); in Iraq the corresponding area cuts through part of Anbar, much of Salah al-Din, and encompassing the entirety of Nineveh governorate.

The Syrian–Iraqi borderlands

Borders provide one key element in the structure of the global system: mapping the number and arrangement of the territorial units upon which all humans live. Borders permit a spatial approach to international or global politics by setting out the location of states and their absolute and relative distances from each other. Borders act as factors of constraint on human interaction, as well as factors that facilitate human interaction. Borders have significant effects on international politics, both by their presence and by their meaning to humans.[1]

Borders and their surrounding borderlands represent a unique geopolitical space within the territorial state system that characterises the globe today. Arguably the most influential legacy of Western imperialism in the Middle East, the territorial nation-state represents a modern-day global framework for existence that fundamentally shapes peoples identities. Yet such a system of bordered lands equating to the limits of sovereignty and national identity—whether legitimate or not—is a product of modernity. Its current hegemonic status alone cannot guarantee its permanency in the future. Indeed, the secessions of East Timor and Eritrea along with the disintegra-

---

1 H. Starr, 'International Borders: What Are They, What They Mean, and Why We Should Care', *SAIS Review*, no. 1, Winter–Spring 2006.

tion of the former Yugoslavia are but three examples of a world in which the permanency of the territorial state has been challenged from within. The emergence of a fracturing civil war in Iraq has proved that if Iraq can be 'invented' as a territorial state, as Toby Dodge has argued,[2] it can equally so be disassembled and rebuilt by the actions of stronger state powers.

Of critical importance in explaining the disconnect between US plans (or lack thereof) and Iraqi reality is what Eric Herring and Glen Rangwala[3] argue is the distinction between 'state building' and 'state formation'. While state building is a conscious programme of organised development, state formation is its reality in practice, where unintended consequences tend to dominate as conflicting state-building strategies and other interests often clash with each other. Despite this kind of disconnect—and with the concomitant reality of state fragmentation and increased regionalism in contemporary Iraq— all parties, internal and external, agree on the territorial unity of the country's external borders. Such a continued stress on national unity is made clear in the Iraqi constitution passed in October 2005, with its preamble to 'preserve the unity of their homeland in a spirit of fraternity and solidarity in order to draw the features of the future new Iraq'.

Indeed Iraq provides an excellent regional focus for the question of the permanency of the territorial state—as a case in which the Western state system was directly imposed through colonialism on a region, and as an area of study where indigenous factors are seen as inherently contradictory to the state system and can be seen to create a 'colonial/indigenous mix'.[4] Of special concern to policymakers in Washington, Damascus and Baghdad alike is the periphery that is

---

2 Toby Dodge, *Inventing Iraq: The Failure of Nation Building and a History Denied*, London: Hurst, 2003.

3 Eric Herring, Eric and Glen Rangwala, *Iraq in Fragments: The Occupation and Its Legacy*, London: Hurst, 2006.

4 Nazih N. Ayubi, *Over-Stating the Arab State: Politics and Society in the Middle East*, London : I.B. Tauris, 1995.

the Syrian–Iraqi border region. This region is today suffering from a crisis of identity born of its inability to fit neatly into a simple ethno-religious framework loosely imposed on the vacuum that came with the final destruction of the Iraqi institutions of state after twenty-two days of war in 2003. It is peripheral from Mosul, which in due turn is peripheral from Baghdad—within which operates what has come to be known as the democratically elected constitutional government of the 'Green Zone' that highlights a state peripheral to an increasingly fragmented Iraqi society.

In its recent history, stemming from the creation of the Iraqi and Syrian states in 1920, no political frontiers, in the European sense of the word, have existed between the two countries that were roughly carved out of the Ottoman Empire. Ease of access across and a diluting of bounded regional sentiment therefore has not only been possible, it has been inevitable. However, border function change mirrors changes in political relationships. We cannot therefore hope to understand the border in a political vacuum. Instead, the reason for the Jazira region's identity crisis lies in the fallout from the 2003 invasion of Iraq and the subsequent disintegration and rebuilding of the Iraqi state. The blame game for the security situation in Iraq has placed enormous pressure on a beleaguered Syria—already facing a shopping list of US complaints—even though it is widely accepted that the foreign fighters who have come to Iraq comprise less than 2,000 in an Iraqi insurgency between 40,000 and 60,000 strong.

During Ottoman times, desert regions such as the Syrian–Iraqi borderland tended to favour tribal autonomy. Mobile, nomadic communities like the Shammar tribe of old, are by their very nature more inclined and able to resist or evade central government. The Ottoman Empire never had more than nominal control over its Arabian subjects, and was never able to collect taxes systematically from desert nomads. Similarly, following World War I, the Arab Syrian government was able to maintain only a thin veneer of authority outside Damascus.

After the Paris peace conference (1919) and the implementation of French and British mandates in the region, the Iraq–Syria boundary was initially defined in a Franco-British convention in December 1920 on certain points connected to the mandates for Syria and Mesopotamia. In 1932, final delimitation details were settled in the League of Nations 'Report of the Commission Entrusted by the Council with the Study of the Frontier between Syria and Iraq'. The carve-up of greater Syria (which also had extensions southwards towards modern Transjordan, and westwards towards Lebanon) caused a fundamental absence of legitimacy in the country's territorial parameters. The Iraq–Syria boundary was an overtly artificial colonial imposition across the Jazira region at a peripheral geo-strategic location vis-à-vis Damascus and Baghdad, the two centres of state power. Both states used tribal proxies to preserve order at the borderland. The emergence of Baathist Arab nationalists from the ashes of colonial rule did not hugely alter this form of relationship. Border areas proved relatively infertile ground for the Baath. Tribal sheikhs continued to play real leadership roles in the community, allowing their co-option to the state in exchange for increased levels of autonomy.

Academic commentators have said that no two Arab states have enjoyed as poor relations as Syria and Iraq. This rather paradoxical conflict between two pan-Arab states lasted from 1968 all the way into the mid-1990s. It witnessed cyclical periods of consolidation and conflict over regional influence and resources. Both sides supported proxies in the other's territory. In the 1980s, Syria backed the Kurdistan Democratic Party (KDP) and the Patriotic Union of Kurdistan (PUK), while Iraq supported the underground opposition Muslim Brotherhood in Syria and backed General Aoun and the Maronites in Lebanon. The states used posturing at the border, arguing over Euphrates water resources and transit costs of Iraqi oil, and at times moved large troop numbers to their respective frontiers. Saddam Hussein was conscious of the divided loyalties of the borderland inhabitants. Having fled across the border in 1959 following

103

the attempted assassination of General Qasim, he knew the border area well. It is reported that in the late 1970s, when Hafiz al-Asad visited Baghdad during a short-lived period of improved bilateral ties, Saddam Hussein enquired about the condition of 'his people in the Jazira'. However, neither state fundamentally altered the peripheral autonomy in terms of the society, economics and movement which existed at the borderland between them. Syrian officials have wryly pointed out that in the 1980s they were unable to stop Saddam Hussein's truck bombs entering from Iraq, and if they could not protect themselves, then what makes Washington think that they can protect Iraq?[5]

The boundary itself is around 600 kilometres in length, stretching from the Turkish to the Jordanian tripoints. Yet since the boundary's creation, it has never existed as a true zone of separation, despite the woeful relations between the two states. As observed by a number of regional tribal leaders, 97 per cent of residents in Syria's eastern provinces have relatives in Iraq;[6] this is of critical importance in understanding the connections between the respective national peripheries in existence in the Jazira area. The family connections are most viscerally explained through a tribal outlook, although the building of the respective states and the settling of the Arab Bedouin communities has affected radical change of this mode of life—regulating it to an important identity, but one that still sits below, for a number of reasons, the people's nationality. However, in light of the essentialist outlook that is often seen as the only means by which to understand post-2003 Iraqi society, the views of Syrian tribal leaders provide interesting insights. In an interview in 2006, Sheikh 'Adi Mazar al-Madlul, a leader of the Shammar, Syria's largest Arab tribe, outlined how religious identity is not as important as blood connections: 'We are Sunni here in Syria, but some of our relatives in Iraq are Shiites.'

5 Interview with Syrian official, July 2005.
6 Interviews with tribal leaders in the Jazira region, 2005–6.

He later went on to describe how he saw the war in Iraq as 'political, not tribal'.[7]

Before the 2003 invasion, a black market economy, largely based on oil, existed across the border mainly between Aleppo and Mosul, setting up a network whose annual worth amounted to at least $2 billion. This gave the local economy a distinct structure born from historic cross-border relations. Although today's illegal trade is a fraction of pre-war times it still keeps afloat a desperately poor local economy, where people earning $10 a month are easily tempted into smuggling people across into Iraq.[8] To fundamentally alter the dynamics of such a border requires a long-term policy with a cornerstone of communication between the respective sides. However, today such communication is glaring in its absence. At a 2005 conference in Jordan concerning Iraqi border security, the US Secretary of Defence Donald Rumsfeld personally vetoed the attendance of a Syrian (as well as an Iranian) delegation. At a tactical level there is a complete absence of communication between the Syrian and US/Iraqi border patrol. Syrians bemoan this fact. In the words of President Bashar al-Asad: 'Who to co-operate with? If you go to the border there are Syrian guards on our side. But if you look at the Iraqi side there is nobody.'[9] Certainly it seems as if the Iraqis are another one and a half to two years away from total border guard deployment following Paul Bremer's ill-fated decision to disband the Iraqi armed forces, including a 35,000 strong border guard.

Transnational trends and a history of boundary building

Despite internal divisions and the persisting challenge from civil conflict, the continued territorial integrity of Iraq following the US

---

7 Interview September 2006.

8 CSIS estimated Saudis crossing the border to be willing to pay thousands of dollars; CSIS, 'Saudi Militants in Iraq: Assessment and Kingdom's Response', 19 September 2005.

9 President Asad speech, 5 March 2005, from the official Syrian news agency website at http://www.sana.org.

invasion in 2003 and the subsequent disintegration and rebuilding of the state is a testimony to both the hegemony of the territorial state system in the present international order, as well as its imperfect reality in practice.

Such continued territorial integrity is accepted by all of Iraq's six neighbouring states, none of whom wishes to redraw the colonial lines that demarcated their zones of national sovereignty. However, what is also clear is that, since 2003, the nascent Iraqi state has had neither the ability nor the uncontested desire to exercise unchallenged sovereignty within its borders. Yet whilst no state today may wish to alter the Anglo-French Sykes–Picot Agreement of 1916 and its fundamental axiom of east/west separation between Iraq and Syria, the history of sovereignty in the region following colonial rule has shown numerous cases of state interference in neighbouring states; whether through war (Arab–Israeli wars 1948, 1967 and 1973; the Iran–Iraq conflict 1980–8), attempted annexation (Iraq versus Kuwait, 1990), or the use of proxies as a means of pursuing political agendas (cyclical usage of Kurdish groups; the proxy battles of the Lebanese civil war).

The nature of territorial state order in the Middle East was shaped by Anglo-French treaties which carved up the region in the early part of the twentieth century, creating initially weak and unstable states which lacked legitimacy and had frontiers that were 'arbitrary, illogical and unjust, giving rise to powerful irredentist tendencies'.[10] Whilst in some cases these tendencies would give rise to conflict concerning the exact position of borders (Iran–Iraq and the Shatt al-Arab) or wider territories (Iraq/Kuwait, Israel/Palestine), the Syrian–Iraqi border has been subject to strategic functional disputes (over migration, trade, border security, oil and Euphrates water resources) as well as revolutionary disputes (concerning the competition for Baathist pan-Arab state legitimacy). The dispute over regime legitimacy, despite occurring in states with little or no history of democratic politics based on the rule of law, is evidence of the challenge facing

---

10 Avi Shlaim, *The Iron Wall: Israel and the Arab World*, London: Allen Lane, 2000.

externally created states in imposing sovereignty over a population within arbitrarily imposed national borders. This struggle lies at the heart of understanding the development of the political systems that have evolved in the Nineveh governorate and in the Jazira area in proximity to the international border. What this chapter proposes is that despite inter-state relations being characterised by animosity and various forms of political rivalry, the borderland milieu in the area surrounding the international border that separates the two countries displays both local and supra-state characteristics of its own.

The peripheral geographical location of the Syria–Iraq borderland has posed a continued challenge and a dilemma for both states in terms of their ability to integrate their respective populations horizontally. The long desert border stretches over 600 kilometres, and is a perfect reflection of the European-derived model of the territorially limited 'ethnically homogenous nation-state'[11] not suiting the realities on the ground. Along the border, people migrate regularly across a line that was determined between 1918 and 1920, when Iraqi officers serving in the Syrian army brought about the annexation of Dayr al-Zur (originally designated for British-occupied Iraq) to King Faysal's Arab government in Syria.[12] Across the Euphrates section are members of the Dulaym tribal confederation, which includes the tribes of Albu Nimr, al-Mahamda, al-Falahat, Albu Fahad, Albu Dhiyab, Albu Issa, al-Karabila and Albu Assaf. Heading north the borderland divides the large Shammar tribe, before the area around the Sinjar mountain range sees the Tayy tribe; in the northernmost section a number of Kurdish tribes are found, including the Dizai, Zangana, Barwari, Khushnow, Shwan, Mizuri, Barzani, Zibari, Shikhan, Surchi, Baban, Baradast and Hamawand.

David Fromkin has referred to the World War I peace treaties as 'a peace to end all peace'. Certainly the Sykes–Picot exchange would

---

11   Rashid Khalidi, *Resurrecting Empire: Western Footprints and America's Perilous Path in the Middle East*, Boston: Beacon Press, 2004.

12   Eliezer Tauber, *The Formation of Modern Syria and Iraq*, Ilford: Frank Cass, 1995.

set in motion the development of a series of imperfect realities, of western territorial concepts imposed on the periphery of the periphery: the relatively sparsely populated Jazira region. At the very heart of this crucial exchange of letters between France and Britain is the division of territory into areas in which the two states are able to 'establish such direct or indirect administration as they desire',[13] with blue used to indicate French areas and British areas coloured in red.

There would be no internal boundaries or interior custom barriers between the two areas, but both governments agreed to guarantee external boundaries that could be used to control the importation of arms. Of key interest to Britain in the early stages of this dialogue was the establishment of free ports and the creation of railways that could link Mesopotamia to the Mediterranean. Yet exactly how the territory would be administratively split was far from clear. In November 1918, the British foreign secretary wrote of Colonel T.E. Lawrence's plan to form three separate Arab states outside of the Hijaz (Syria, Upper Mesopotamia and Lower Mesopotamia), with the boundary between the latter two running from the confluence of Diyala river and the Tigris to Ana on the Euphrates. Yet Lawrence's cultural sensitivities as to how much land to carve from the Arabs was trumped by the strategic value of Mosul that had been identified in 1915.

Nevertheless, the 'territorial compromise between the vested interests of outside powers and the aspirations of the indigenous population'[14] was still the theoretical bedrock of the British approach to drawing post-war boundaries. The seeming incompatibility between outside interests and indigenous aspirations was reconciled by the British belief in the benefits of their own presence to the mandated population, and by their perception that relations with the native

---

13 Sir Edward Grey, Sykes-Picot correspondence, May 1916, quoted in Richard Schofield (ed.), *Arabian Boundary Disputes*, Farnham Common: Archive Editions, 1992, vol. 8, p. 56.

14 Political Intelligence Department Memorandum (November, 1920), quoted in Schofield, *Arabian Boundary Disputes*, vol. 8, p. 64.

population of Mesopotamia 'grow closer every day, and is certainly not incompatible with their national aspirations'.[15] In a correspondence with King Hussein of Hijaz concerning the *vilayet*s of Baghdad and Basra, Sir Henry McMahon made clear that the Arabs had to recognise the 'established position and interests of Great Britain', which would 'necessitate special measures of administrative control to secure the territory from foreign aggression'.[16]

In respect of the administration of the borderland between mandated Syria and Mesopotamia, Gertrude Bell and A.T Wilson presented the reality of what was likely to occur at the periphery of both administrations control:

It is clear that no Government will exercise effective control over Syrian desert. Governments are concerned only with the administration of settled districts, and the relations of tribes to borders of cultivated land.[17]

Then, following the acquisition of mandates from the League of Nations at San Remo, in December 1920 a Franco-British convention on 'Certain Points Connected with the Mandates for Syria and the Lebanon, Palestine and Mesopotamia' for the first time discussed a more precise agreement on future boundaries:

On the east, the Tigris from Jeziret-ibn-Omar to the boundaries of the former vilayets of Diarbekir and Mosul. On the south-east and south, the aforesaid boundary of the former vilayets southwards as far as Roumelan Koeui; thence a line leaving in the territory under the French mandate the entire basin of the western Kabur and passing in a straight line towards the Euphrates, which it crosses at Abu Kemal.[18]

Interestingly, the initial approach to division adopted by the British and the French was to try to use previous Ottoman *vilayet* boundaries

15 Ibid.

16 Letter from Sir H. McMahon to King Hussein, 24 October 1915, quoted in Schofield, *Arabian Boundary Disputes*, vol. 8, p.361.

17 Note by India Office on Foreign Office Memorandum (November, 1918), quoted in Schofield, *Arabian Boundary Disputes*, vol. 8, p. 368.

18 Franco-British Convention 1920, reproduced in Schofield, *Arabian Boundary Disputes*, vol. 8, p. 66.

as a blueprint for imposing their own spheres of influence. Article 2 of the convention promised to establish a commission to 'trace on the spot the boundary line'. Article 3 was to be a harbinger of future functional border issues: it outlined the need for an agreement over irrigation plans and the use of Tigris and Euphrates water, in order to avoid the French 'diminishing' Mesopotamian supplies.

Functional agreements were also outlined in respect to railway networks with the British securing 'the right to transport troops'[19] across French mandated territory. The 1920 convention went so far as to grant railway lines their own 'extra-territorial' status; such was their importance to British strategic thinking. Yet for more than a decade, the rather grandiose ambitions of the 1920 convention had only limited impact on what was supposed to be the Syrian–Iraqi border. In 1921 a British–French commission working along the southern border between Syria and Palestine/Transjordan found it impossible to establish a line from the Mediterranean as far as El Hamme, due to 'the difficulty of establishing a line which should take into account local conditions'.[20] The commission discovered similar problems that halted work along the Syrian–Iraqi border. One factor in particular prevented this border from being properly delimited: the final assignment of the *vilayet* of Mosul was still 'in suspense'[21] and was not settled until December 1925. The Syrian–Turkish border was only fixed by a Franco-Turkish protocol of 22 June 1929.

Meanwhile, in 1928 the British government took the initiative with an idea to deal with the boundaries of Syria–Iraq/Syria–Transjordan as a whole. By 1931 the British-backed government of Iraq attempted to address the issue in a more exact manner, criticising the 1920 convention for providing 'little more than a sketch map'.[22]

---

19 Ibid., p. 67.

20 Draft for combined reference to the Council of the League of Nations 1931, reproduced in Schofield, *Arabian Boundary Disputes*, vol. 8, p. 147.

21 League of Nations Boundary Commission, 1932, reproduced in Schofield, *Arabian Boundary Disputes*, vol. 8, p. 259.

22 Government of Iraq Statement 1931, reproduced in Schofield, *Arabian*

This sketch map would require 'substantial modifications...unless a totally unworkable frontier were to be imposed on the two States concerned'.[23] With the creation of a functionally workable boundary line in mind, the Iraqi government set about describing—through the use of maps and geographic reference points—where exactly the boundary line would be. This delimitation would be 'based firstly on the Convention of 1920',[24] but would go further to take into account socio-geographic factors.

Geographically, the 1931 delimitation utilised recent surveys undertaken to better understand the topography of the 600 kilometres of border. Interestingly, those surveys also examined considerations of tribal needs as well as questions of administrative convenience. The approach taken by the British recognised that hermetical sealing of the terrain was impractical as well as unfeasible when it came to regulating the movement of nomadic Bedouin tribes (as Gertrude Bell had said back in 1918). The compromise solution was an understanding that 'no frontier can be drawn which need not be crossed by the Bedouin and similar tribes of wide range of migration: nevertheless the fewer the sections that have to cross the frontier the better the frontier is'.[25] At first glance, such anthropological sensitivity would appear to contrast with the 'security first' approach of earlier British policy-makers. Yet, in reality, administrative concerns with security would best be served with an understanding of the nature and identity of the population of the borderland, especially in regard to nomadic movement that would invariably challenge the presence of the border.

For the initial delimitation the British chose five sectors snaking their way from the Turkish tripoint southwards to the Syrian desert. Each section analysed by the surveys was examined in terms of the population that would be affected. What this analysis of the

---

Boundary Disputes, vol. 8, p. 71.

23 Ibid.
24 Ibid., p. 73.
25 Ibid.

border sectors shows is the benefits of a culturally sensitive and realistic approach to demarcating an imaginary line in the sand. Critically, however, the delimitation was seen only as a rough guide to larger power politics, and the carve-up of territory between France and Great Britain ultimately neglected many of the survey's findings. Indeed, as the delimitated line was essentially a highly artificial entity, it was only when the border's function was challenged that flaws found within the final 1932 League of Nations report would be uncovered.

FIRST SECTOR—TIGRIS TO TALL DALSHA: 'THE ZUMMAR'

Known as the 'Zummar' area, the population affected included partly settled, partly nomadic tribes such as the Gargariyya, Juhaysh, Sharabiyyin, Hasan, Miran and Shammar. Divisions within each tribe meant that the proposed boundary line would split ones on either side of the Tigris for example. Agricultural patterns were such that the boundary line would also divide a tribe's spring destination from its winter pastures. In terms of ethnicity the sector was surveyed as predominantly Kurdish (in terms of numbers of counted tents).

The Shammar Bedouin Arabs play a key part in the narrative of the Syria–Iraq border from inception to the modern day. As several surveys recognised, the Shammar 'are affected by the frontier almost throughout its length from the Tigris to the Euphrates, since any frontier between Iraq and Syria must cut across their traditional pastures'.[26] In the last years of the Ottoman Empire the Shammar were split between the Shammar of Dayr al-Zur under Sheikh Faris and the Shammar of Mosul under Sheikh Farhan. Respective Iraqi and Syrian governments appointed the sheikhs as chiefs of their regions, and although it was understood that the *de facto* international boundary did not align with the existing tribal dividing lines, the British expected greater recognition and incorporation of the boundary into people's minds once the line was actually fixed.

---

26 Ibid., p. 76.

In demarcating the 1920 agreed line, the issue of *vilayet* boundary suitability was often raised, especially when villages that represented border towns no longer existed and agricultural patterns had changed. For example, the survey team had to make a best guess as to which of two sites was the village originally referred to as 'Roumelan Koeui'. As the area in sector one was largely reliant on plentiful water for agriculture, an understanding of how tribal movements adjusted to this was critical in evaluating the impact of the planned hardening of the frontier. For example, while the Syrian side had plentiful water supplies all year round, the Iraqi side would struggle during the summer months. However, as the watershed represented the boundary line at this point, it was suggested that Iraqi tribes be allowed access to cross-border enclaves free of a grazing tax. It was also recognised that 'elements of the Miran, Sharabiyyin and Khurusa (of Shammar) are the only tribesmen who will frequently cross the proposed line'.[27]

SECOND SECTOR—TALL DALSHA TO GUSAIBA: 'THE SINJAR'

Known as the Sinjar area in reference to the Jabal Sinjar hill range, forty of the sixty villages were identified as predominantly Yazidi. As with the first sector, concerns over agricultural patterns dominated. The survey identified the Syrian Tayy tribe that would travel to Iraq for 'about three months in the winter when the Wadis of the Khabur are boggy'.[28] The discussion of the boundary line aimed to 'ensure the unity of the administration of the Yazidi tribes'[29] and their respective agricultural spaces. However, once again anthropological sensitivities against splitting tribal lands were usurped by the final delimitations decisions taken subsequently.

THIRD SECTOR—GUSAIBA TO BAGHUZ: 'THE JAZIRA'

The main focus of boundary line discussion again focused on causing the least possible interruption to traditional Shammar movements.

---

27 Ibid., p. 79.
28 Ibid., p. 80.
29 Ibid.

Interestingly, in this case, the name 'Jazira' referred to as a very specific area of land intersecting across the borderline that was being investigated by the commission. Such a narrow definition contrasts with its usage today (as well as with the more common historical usage), in which it connotes the far wider area of eastern Syria between the Euphrates and Tigris rivers and eventually funnelling into Iraq southwards to the northern reaches of Baghdad.

FOURTH SECTOR—THE EUPHRATES AT ABU KEMAL

The Agaidat and Dulaym tribes dominated this area at the time of the British surveys. Crucial for boundary makers was the fact that the Agaidat were a tribe of cultivators who sometimes moved up to 50 kilometres east of the proposed frontier. This was an acceptable requirement of movement that allowed Abu Kemal to stay as a united town and not one split down the middle. Of course the splitting of the islands in the middle of the Euphrates was more of an imprecise science. Indeed decisions made in the 1920s and 1930s could not help but be changed over time as natural river processes took place, carving up a more convoluted sense of territorial jurisdiction that would create problems for US military personnel working in the area from 2003.

FIFTH SECTOR—THE SYRIAN DESERT

The desert area was characterised as having a minimal Bedouin population that relied on certain topographically located swathes of shrubs to maintain camel caravans. Travel routes were therefore to and from principal market towns. Since the population was of a purely nomadic character, it was decided that there was no need to make any 'substantial modification of the straight line'[30] that would connect Abu Kemal to the then Transjordan tripoint.

However, beyond the 1931 micro-management of the boundary lines and the minutiae of tribal migrations, more far-reaching iden-

---

30 Ibid., p. 84.

tity issues lurked. Jazira identity cannot truly be appreciated without taking into account the important role of Mosul, the economic hub for so much of the population in this region. Key to its Jazira identity was that the city looked west to Aleppo for its trade relations rather than south to Baghdad. Iraqi writer Nibras Kazimi wrote about how the relationship between the two cities highlighted a 'loose and grey kinship' that existed across a previously united region. Kazimi went on to tell the story of how 'the men of Mosul had been conducting a centuries-old experiment in genetic improvement by marrying the legendary beauties of Aleppo until Britain and France decided to create the national states of Iraq and Syria'.[31]

These more fundamental issues were not addressed by the 1931 demarcation, whose sponsors had already decided that a region with centuries-long traditions was to remain bisected in the modern state system of the Middle East. But for the remainder of the twentieth century, Mosul's sense of attachment to a wider regional community would continue to assert itself periodically, both in the city itself and in its hinterland. To the west of Mosul, already in the 1930s, Yazidis were implicated in a movement that sought to make their lands part of French-controlled Syria and, a few years later, a civic, joint Kurdish–Christian 'regionalist' initiative materialised on the Syrian side of the border.[32] And Mosul itself played a leading role in what Iraq historian Hanna Batatu has described as a wave of pan-Arabism directed by descendants of families who were adversely affected by the artificial closure of the intra-regional arteries of the Jazira region in the twentieth century. According to Batatu, 'the officer corps of the Baath drew many of their restless elements from the northern Arab families, who had moved to the capital and whose traditional economic life had been disorganised by the hindrances of the new frontiers with Syria'.[33]

---

31 Nibras Kazimi, 'The Syrian Blink', *The New York Sun*, 6 January 2005.

32 Nelida Fuccaro, *The Other Kurds: Yazidis in Colonial Iraq*, London: I.B. Tauris, 1999, pp. 147–55.

33 Hanna Batatu, *The Old Social Classes and the Revolutionary Movements of*

The impact of the 2003 invasion

Security is the top priority and we have to defeat the terrorism both coming
from inside and outside the country and to fortify our borders to stop the
flow of criminals to our country.

Interim Prime Minister Iyad Allawi, 18 January 2005.

Following the 2003 US-led invasion of Iraq, policy in regard to international relations with its six neighbouring states faces changes
to existing boundary disputes and the possible creation of new ones.
The importance of border security to the successive transitional Iraqi
governments was proved by the closure of all of Iraq's borders around
key dates. Borders were closed during the first election of 30 January
2005, over the Shiite holiday of Ashura in February 2005, around the
constitutional referendum date of 15 October 2005 and around the
second election date of 15 December 2005. Yet, in 2004, Mustafa
Alani, then of the Royal United Services Institute, claimed that the
US decision to disband Iraq's border guard (35,000 strong) along
with the rest of the army following the US invasion, would turn Iraq's
3,650 kilometres of international boundaries into an 'open house'.

The consequences of this disintegration of the Iraqi state as well as
the debate over exactly what format the new Iraqi state will take are
likely to shape the future—along with the numbers of the replace-
ment border force and its ability to police Iraq's international borders,
plus the role of international forces. Meanwhile, the insurgency that
emerged following the 2003 invasion, with an estimated strength
that varied between 20,000 to 40,000[34] and as high as 200,000 plus,[35]
crippled American efforts to create a functioning unitary democratic
Iraq. At a workshop held in Jordan in 2005 by the US defence and
energy departments it was realised that border security for the 'new
Iraq' would represent a key priority in state reconstruction. Yet such

Iraq, Princeton: Princeton University Press, 1978, p. 1114.

34 Based on Brookings Institute, *Iraq Index*, 2003–2005.

35 Office of the Iraqi director of intelligence, quoted at Juan Cole's blog
Informed Comment (www.juancole.com), February 2005.

rebuilding must take into account the dynamics of each of Iraq's six borders. This in turn relates to today's politicisation of the border issue: between the 2003 invasion and 2005 Syria would find itself at the epicentre of the 'Iraqi blame game'.

In 2003, in line with both Syria's public opinion and with its geo-strategic interests at the time, President Bashar al-Asad was the region's biggest critic of the US invasion. In December 2004 President George W. Bush urged Syria to 'stop the flow' of jihadists across the border. In January 2005, the Iraqi minister of state for national security accused Iran and Syria of being 'two naughty boys' directly involved in assisting foreign fighters' transit into Iraq.[36] It is widely accepted by reliable sources that busloads of would-be-fighters left from outside the Iraqi embassy in Damascus prior to the outbreak of war; however there is no evidence that Syria directly facilitated even medium-scale fighter transit following the outbreak of hostilities and the fall of the Iraqi regime in April 2003. Instead Syria's immediate reaction was to do its minimum best in regard to border security.

Syria has justified all changes to its side of the border along two lines: firstly that once Iraq regains its security, this can lead to the provision of a timetable for the withdrawal of multi-national forces from the country; secondly, that it is necessary to prevent terrorists from entering Syria from Iraq. In doing this, the regime has taken a number of steps towards what can be described as changing the function of the border from a porous administrative line to a security filter. The basis of the Syrian strategy is the principle that border security starts with a good, solid strategy along the border itself. Syria has constructed 557 border posts along the border. Situated at a distance ranging from one to three kilometres between them as imposed by the typographical nature of the terrain, each post is manned by five to eight soldiers equipped with personal weapons and one fixed heavy weapon.

---

36 Transcript of teleconference with Qasim Dawud, 27 January 2005, at http://www.defenselink.mil/transcripts/transcript.aspx?transcriptid=1672.

The most physical border move has been the construction of a
sand berm—a fence of earth that has been constructed at a height of
between two to four metres along key intersections of the border line.
Syria has also upgraded its official crossing points, although only two
of the three points are actually open: al-Yarubiyya in north-eastern
Syria and al-Tanf in the south. Al-Yarubiyya experiences a massive
rate of transit—much of it made up by construction materials on
their way to Iraqi Kurdistan, which currently experiences a building
boom. There is also a rail service that travels across this border with
two trains a day, mainly carrying freight cargo.

In the northern sector a lightening network of medium voltage
has been laid over a distance of 1,800 metres, beginning from Sim-
alka village towards the northern border triangle. Across the entire
border, Syrian officials claim that fifty moving patrols are conducted
day and night, in which over 800 personnel from the security forces
take part. By early 2006, the overall size of the Syrian border security force was around 10,000, including troops being redeployed
to eastern Syria following the withdrawal from Lebanon. A statistic
that highlights the shift in the importance of the boundary's security
is that the pre-war size of the Syrian border guard along the Iraq
frontier numbered only 700.

Both British and US officials in Syria admit that the Syrians have
a pretty good system of border coverage in place. Crucial for an
understanding of how these successes can be applied on the Iraqi
side is the concept of 'security in depth'. The Syrian interior ministry
in 2005 introduced the development of a new integrated computer
system for all border entry points. This was designed to compensate
for the absence of visa requirements for Arabs to enter the country.
However, in October 2005 the ministry issued a circular inform-
ing immigration and security officers that non-permanent resident
males aged between eighteen and thirty could be denied entry on
a number of pretexts, including travelling alone, having student or
recent graduate status, having residence in a country other than their
own, or having been involved in 'suspicious' travel abroad.

The result of all these actions is that Syria is by no means an easy place from which to enter Iraq. However there are also some glaring negative characteristics of the Syrian border security arrangements. At a tactical level there is a complete absence of communication between the Syrian and the US/Iraqi border patrol. A simple incident highlights this absence of communication. When US forces closed al-Qa'im crossing last year after taking fire from both sides of the border, they communicated the border's closure by using a catapult to send the message to the Syrian side of the border. What is more, it seems that a decision has been made banning local-level communication from Syrian border guards until bilateral relations at the state level are improved. Such an absence of communication has inevitably led to failures of joint intelligence, and the Syrians claim that over one hundred incidents have been recorded of US/Iraqi border guards targeting Syrian forces by accident. In such incidents the Syrian have reported six killed and seventeen injured.[37]

There is also the inability of the Syrian forces to patrol effectively at night due to a combination of poor training and lack of proper equipment. Previous to the assassination of Lebanese Prime Minister Rafiq al-Hariri on 14 February 2005, the British government was involved in a scheme to provide Syria with night vision equipment that could address this shortcoming. But following the killing of Hariri this programme has been put on ice, although speaking in December 2005 British Defence Secretary Des Browne hinted at assisting the Syrians helping secure their border in return for their positive engagement over the issue. Such assistance is certainly necessary. Currently, small patrols are unable or unwilling to challenge well-equipped smugglers who often operate in large numbers. These are serious weaknesses considering that the majority of smuggling occurs at night.

Much of this chapter's main argument over the regional identity of parts of north-western Iraq concerns the shared identity across the international borderline. Religious, tribal, economic and familial

---

37 Interview with Ibrahim Hamidi, *Al-Hayat*, 14 March 2005.

links span across large parts of the Jazira, making the hermetic seal-ing of the line in the sand an unnatural division that is unlikely to be accepted in the long term by the residents on either side. Thus the interdiction of suspected 'jihadists' or 'terrorists' is made difficult precisely because security paradigms often show little consideration to layers of local identity. Even Arabist members of the US military based in the region have bemoaned that they were never sure what layer of identity people in such a periphery were operating on. Many of the terrorists arrested in Iraq after having crossed the Syrian bor-der into the country have no criminal record, and, if stopped at the border, would not be in possession of any incriminating evidence of intent such as weaponry or training manuals.

The hardest stage in the interdiction of unwanted personnel into Iraq concerns the physical stage of flight and crossing of the border. It is easy to transverse sand berms on foot (as an al-Jazeera investi-gative reporter proved), and according to defence analysts, it is not particularly hard work with a shovel to secure 4WD access. This was proved in 2005, when an Iraqi patrol crossed the border to pursue suspected insurgents and ended up capturing a British embassy ve-hicle which was subsequently returned with much embarrassment. Also the berm has been in place for nearly three years now and has suffered a large degree of natural weathering: the border is literally 'blowing away'—also an apt metaphor for how local residents on either side perceive it.

Conclusions

There is recognition from informed quarters that the Syrians have done as much as they can unilaterally to secure their border with Iraq. The reality is that their Iraqi counterparts are a long way off. General John Abizaid, the head of the US Central Command, has reportedly admitted that 'the Syrians ... moved against the foreign fighters',[38] and yet the political expediency of isolating Syria and ex-

---

38 Confer the press report quoted at http://www.free-lebanon.com/LFPNews/2006/March/Mar19/mar19a/mar19a.html.

MOSUL, THE JAZIRA REGION AND THE SYRIAN-IRAQI BORDERLANDS

cusing the poor situation in Iraq by blaming Damascus saw President George W. Bush in a speech in March 2006 describe al-Qaida fighters coming in from Syria as the enemy that US troops are presently engaged with. The Syrians have pushed border security high up on their reform agenda, and their current approach can be characterised as a transition from the 'stone age to the space age'. In terms of border security the next step for the Syrians has been to request the assistance of Westminster International. This British security solution provider firm was contacted by the Syrian interior ministry with the question 'what can we do to improve border security?' The firm suggested the Syrians should acquire a full border perimeter security solution featuring a three metres high double-line security fence fitted with micro-strain fibre-optic sensing equipment. This would be monitored by thermal imaging surveillance cameras which would transfer information to a net-workable command and control centre.

Yet although a focus on border securitisation is both necessary and understandable, it deflects attention away from the surrounding region, its identity and its transnational character. To address these issues, a normalisation of inter-state relations including management of border crossings—rather than a perfection of surveillance technology—would seem the most promising path ahead.

121

6
KURDISH OR KURDISTANIS?
CONCEPTUALISING REGIONALISM
IN THE NORTH OF IRAQ

Gareth Stansfield and *Hashem Ahmadzadeh*[1]

In recent months, if not years, a new way of discussing political affiliation has gained prominence in the north of Iraq. This is to refer to 'Kurdistanis', presumably in a manner that reflects a general subscription to the notion of 'Kurdistan' as an institutionalised entity—not only in political and administrative terms (which it is, according to the constitution of Iraq), but also in an 'imagined' sense whereby the ethnic identities of Kurds, Assyrians, Turkmens, and Arabs are subsumed under one all-encompassing 'Kurdistani' vision. But to what extent is it correct to talk about a 'Kurdistani' identity in the north of Iraq—the territorially disputed region commonly referred to as 'Kurdistan'? The name implies not only an attachment to territory and an acknowledgment of the location of this territory, but, more importantly, an acceptance of the concept by non-Kurds in particular.

However, if a region had to be identified in post-Saddam Iraq as being distinctly 'ethnic' in terms of its political mobilisation and character, then it would be the Kurdistan Region that exists in the north of the country. Indeed, the Kurds display the clearest case of political mobilisation in Iraq occurring according to ethno-sectarian

1 Gareth Stansfield would like to thank the United States Institute of Peace for supporting aspects of this research through its award of grant USIP -250-04F, 'Investigating Political Mobilization in Iraqi Kurdistan'.

identities. The evidence is also not limited merely to the period of the *de facto* Kurdish state established in 1991—indeed, a case will be made that the political leadership of the Kurdistan Region has sought to distance itself, at least nominally, from being seen to be overtly 'Kurdish'. The years of rebellion against the Iraqi government since the early years of the history of Iraq as a modern state (they include the revolt of Sheikh Mahmud Barzinji in the 1920s as well as that of Mulla Mustafa Barzani in the early 1940s and later on in 1960s) combined with the emergence of a *de facto* Kurdish state after the Gulf War in 1991 all suggest that any attempt to envisage the Kurdish position in Iraq as being anything other than ethnically-based would be somewhat futile. But Kurdish politicians are keen to do exactly this and choose to refer to the regional government established since 1992 as the 'Kurdistan' Regional Government, rather than use the ethnically exclusive term 'Kurdish'.[2] Why this should be the case is clear: the Kurdish political leadership recognises the problems of being seen as an ethno-nationalist movement, particularly by regional Middle East powers, and are therefore promoting the idea that the 'Kurdistan Region' is a geographic construct to which peoples of any ethnicity or creed can subscribe. The term 'Kurdistan' is therefore being employed in the Kurdistan Region of Iraq as a means to construct a non-ethnic Kurdistani nationalism.

However, 'Kurdistani' has an older, and contrary, meaning in Kurdish political discourse, and one which has quite different implications when discussing regionalist tendencies among the Kurds. Far from being a tool to engineer some form of civic nationalism among a wide range of peoples living in the Zagros mountains, the original 'Kurdistani' idea was distinctly ethnic in outlook and focused upon the promotion of a pan-Kurdish nationalist ideal, irrespective of international boundaries. Kurdistan was, quite literally, the 'land

2 However, the practice of referring to the 'Kurdish Regional Government'—whether by accident or choice—by journalists, academics, and politicians, continues to weaken any KRG strategy of promoting itself in a manner that strengthens the notion of a civic, cosmopolitan, cohesiveness in the Kurdistan Region of Iraq.

of the Kurds' and its adjective merely served to promote this idea in nationalist terms.

In the contemporary Kurdistan Region of Iraq, a struggle is evident over how the terms 'Kurdish', 'Kurdistan', and 'Kurdistani' should be used and to what they refer. The struggle can be seen taking place in the wide range of newspapers and journals now being published in Erbil and Sulaymaniyya, and also between and within both Kurdish and non-Kurdish political parties as they attempt to promote or deny being 'Kurdistani' either in an Iraqi-regional, or a pan-Kurdish sense. Indeed, there are signs that the tension evident in the semantics of the term 'Kurdistani' haunts the leaderships of the major political parties (namely, the Kurdistan Democratic Party (KDP) and the Patriotic Union of Kurdistan or PUK) as they, as not only Iraqi Kurdish leaders but now national symbols of a wider Kurdish community, seek to balance the political realities of existence in post-Saddam Iraq with the expectations of Kurds in Iraq, Turkey, Iran, Syria, and the often ultra-nationalist diasporic community. Division can also be seen within the Turkmen and Chaldo-Assyrian (Christian) communities of northern Iraq, with some embracing the concept of being 'Kurdistanis', and some avowedly, and at times violently, opposing it.

The question of 'Kurdish' and 'Kurdistani' regionalism will therefore be addressed in this chapter, with a focus on how Kurdish political parties have attempted to promote a regional vision of Kurdistan in Iraq as home to Iraqis who live in the north of the country, and whether their attempts have succeeded or failed. First, the term 'Kurdistani' needs to be contextualised historically as neither of these two uses of the term 'Kurdistani' is new. Indeed, as will be seen, both have long histories. What is quite different in the current period, however, is the tension that now exists between those advocating a 'Kurdistani' region in Iraq, in terms of being acceptable in a regional sense to Kurds and non-Kurds alike, and those who continue to view 'Kurdistani' as being in reference to the wider Kurdish community of an ill-defined greater Kurdistan.

Early notions of 'Kurdistan' and being 'Kurdistani'

The earliest stirrings of Kurdish nationalism and the vision of 'Kurdistan' came about in the mid to late nineteenth century, in keeping with the nationalist thinking emerging from within Arab and Turkish intellectual circles.[3] Before this period, it is unlikely that the term 'Kurd' was used by the indigenous people. Rather, it seems likely that it was an 'outsider's term' used by Arabs and Persians, with indigenous names being of tribal or geographic origin.[4] However, it remains the case that nationalist thought began to coalesce at least among intellectual groupings of Kurds in the nineteenth century, and it is a useful task to contextualise the setting in which early Kurdish nationalist thought developed, rather than merely dismiss Kurdish nationalism as a twentieth-century phenomenon.[5]

Before the nineteenth century, the Kurdish regions of the Ottoman and Qajar Empires had enjoyed relatively high levels of autonomy from the imperial centres. Far from being the obscure back-

---

3 This is an important fact to recognise. Far from being 'late starters' in the creation of a nationalist project, the efforts of Kurds or, more accurately, Kurdish intellectuals, commenced at a comparable time to that of other mobilising nationhoods in the Ottoman Empire. What is perhaps a more accurate depiction of the progression of Kurdish nationalism is that its subsequent development suffered from interruptions caused by the failure of the Kurds to secure a state of their own in the 1920s. While Kurdish nationalism was not the product of a Kurdish state, prospects for its consolidation and strengthening were diminished in the absence of a state.

4 Hakan Özoglu, *Kurdish Notables and the Ottoman State: Evolving Identities, Competing Loyalties, and Shifting Boundaries*, Albany, NY: State University of New York Press, 2004, p. 27.

5 Janet Klein presents a highly nuanced understanding of Kurdish nationalism in the late Ottoman Empire as being more accurately 'Kurdism'. 'Nationalism' was seen by Kurdish intellectuals as an Ottoman tool to strengthen their hold on power, whereas 'Kurdishness' was focused on 'the rights of the Kurds', with particular reference to protecting the privileges Kurdish tribal chiefs enjoyed under the Ottoman sultan, and which were threatened by the process of modernisation. See Janet Klein, 'Kurdish Nationalists and Non-Nationalist Kurdists: Rethinking Minority Nationalism and the Dissolution of the Ottoman Empire, 1908–1909', *Nations and Nationalism*, vol. 13, no. 1, 2007, pp. 135–53, quote at p. 137.

water territory of these vast empires, the mountainous borderlands were divided into several Kurdish emirates, including Baban, Botan, Hakkari, and Soran.[6] These Kurdish emirates were able to maintain their autonomy from the two empires because they were located in inhospitable terrain far from the imperial centres, and the preferred method of dealing with them was to empower local leaders and to then exact tribute from them. However, in a bid to modernise in order to keep pace with European imperial powers that were deemed threatening to the integrity of the Ottoman Empire, an extensive set of nineteenth-century reform programmes, known as the *nizam-i cedid* (New Order) and then the *tanzimat* reforms sought to modernise the empire both in terms of regulating and centralising its administrative structures and procedures, and improving communication and transport networks. With these changes, the Kurdish emirates began to be seen as anomalies in need of removing.

The process of transforming the empires therefore brought the Kurdish emirates into conflict with imperial forces. But it was a struggle that the provincial emirs had no hope of winning, with the result that the Kurdish emirates were reincorporated into the empires and ceased to exist by the middle of the century. However, the abolishing of the emirates did not result in the demise of the embryonic nationalist sentiment. Rather, it acted as a catalyst. While the Kurds had often revolted against the yoke of the imperial centre, such rebellions were of a local, often tribal, nature, with little or no interest given to the idea of a wider nationalist project. But this began to change, slowly at first, in the years following the end of the autonomous emirates. In 1880, a revolt under the leadership of Sheikh Ubaydullah Nahri marked a significant change in how Kurds perceived themselves as part of a wider ethno-linguistic community.

---

6 See Hakan Özoglu , 'State–Tribe Relations: Kurdish Tribalism in the 16th- and 17th-Century Ottoman Empire', *British Journal of Middle East Studies*, vol. 23, no. 1, May 1996, pp. 5–27. For a description and analysis of the history of the Kurdish emirates, see Martin van Bruinessen, 'Kurds, States and Tribes', in Faleh Jabar and Hosham Daoud (eds.), *Tribes and Power: Nationalism and Ethnicity in the Middle East*, London: Saqi, 2003, pp. 165–83.

Although the movement had still the signs of localism and traditional leadership, its aims were altogether wider—to fight for the creation of a greater Kurdistan, overriding the borders of the extant Ottoman Empire. The forces of Sheikh Ubaydullah succeeded in occupying a large part of what is now Iranian Kurdistan, with the aim of unifying it with the Kurdish region of the Ottoman Empire. While the uprising ultimately failed, it still should be recognised as being a seminal moment in the development of Kurdish nationalism.[7]

By the end of the nineteenth century, a noticeable body of Kurdish intellectual activity had emerged that focused mainly on the distinctiveness of Kurdish culture, language, and ethnic identity. For them, the label 'Kurdistan' was considered to be the 'land of the Kurds', and the use of the 'Kurdistan' term was a prominent feature of their cultural and political publications—indeed, the first Kurdish newspaper published by the Kurds in the Ottoman Empire, in Cairo in 1898, was simply called *Kurdistan*. But it was in Istanbul that the most prominent Kurdish intellectual circles established themselves, again having an initial cultural focus, but developing political agendas very quickly.

But, even at this point of origin, division characterised the debate about the idea of an independent Kurdistan. The differences between the prominent Kurdish leaders within the early Kurdish organisations in Istanbul provide stark evidence of this. During the years following the Young Turk revolution of 1908, several Kurdish organisations formed with the intention of promoting 'Kurdish rights'. Among the Kurdish notables of Istanbul were two influential figures—Sheikh Abd al-Qadir Nahri, who was the son of Sheikh Ubaydullah, and Amin Ali Badr Khan. Each sought to outdo the other in their attempts to have the most popular Kurdish journal.[8]

---

7 See Denise Natali, *The Kurds and the State: Evolving National Identity in Iraq, Turkey, and Iran*, Syracuse, NY: Syracuse University Press, 2006, pp. 10–11.

8 See David McDowall, *A Modern History of the Kurds*, London: I.B. Tauris, 1996, pp. 93–4.

This confusion between the use of 'Kurdistan' or 'Kurd' in Kurdish political and intellectual discourse continued into the twentieth century and it is possible to see the continued dual and shifting use of these terms among Kurdish organisations in the years before the fall of the Ottoman Empire, with them used interchangeably. Ironically, one of the first modern Kurdish organisations that was established in Istanbul in 1908 was the Kurd Teavün ve Terakki Cemiyeti (Kurdish Mutual Aid and Progress Association)—a Turkish name utilising Arabic words, with no Kurdish words present at all apart from the use of *Kurd* itself. But, other publications from this association did employ the Kurdish language, and continued to have 'Kurd' in their titles. These included *Roja Kurd* (The Day of the Kurds), and *Hetawe Kurd* (The Sun of the Kurds). A further organisation was established in 1912 in Istanbul, this time called Kurdistan Muhibbun Cemiyeti (The Kurdistan Friends' Association), with its newspaper called *Hevia Kurd* (Kurdish Hope). While the terms 'Kurd', 'Kurdish' and 'Kurdistan' were used somewhat freely and interchangeably, it seems that there was little political meaning in doing so. Rather, both were seen to be an expression of the same nationalist idea of an ethnically coloured vision of Kurds and Kurdistan.

Even though the Kurds had advanced considerably their nationalist ideas in the early years of the twentieth century, they proved unable to convert these developments further following the defeat of the Ottoman Empire in World War I. The main reason was that Kurdistan and the Kurds were divided by European imperial actions, and then targeted by the dominant nations in the countries they eventually found themselves in.[9] While the 1920 Treaty of Sèvres (and, in particular, articles 62, 63, and 64) made provision for the establishment of a Kurdish state in south-east Anatolia and with the

9 The term 'dominant nationhood' refers to situations whereby the nation, even if identified as 'civic' rather than 'ethnic', becomes coloured with ethno-cultural semantics that indicate the dominance of one particular grouping in the state. See Andreas Wimmer, 'Dominant Ethnicity and Dominant Nationhood', in Eric Kaufmann (ed.), *Rethinking Ethnicity: Majority Groups and Dominant Minorities*, London: Routledge, 2004, pp. 40–58.

Kurds in the former Mosul *vilayet* given the option of a plebiscite to decide whether or not to join, the rise of the Turkish nationalist Mustafa Kemal Atatürk forced the British overlords of Mesopotamia to back down from these promises. The establishment of the Republic of Turkey and the abolishing of the caliphate also saw new emphasis placed on the 'Turkishness' of the new state— thereby depriving the Kurds of the political space essential for the promoting and objectifying of Kurdish nationalism. Elsewhere, while a part of Kurdistan came under British colonial management, the rest of Kurdistan suffered from the absolute lack of any effective political organisation to fight for the rights of the Kurds.

The result of these early twentieth-century developments is now well known. While nation-states reflecting the predominant nations of the region (i.e. Arab, Persian, and Turkish) were created in the subsequent drawing of the political map, the Kurds failed to secure, or rather were not granted, such an entity. The result saw them physically divided between four countries, i.e. Turkey, Iran, Iraq and Syria, but also saw the beginnings of a psychological division, as Kurds in different states became drawn into the orbits of state structures dominated by different ethno-nationalist projects.

The emergence of these new, vigorous nationalisms had the counter-effect of strengthening nationalist feeling among the Kurds. The first serious reaction towards the establishment of the Republic of Turkey was led by Sheikh Sa'id Piran in 1925.[10] This revolt was as much tribally motivated as national, and was quickly defeated by Turkish forces and its leaders hanged. But, while unsuccessful, Sheikh Sa'id's revolt was an important watershed in one regard—it marked the beginning of a process by which leadership of the Kurd-

---

10 For accounts of the rebellion of Sheikh Sa'id Piran, and the subsequent rebellions of Mount Ararat and Dersim, see Robert Olson, *The Emergence of Kurdish Nationalism and the Sheikh Said Rebellion: 1880–1925*, Austin: University of Texas Press, 1989; idem, 'The Kurdish rebellions of Sheikh Said (1925), Mt. Ararat (1930), and Dersim (1937–8): Their Impact on the Development of Turkish Air Force and on Kurdish and Turkish nationalism', *Die Welt des Islams*, vol. 140, no. 1, March 2000, pp. 67–94.

ish national movement would move from being the preserve of tribal leaders, to being led by figures with wider nationalist agendas in mind. But, while the 'vision' of Kurdish nationalism began to emerge following Sheikh Sa'id's parochial insurrection, the opportunity to act 'nationally' had been considerably weakened by the effect the newly-drawn borders had on mobility and linkages between communities. It also meant that Kurdish nationalists no longer had one, or two, enemies to contend with (i.e. the Ottoman and Qajar Empires). Rather, they had as many as three or four, with state armies that were far better equipped than the nineteenth-century armies of the old empires, or, in some cases, supported by the technologically advanced nations of the West. The revolts of Ismail Agha Simko in Iranian Kurdistan against the Pahlavi dynasty, and Sheikh Mahmud Barzinji's fight to establish a Kingdom of Kurdistan in Iraq in the 1920s illustrate clearly the fragmentation of Kurdistan and the effect of this on its national movement(s).[11]

The effect of being subject to four different newly emerged nation-states imposed a secondary form of nationalism upon the Kurdish movements that was effectively a function of their geographic location. Although the ideal of Kurdishness and the dream of a greater Kurdistan continued in Kurdish cultural and political discourse, in reality the boundaries drawn between different parts of Kurdistan hampered any effective and successful struggle towards the realising of such a dream. From the mid-twentieth century onwards, pan-Kurdish political formations struggled to organise themselves (the need to build linkages bringing together Kurds living in different states proved to be a debilitating task), particularly as most politically-minded Kurds became focused increasingly on combating the most immediate threat—which was almost always the government of the state in which they resided. Only once these immediate threats

---

11 For details of Ismail Agha Simko's revolt see Natali, *The Kurds*, pp. 118–19; David Romano, *The Kurdish Nationalist Movement: Opportunity, Mobilization and Identity*, Cambridge: Cambridge University Press, 2006, pp. 222–4. For details of Sheikh Mahmud's revolts, see Gareth Stansfield, *Iraq: People, History, Politics*, Cambridge: Polity Press, 2007.

were removed could Kurdish political parties then turn their collective attention to the wider Kurdish situation, but this rarely happened as it was simply impossible for the limited Kurdish parties to challenge the might of the states.

But, even if rarely, Kurdish nationalism did manage to rear its head and threaten to redraw regional boundaries. Benefiting from the weakening of regional powers during World War II, the Kurds of Iraq and Iran were given a unique opportunity to convert the burgeoning rhetoric of Kurdish nationalist discourse into a physical state on the ground. The 1930s had witnessed a blossoming of Kurdish political and cultural activities, and, with the occupation of northern Iran by Russian forces taking place during the early years of the war, the Kurds began to organise themselves in a more effective and aggressive fashion.

One of the most influential Kurdish intellectual organisations, J.K.[12] was founded in 1942 in Mahabad—the main Kurdish city in Iran whose name would become synonymous with the Kurdish desire for independence.[13] This organisation marked a new era in the Kurdish nationalist movement as it brought together several different poles of Kurdish intellectual thought. It was, in effect, the result of a new socio-economic and political environment, with the founders of the body coming from the educated urban lower middle classes. Unusually, and perhaps due to the amount of political space that existed in Kurdistan during the war, the group had ambitions far greater than merely promoting the rights of the Kurds in Iran.

---

12 Otherwise known as Komalay Jiyanaway Kurd (The Society for the Revival of the Kurds), J.K. was established in September 1942. The equivalent of the initials of J.K. has been an issue of disputation among scholars, who interpret 'K' both as 'Kurdistan' and 'Kurd'. For a detailed list of different views concerning the equivalent of J.K., see Hasan Qazi 'Znjiray Komarnasi (3): Sabarat ba newi Komalay J.K.' [Article series about the republic: about the name of J.K.], *Gzing*, no. 18, 1998, pp. 46–7. Qazi lists thirty-three sources and refers to their various ways of interpreting J.K.

13 Since the establishment of the Democratic Republic of Kurdistan in January 1946 and its collapse in December of the same year, Mahabad has occupied a central position in Kurdish nationalist discourse.

Instead, J.K.'s political platform was one that focused upon the promotion of a greater Kurdistan. The pinnacle of this ambition was realised in a famous 'three-borders meeting' that was held in Dalanpar where the borders of Iraq, Iran and Turkey meet, bringing together representatives from Iraq, Iran, and Turkey.[14] The evidence of J.K.'s pan-Kurdish aspirations was not merely limited to the occasional meeting. A survey of J.K.'s journal, *Nishtiman* (Motherland), shows how the idea of Kurdishness and a greater Kurdistan was being actively discussed, and the *nishtimani* aspirations of the organisation were proudly displayed in its motto of "Long live greater Kurdistan", printed on the front cover of the journal itself.

The importance of J.K., however, is not to be found purely in an appreciation of its nationalist ideas. It also formed a leading part of an intellectual milieu that led to the formation of a new political organisation—the Kurdistan Democratic Party or KDP—in October 1945. The leader of the KDP, Qazi Muhammad, was an influential cultural and religious figure who later became the president of the Democratic Republic of Kurdistan (commonly if erroneously referred to as the 'Republic of Mahabad') in January 1946.[15] From an initial 'Iranian' Kurdish initiative, the new republic rapidly took on a pan-Kurdish colour when Kurds from other parts of Kurdistan, especially from Iraq, pledged their support. The most important of these figures was Mustafa Barzani, a tribal leader who had organised several revolts against the Iraqi government and their British backers throughout the 1940s. Barzani headed a large group of Iraqi Kurds who then formed the backbone of the military force of the Democratic Republic.

In the same year, while the Democratic Republic of Kurdistan was establishing its various institutions, some of Barzani's followers decided to form an Iraqi version of the KDP—against the wishes of Qazi Muhammad—by bringing together various organisations that

---

14 McDowall, *A Modern History*, p. 237.

15 The Kurds never used this name; instead they referred to the Democratic Republic of Kurdistan.

STANSFIELD AND AHMADZADEH

had begun to emerge in the 1930s (such as Darkar and Hiwa) with the traditional tribal groupings.[16] The establishment of an Iraqi KDP showed the bitter reality of Kurdistan, and its national movement, becoming by necessity fragmented. From this point on, Kurdish political forces in each country increasingly developed independently of each other.

The 'Kurdistani vision' of Kurdish parties

The division of Kurdistan between Iran, Turkey, Iraq and Syria burdened the Kurds with a structural weakness when it came to promoting an ethnic (i.e. pan-) Kurdistani agenda. Quite simply, it would prove impossible for the Kurds to act in a unified manner against the combined interests of Tehran, Baghdad, Ankara and Damascus (and also the rest of the international community), which meant that each of the Kurdish movements in each of the states in which they resided developed their own, local, political colouring, agendas, and ideas. However, the vision of a greater Kurdistan region has continued to survive. In the programmes of most of the established and well-known Kurdish political parties, it is commonly mentioned that Kurdistan is the country of the Kurds. However, they also acknowledge that this *nishtiman* (country) has been divided between four states. The dilemma of how to combine the need to be seen as acting in a *nishtimani* fashion while developing a political programme focusing on immediate regional concerns has seen the Kurdish parties embark upon a tortuous process of balancing names, hyphens, suffixes and affixes. For instance, the original KDP, established in October 1945 in Iranian Kurdistan, did not have any affix that could show its affiliation to Iran. It was only in 1973 that it was decided to add Iran to the name of the Iranian KDP. Similarly, the KDP then established in Iraq did not carry anything to denote its geographic area of interest as being limited to one part of Kurdistan. Instead,

---

16 For an account of the emergence of Iraqi Kurdish political groupings, see Gareth Stansfield, *Iraqi Kurdistan: Political Development and Emergent Democracy*, London: RoutledgeCurzon, 2003, pp. 63–6.

at its moment of establishment in August 1946, the name of the party signified a distinctly ethnicised agenda, with its name being the 'Kurdish' Democratic Party (Parti Demokrati Kurd). This was changed in the KDP's congress of 1953, when *Kurd* was changed to *Kurdistan* as a means to broaden its appeal to non-Kurds living in Kurdistan.[17] Again, however, there was no attempt to denote the 'Iraqi' location of the party.

Similarly, the second of the two major Iraqi Kurdish parties has no reference to Iraq in its name, and is even more tied to the notion of the greater Kurdish *nishtiman*. The Yaketi Nishtimani Kurdistan, otherwise known as the Patriotic Union of Kurdistan (PUK), appeared in 1975 following the collapse of the Kurdish rebellion in Iraq. While its name is often said to refer to the union of three political groupings that formed the basis of the PUK, it is also possible to argue that its name refers to greater Kurdistan. This argument is particularly persuasive when it is realised that the founders of the PUK were not wholly from the region of Iraqi Kurdistan. The same tendency can be seen with reference to the Parti Karkaren Kurdistan, known in English as the Kurdistan Workers' Party (PKK), which makes no reference to Turkey (nor to any limited part of Kurdistan) in its name. The KDP of Iran is now something of an exception. In the case of the KDP of Iran the affixation of Iran to the name of the party has been subject to political and ideological ebbs and flows. The party did not carry the designation of Iran for many years. The first issue of its journal, *Kurdistan*, which was published after the second conference in January 1971, states that the paper is 'The organ of the Central Committee of the Kurdistan Democratic Party', for example. However, by the time of the third conference, held in Baghdad in 1973, a change could be seen, with 'Iran' being mentioned more prominently, even in the journal *Kurdistan*. The end result of this trend saw the KDP become the Kurdistan Democratic Party

---

17 See Stansfield, *Iraqi Kurdistan*, p. 66. For a detailed account of the formation of KDP-Iraq see Ibrahim Ahmad, 'From My Memories: The Establishment of J.K.'s Branch', *Gzing*, no. 13, autumn 1996.

(Iran)—clearly emphasising the division of the Kurds. The party would then alter its moniker to Hizbi Demokrati Kurdistani Iran (Democratic Party of Iranian Kurdistan, or KDPI). By the start of 2007, the KDPI split into the KDPI and the KDP-I. The meaning of the hyphen is still unclear. Perhaps it has no use beyond differentiating the name from the KDPI. However, the fact that the Iranian suffix still survives is indicative of the manner in which political elites in Kurdistan still view their struggle, and how their wider view of Kurdistani-ness is constructed.[18]

Kurdistani civic nationalism in Iraq: reaching out to Assyrians and Turkmens?

The early intellectual emphasis on the idea of Kurdistan as being the country of the Kurds can be seen in political parties across Kurdistan regardless of its politically divided nature. Indeed, the politics of these Kurdish political parties have been practically shaped by the fact that they find themselves in the first hand bounded to the idea of the greater Kurdish *nishtiman*. Yet, increasingly, a 'Kurdistani' discourse became associated with an endeavour to construct a civic or territorial nationalism rather than an ethnic one. The Kurdistan region of Iraq, from 1991, became the flag-bearers of Kurdish nationalism due to the carving out of a *de facto* Kurdistan Region under the protection of the US- and UK-policed 'no-fly zone'.[19] Yet, far from pursuing a policy of promoting a wider *nishtimani* policy, the Kurdish

---

18 In December 2006 most of the prominent leaders of KDPI including Abdullah Hasanzadeh (who was the leader of the party from 1993 to 2005), split from the KDPI and built up the KDP-I.

19 For analyses of the formation and development of the *de facto* state, see Michael Gunter, *The Kurds of Iraq: Tragedy and Hope*, New York: St. Martin's Press, 1993; Sarah Graham-Brown, *Sanctioning Saddam: The Politics of Intervention in Iraq*, London: I. B. Tauris, 1999; Denise Natali, *International Aid, Regional Politics and the Kurdish Issue in Iraq after the Gulf War*, Abu Dhabi: Emirates Center for Strategic Studies and Research, 1999; Gareth Stansfield, *Iraqi Kurdistan*; Brendan O'Leary, Khalid Saleh, and John McGarry (eds), *The Future of Kurdistan in Iraq*, Philadephia: University of Pennsylvania Press, 2005.

leadership in Iraq remained distinctly aloof from—even antipathetic toward—their ethnic kinsmen across the borders in Turkey, Syria, and Iran. Rather, the emphasis of the Iraqi Kurdish leadership was focused more upon consolidating their gains in Iraq, which meant, by necessity, that non-Kurdish peoples living within their newly-gained domains would have to be accommodated, or coerced. Two non-Kurdish peoples in particular stand out as being targets in this regard—the Chaldo-Assyrian and the Turkmen communities. Due to their relatively large numbers and the fact that they tied into wider regional and diasporic communities (with the Turkmens being intrinsically linked with Turkey, and the Chaldo-Assyrians having a strong and influential lobbying operation in North America), the Kurdish leadership had to try, at least, to bring their political leaders into what had initially been referred to as 'Kurdish' self-rule—but soon began to be euphemistically referred to as an ethnically neutral 'democratic experiment'.

The Turkmen community claims links to the wider Turkic family of peoples which trace their origin to Central Asian tribes who migrated into areas of the modern Middle East region and Turkey. But their exact origins are disputed, with some scholars claiming that the forerunners of today's Turkmen community first came to Iraq in the seventh century as soldiers recruited into the Muslim army.[20] Turkmens then assumed positions of military and administrative responsibility in Iraq which peaked during the Ottoman Empire, when Turkmens found that their ethnicity granted them privileged status within the state bureaucracy. However, while this is a relatively persuasive scenario, it is not clear that the process was quite so simple, nor that Turkmen identity can be described in a manner which implies such clear ethnic distinctiveness. While the evidence that migrations of Turkic peoples occurred in the distant past seems to be reasonably clear, it is not clear how today's Turkmen community descended from them. Indeed, these communities did not live in isola-

20 Ershad al-Hirmizi, *The Turkmen and Iraqi Homeland*, Istanbul: Kerkük Vakfı, 2003, p. 16.

tion from those around, and assimilated with the Arab communities of the region, with Arabic becoming their native language. Also, the label 'Turkmen' could refer to something other than ethnic origin in the Ottoman context. Rather, it was also used to refer to those 'non-Turkmen' employed within the Ottoman bureaucracy that had effectively becoming 'Turkified' by taking on Turkic customs and language as they undertook their work in the institutions of state.[21]

In contemporary Iraq, the Turkmen people can be found mainly in the urban centres of the north.[22] But this is all that can be stated with any accuracy as no accurate statistics exist that indicate the size of the Turkmen community (indeed, no accurate statistics exist on any subject in the Iraqi state at present). Turkmen scholars who are keen to emphasise the importance of the community estimate that they make up an unrealistic ten to fifteen per cent of Iraqi society, but other Iraqi and Western sources believe the figure to be less than five per cent.[23] Whatever the actual percentages are, it is clear that there are prominent populations in towns such as Talafar, Mosul, Erbil, Altunkupri and Kirkuk, with a sizeable population also in Baghdad. Because of this, there is competition between Turkmens and Kurds in some of these towns, as Turkmens, with their history of being based predominantly in the urban areas, consider the cities to be historically 'theirs', with the Kurdish presence being the result of later rural–urban migration for economic reasons, or, in the case of Kirkuk, the 'Kurdification' of the city following the end of Saddam Hussein's regime.

The Chaldo-Assyrian community in Iraq is equally difficult to gauge in terms of its size.[24] Most scholars treat it as as being synony-

21 Stansfield, *Iraq: People, History, Politics.*

22 H. Tarik Oguzlu, 'The "Turkomans" as a Factor in Turkish Foreign Policy', *Turkish Studies*, vol. 3, no. 2, 2002, pp. 139–48, reference at p. 142.

23 Ibid., p. 143.

24 The Assyrian-Chaldean division has its origins in the earlier divide that existed between Chaldeans and Nestorians. Considered as separate religious communities until the early twentieth century, Nestorians began to view their association with the ancient Assyrian empire with more vigour—to the

mous with the 'Christian' community of Iraq, which is estimated to number no more than one million persons. But, unlike the Turkmen community, there are no major population concentrations existing beyond the presence of some Christian quarters in major towns in the north of the country (and particularly in Erbil, Dohuk and Mosul), with the majority of Christians still living in Baghdad.[25] The Christian community is characterised by its own internal divisions which have both sectarian and ethnic dimensions. The majority are Catholics of a wide range of denominations, with a smaller grouping of Eastern Arab Orthodox Christians. In practice, the Chaldean Catholic Church is by far the largest and most influential in the Christian community with perhaps as many as 70 per cent of Iraq's Christians belonging to it. However, whereas Chaldeans are keen to emphasise their religious (and not ethnic) identity, the Assyrians are keen to associate themselves with the glories of the ancient Assyrian Empire, and describe themselves as being the 'original' inhabitants of Iraq.[26] While some probably are descended from people living in the region several thousand years ago, it is impossible to prove such claims. Indeed, it is probably more accurate to point to the settling of some 20,000 Assyrians in Iraq from the Hakkari region of southwest Turkey by the British army during World War I. But, it remains the case that the modern Assyrians continue to assert that they are a primarily an 'ethnic' community, which has prompted considerable arguments within the Christian/Assyrian community between Chaldeans and Assyrians, over how their identity should be described. Generally speaking, Chaldeans have preferred to identify themselves more closely with their religious, Christian, beliefs, whereas the Assyrian community promotes itself as an ethnically distinct people

---

extent that the 'Assyrian' component of their identity began to be commonly emphasised—by the time of the formation of the modern state of Iraq.

25 Anthony O'Mahony, 'Christianity in Modern Iraq', *International Journal for the Study of the Christian Church*, vol. 4, no. 2, 2004, pp. 121–42; Stansfield, *Iraq: People, History, Politics*.

26 See, for example, the website of the 'Assyrians of the United States', http://www.nineveh.com/whoarewe.htm.

descended from the ancient Assyrian empire. With the removal of Saddam Hussein, leadership of both sides recognised that it was now essential to present a unified front in order to promote their common interests, and, on 24 October 2003, the final declaration of the Chaldean Syriac Assyrian General Conference stressed the unity of all Christians in Iraq while agreeing to the name 'Chaldo-Assyrian' and recognising that they are 'an indigenous nationality (people) on a par with the rest of the Iraqi ethnic nationalities'.[27]

The Kurdistan Region of Iraq—the failure of civic 'Kurdistani-ness'

Within the Kurdish political parties the differences over the definition of 'Kurdistani' occasionally broke down into violence, as happened within the PUK in the 1980s. However, in most respects the issue over whether the term 'Kurdistan' was used in a distinctively 'Iraqi' or a wider *nishtimani* context was largely academic, as the Kurdish parties did not control large swathes of territory containing other peoples. This was to change following Saddam Hussein's ill-fated invasion of Kuwait in August 1990 and the subsequent defeat of the Iraqi army in Kuwait.

While the path to *de facto* statehood for the Kurds was traumatic, with Kurds and Shiites being encouraged in 1991 by US President George Bush to rise up against the Baath regime before being left to the mercy of the regrouped Iraqi republican guard, the leadership of the Iraqi Kurdistan Front (IKF—which included the Assyrian Democratic Movement alongside the regular Kurdish political parties) managed to turn a dangerous limbo situation (IKF *peshmerga* (militia) and Iraqi military forces were face to face in the streets of the cities of Kurdistan) to one where the Baath regime—perhaps in the knowledge that it needed to consolidate its power in the more important centre of the country and the sensitive south—withdrew its military units and administrative personnel from Kurdistan, leav-

---

27 Stansfield, *Iraq: People, History, Politics.*

ing a vacuum that the leading Kurdish parties were naturally placed to fill.

In what still remains a notable achievement reached in chaotic circumstances, the leadership of the IKF managed to organise itself and formed an emergency administration for the region evacuated by Iraqi state forces. In May 1992, elections to the Kurdistan National Assembly (KNA) were held alongside the election for who should be president of the Kurdistan Region. The elections and the structure of the KNA did pay at least lip-service to the notion of representing all peoples who lived in the 'Kurdistan Region' rather than only 'Kurds', by ring-fencing five out of the 105 seats in the assembly for representatives elected from Chaldo-Assyrian parties, and by including Assyrians in the first cabinet of the Kurdistan Regional Government (KRG).

It is perhaps these and other subsequent examples of Kurdish inclusiveness that led some academics to suggest that a civic nationalism that transcended the seemingly deep ties of ethnicity began to develop in the Kurdistan Region. Noting that her findings were based upon fieldwork conducted in 2002, Carole O'Leary, for example, wrote, 'I would further suggest that a second unintended but welcome consequence of the establishment of the safe haven is an experiment in pluralism that is encouraging the emergence of a communal identity shared by Kurds, Assyrian-Chaldeans and Turkmens'.[28] However, based upon the authors' own visits to the region from 1997 through to the present, we suggest that the emergence of this communal identity—while certainly promoted by the leading Kurdish political parties—remains at best only partially subscribed to by non-Kurdish peoples, and then mainly for politically associated reasons.

Among the Assyrians, the most prominent political party to participate in the KRG was, and continues to be, the Assyrian Demo-

---

28 Carole O'Leary, 'The Kurds of Iraq: Recent History, Future Prospects', *Middle East Review of International Affairs (MERIA) Journal*, vol. 6, no. 4, December 2002.

cratic Movement (ADM) led by Younadem Youssef Kana. The ADM has been a perennial member of the cabinets of the KRG, with the leader himself at times taking on ministerial responsibilities. However, such involvement does not necessarily mean that there is wider acceptance among the Assyrian community of a 'Kurdistani' identity. Indeed, it would seem to be the case that the overwhelming sentiment is against such an idea, with Assyrians in Erbil and Dohuk in particular remaining keen to preserve their distinctiveness in the face of what many consider to be the overwhelming dominance of the Kurds in the institutions of the *de facto* state. But the KDP in particular has a long history of interaction with the Assyrian community due to most Christians/Assyrians living in territories that constitute the heartland of the KDP, around Dohuk and the Bahdinan region of Kurdistan. There is a long history of Christians/Assyrians joining the *peshmerga* forces of the KDP in their struggles against the Iraqi government, with several well-known leaders and personalities continually referred to in contemporary KDP writings, including the female *peshmerga* Margaret George and, in more recent years, the late governor of Erbil, Franso Hariri.[29] With this history of interaction, it has been a logical move by the KDP to include within its leadership prominent Assyrian politicians. Some observers view this in a cynical light. The appointing of Sarkis Agha Jan Mamendu to the important position of minister of finance and economic affairs in the fifth cabinet of the KRG can be viewed as either a commitment by the KDP to bringing in non-Kurds to prominent positions, or a cynical attempt to win Assyrian support by the appointing of a figure who is known to have strong links to the KDP leadership. There is, perhaps, truth in both statements.

---

29 Franso Hariri had joined the KDP in the 1960s and became close to Mulla Mustafa himself. He gained increasingly important positions of responsibility within the KDP—culminating with membership of its central committee, being head of the KDP block within the KNA, and governor of Erbil. He was assassinated on 18 February 2001 by members of the radical Islamist group Ansar al-Islam while travelling to the governor's office in Erbil.

Yet, it is clear that there remains considerable opposition among the Assyrian community toward the notion of a 'Kurdistani' identity. This opposition can be seen in the publications of the ADM, and in many of the pronouncements that come from the Assyrian diaspora community. Indeed, relations between the ADM and the Kurdish parties have become so poor following the Iraqi elections of December 2005 that the ADM chose to join forces with the Shiite-dominated United Iraqi Alliance (UIA), rather than remain under the wing of the Kurds. This was a considerable blow to the Kurds. It impacted upon their performance in the election, but it also dealt a blow to their claim that they were successfully building a 'Kurdistan' rather than a 'Kurdish' region in the north of Iraq. The ADM position developed even further following the election. With Christians being increasingly targeted by Islamists in Iraq, and being unimpressed by the idea of living in a region dominated by the Kurds (indeed, the ADM claimed that KDP security forces were actively harassing Assyrians living between Mosul and Erbil), the ADM leadership came to the conclusion that the only solution that could guarantee their future was for the Assyrians to have their own 'Assyrian Administrative Region', with its centre being the town of Bakhdeda, east of Mosul.[30]

From the perspective of the Kurdish leadership, the Assyrians are of secondary importance in terms of winning them over to the idea of being 'Kurdistanis'. Apart from their possible ability to influence US politicians by appealing to their Christian solidarity, the Assyrians remain distinctly less important than the Turkmens when considering regional dynamics from a Kurdish perspective. With Turkey watching what the Kurdish leadership in Iraq is doing and with the Turkish military command ready to order the invasion of the Kurdistan Region if it is seen to be moving toward a position where

---

30 See *The Mesopotamian*, vol. 1, no. 2, December 2004; Iraq Sustainable Democracy Project, 'An Assyrian Administrative Unit: Ending the Exodus of Iraq's Most Vulnerable', *Policy Brief*, February 2006, http://www.aina.org/reports/isdppb20060802.pdf.

secession from Iraq becomes a possibility, any conceivable trip-wire that could be used to legitimise an intervention has to be carefully managed. For the Kurds, the Turkmens are this trip-wire.

The Kurdish strategy toward the Turkmens has been one of seeking to divide them politically and to isolate the most anti-Kurdish and pro-Turkmen elements—and it has achieved some successes. The most notable move was KDP's role in establishing a new Turkmen political party as a means to weaken the pro-Turkish Iraqi Turkmen Front (ITF), which is considered to have very close links with Ankara and to be highly antipathetic toward the establishment of a Kurdistan Region in Iraq. The ITF formed in 1995 as a political front of twenty-six groups aiming to represent the Turkmen community in Iraq and challenge the authority of the Kurdish parties as they continued to consolidate their hold on power by further institutionalising the KRG. The ITF proved to be a considerable problem for the Kurdish parties, particularly as it often acted as the *de facto* representative of the Turkish government in Erbil and Sulaymani-yya, granting visas to individuals wishing to travel to Turkey, and registering people (of whatever ethnic background) as Turkmens.[31]

In 2002 came the announcement that five parties had split from the ITF to form the Turkmen National Association (TNA), which adopted a far more conciliatory position toward the KRG and particularly the KDP, with some speculation existing about the KDP financially assisting the TNA.[32] Indeed, the leader of one of the constituent parties of the TNA, Jawdat Najjar of the Turkmen Cultural Association, was made a regional minister (without

31 While most problems between Kurds and Turkmens (outside Kirkuk) happen in Erbil, this does not mean that the KDP position toward the Turkmens is in any way different to that of the PUK. Rather, the prevalence of problems in Erbil relates to the simple fact that there are less Turkmens living in Sulaymaniyya than there are in Erbil. If the PUK happened to be the leading political party in Erbil, then it is likely that the problems there would still remain.

32 The five parties that form the TNA are the Turkmen Cultural Association, the Turkmen Brotherhood Party, the Turkmen National Liberation Party, the Iraqi Turkmen Union Party and the Kurdistan Turkmen Democratic Party.

portfolio) in the KRG. While the TNA has proved able to gain considerable support especially in Erbil, the strategy to gain Turkmen support for the Kurdistani initiative failed due to the problems created between the communities by the situation in Kirkuk. With the Kurdish leadership demanding the inclusion of Kirkuk into the Kurdistan Region of Iraq, and insisting upon not only its modern Kurdish character, but its more ancient Kurdish origins, the Kurds found themselves an implacable foe in the form of the Turkmens of Kirkuk. With the Kurds seeking to reverse Saddam Hussein's policy of Arabising Kirkuk by assisting in the return of Kurdish families to the city, the Turkmens accused the Kurdish leadership of attempting to 'Kurdify' Kirkuk just as Saddam had 'Arabised' it, with Turkmens being targeted by Kurdish security forces as the Kurds sought to create facts on the ground before any process of normalisation would decide Kirkuk's fate. With the constitution of Iraq outlining a procedure by which Kirkuk's future will be decided—by the end of December 2007 if it is followed—the opposition of Turkmens toward Kurdish plans grew considerably, with them accusing the Kurds of not wanting to build a civic national project to which all Iraqis could subscribe, but rather to create an independent Kurdish state that would secede from Iraq. As such, while advances had been made in the relationship between Kurds and Turkmens, the question of Kirkuk brought deeply-rooted mistrust to the surface and fundamentally undermined the idea that the notion of 'being Kurdistani' was widespread among the Turkmen community.

The resurgence of traditional Kurdistani-ness

While the policy of building a civic Kurdistani identity faltered in the post-Saddam period, or at least became complicated by competing agendas, there has been a resurgence, among Kurds, of the traditional idea of 'Kurdistan'—that is the idea of a greater Kurdistan entity as the homeland of all Kurds no matter where they reside. This resurgence has happened independently of, and perhaps even against, the wishes of the leaderships of the KDP and PUK, and is rather the result of the continued pressure of the Kurdish diaspora and the heightened expectations of Kurds following the survival of the Kurdistan Region in Iraq since 1991.[33] The fall of Saddam Hussein's regime further magnified Kurdish nationalist sentiment, with a harder nationalist line emerging that questioned the state-less condition of the Kurds and saw changes in the geopolitical circumstances of the Middle East as perhaps opening the door to statehood that had been so effectively closed in the 1920s.

In the diaspora, groups such as the US-based Kurdistan National Congress (KNC)[34] and cultural bodies located in Western capitals all served to nurture the idea of Kurdistan in its entirety rather than of its parts, with conferences and gatherings taking place that focused on the right to statehood of the Kurds, and the promotion of federalism—not for Iraq, or even Iran, but for the proposed Kurdish state itself. Recognising, perhaps with some accuracy, that the political and socio-economic trajectories of Kurds in their four locations have been different if not divergent since the 1920s, diaspora organisations built upon the idea of federalism (which was being discussed by the Iraqi Kurdish leadership as appropriate for Iraq) and presented it as potentially a good idea for Kurdistan, with what would be a very large federal state assembled from the as yet undefined Kurdish regions of Turkey, Syria, Iraq, and Iran.

Among Kurds in Iraq, including many members of the KDP and PUK, a reinvigorated pan-Kurdish nationalist idea could be seen. New publications that existed increasingly independently of the KDP and PUK talked openly about the situation of Kurds in Iran and Turkey,

---

33 The expectations of Kurds in the diaspora are clearly displayed in the vast range of internet sites that have emerged in the last decade. These sites are often independent of any political party—and often take a highly critical line against the KDP and PUK. Consider, for example, www.kurdishmedia.com, or www.peyamner.com. The latter in particular is interesting in the manner that its content is organised with 'World' and 'Iraq' news sections, but with Kurdish news being labelled 'National'.

34 See www.knc.org.uk.

while publishing letters and comments about the failure of Iraq and the need for the Kurdish leadership in Iraq to declare its independence. These ideas, that are common among young Kurds between the ages of fifteen and thirty-five, are also driven by the immense expansion of Kurdish weblogs and websites focusing upon Kurdish issues and rediscovering the linkages between Kurds in different countries that had been weakened throughout the course of the twentieth century. The community may be imagined, and even virtual, but it is also increasingly influential and has given the KDP and PUK a public relations problem that they both now struggle to deal with. The most obvious manifestation of this trend could be seen during the 30 January 2005 elections in Iraq. Held alongside the elections was an unofficial referendum, organised by the Kurdistan Referendum Movement. Asked to choose one option of 'I want Kurdistan to stay part of Iraq', or 'I want Kurdistan to be independent', 98.8 per cent of a total of 1,998,061 participants voted for secession.[35]

From being 'Kurdistani' parties in the traditional sense of the term, the KDP and PUK by necessity became 'Iraqi Kurdish' then 'Iraqi Kurdistani' parties due to the pressures imposed upon them by their immediate political parameters—i.e. by existing in Iraq. As such, they are closely tied into Iraqi politics and now have a vested interest in seeing US policy in Iraq succeed and, ultimately, Iraq survive. It is now very difficult, if not near impossible, for either Jalal Talabani or Massoud Barzani to openly talk about seceding from Iraq (even though Barzani at times comes close), and it is certainly not possible for them to mention the option of a greater Kurdistan appearing on the map anytime soon (or ever, if Turkish sensitivities are to be avoided). Yet, it is exactly these sorts of ideas that the active political classes in Iraqi Kurdistan now wish to hear, and this is one of the main reasons (along with the issue of corruption) why the leadership of the KDP and PUK is routinely and powerfully criticised. They are accused of wasting the best chance the Kurds have ever had of being

---

35 The Kurdistan Referendum Movement maintains a website at www.kurdistanreferendum.org.

independent, at least since the 1920s, and of turning their backs on their ethnic kinsmen in Turkey, Syria, and Iran.

Conclusion

Regionalism in the north of Iraq can be considered in one of two ways. It can either by seen as an attempt to build a civic nationalist project that encompasses all peoples regardless of their ethnicity in a framework that formally does not have a dominant nationhood underlying it. This has been the strategy, seen toward the end of the 1990s, of the Kurdish leadership in Iraq that has promoted the idea of a 'Kurdistani' identity to which Arabs, Turkmens, Assyrians and, of course, Kurds, could subscribe. This policy, while gaining some support from Turkmens and Assyrians, has largely failed due to the political pressures that exist in modern Iraq (particularly over issues such as the status of Kirkuk) and the latent suspicion that continues to exist between Kurds, Assyrians, and Turkmens.

The second way that regionalism can be seen as existing in the north of Iraq goes well beyond the boundaries of the state and encapsulates the entirety of the undefined area in which Kurds live—otherwise known as Kurdistan. While this regionalism has a long history that can be traced back to the first Kurdish intellectual groups that began discussing their ideas on nationalism and Kurdish statehood, the imposition of international boundaries that divided mythical Kurdistan between Iran, Turkey, Iraq and Syria served to undermine the unity of the Kurdish nationalist project and instead forced Kurds to engage the states in which they lived—often bringing them into opposition with each other. While parties such as the PUK and KDP retained a commitment to the idea of Kurdish unity, it increasingly became symbolic, with their actions governed by achieving their aims of autonomy within the framework of the Iraqi state. This tendency peaked with the formation of the Kurdistan Region of Iraq in 1991, and then combined with the need to promote a civic 'Kurdistani' identity.

Kurdistan has now entered a third phase in its nationalist development, and this is the rediscovery of the true *nishtimani* idea of unity among Kurds across boundaries. Driven by the post-2003 changes in Iraq and empowered by Kurdish autonomy there since 1991, but further sensitised by what is now perceived to be the slipping away of opportunities, the regional idea in Kurdistan is now very much greater than the idea of a Kurdistan Region in Iraq. It is the idea of a greater Kurdistan.

7

AL-IRAQ AL-ARABI: IRAQ'S GREATEST REGION IN THE PRE-MODERN PERIOD

Alastair Northedge

A major question of debate recently has been whether Iraq is a real and historical entity or an artificial creation by the British in the wake of the First World War—amalgamated from the three unconnected and disparate Ottoman *vilayet*s of Mosul, Baghdad and Basra.

There is no doubt that the origin of the idea that Iraq is an artificial creation stems from the work of many contemporary historians, who begin their work on Iraq with the depiction of the late Ottoman situation where Iraq is divided into three *vilayet*s. For example, Charles Tripp, in his well-known and excellent *A History of Iraq*, begins with the statement, 'During the sixteenth and seventeenth centuries, the lands that were to become the territories of the modern state of Iraq were gradually incorporated into the Ottoman Empire as three provinces, based on the towns of Mosul, Baghdad, and Basra.'[1] There is evident scepticism about the reality of the country, but he, rightly, has doubts, as he goes on to state that the name Iraq has been used since the eighth century to represent the alluvial plain of the south of the country.

Clearly, modern-day ideas of national identity and identification with a territory did not exist before the nineteenth century. Much of the reason for the lack of such an identity before then is to be connected with the more isolated lives that most people led in ancient

---

1   C. Tripp, *A History of Iraq*, Cambridge: Cambridge University Press, 2002, p. 8.

and medieval times. Fewer people travelled outside their home region, mainly merchants, armies and the occasional traveller.[2] Unless there is awareness of the 'other', no self-identification is necessary. The earliest denomination of the land of Mesopotamia is *kalam* in Sumerian (literally, the 'land'). Over the centuries, and millennia, trade and travel links with other territories developed and local awareness became more essential. This was an incremental factor over time. It is evident that in early times such awareness was nascent and ill-defined.[3] So it is necessary to look at the sources of cultural unity, in the physical environment, social and economic history, and in the building blocks of human interaction—language and religion.

The natural environment

Southern Iraq is an alluvial plain, the extension to the north of the Gulf, filled up by the sediments deposited by the rivers Tigris and Euphrates. In the Sumerian period (third millennium BC), the head of the Gulf lay certainly further north than today, perhaps 100 kilometres further north. The cities of Sumer, now in the desert, lay on or close to the shores of the Gulf. The environment is naturally a desert, with 150 millimetres of rain each year at Baghdad. 250 millimetres of rain a year is necessary for minimal rain-fed cultivation. Irrigation from the Tigris or the Euphrates is obligatory. Irrigated agriculture offers around twice the yield of rain-fed winter wheat in the Middle

---

2 The travels of Muslims for the Hajj pilgrimage to Mecca are an important exception. Not only are there many texts describing journeys, e.g. Ibn Battuta and Ibn Jubayr, but there is also archaeological evidence which can only be ascribed to the mixing effect of these travels, notably the introduction of a Central Asian technique of decoration on the pottery of the Middle Euphrates in the eleventh century; A. Northedge, A. Bamber and M. Roaf, *Excavations at 'Ana, Qal'a Island, Iraq* (Archaeological Reports, 1), Warminster: Aris and Phillips, 1988, p. 94.

3 Obviously, a territory situated in a continental land mass has greater problems of self-identity than one with clear natural boundaries—sea, mountains or deserts.

East, with greater reliability,[4] and this in itself explains the success of ancient Mesopotamian civilisation. However, ancient peoples were not aware that excessive irrigation in a hot climate leads to salinisation of the soil, and civilisation centres withdrew from Sumer to the north, to Babylon, and eventually Baghdad. In this flat plain, the courses of the Euphrates and the Tigris moved much in historical times, the Euphrates to the west, and the Tigris to the east below Kut al-Amara. The limits to the north of the Mesopotamian plain are located 17 kilometres south of Samarra on the Tigris, and at Falluja on the Euphrates. It should be emphasised that the Mesopotamian plain is a highly distinctive physical environment, quite different from surrounding regions, and only to be compared with the Nile valley in Egypt, both in its agricultural potential and annual floods in pre-modern times, two major factors in wealth production in the days of agricultural empires.

Above Falluja, agriculture takes place in the increasingly narrow plain of the Euphrates, which narrows from 30 kilometres at Falluja to 2 kilometres at al-Qa'im. This zone also includes the desert to the west, and the Jazira steppe to the north as far as the Tigris. To the north along the Tigris, the river plain is narrow, past Samarra, Tikrit and Bayji, until it reaches the second major cultural area of ancient and modern times, the plains around Mosul. In ancient times, the economy was based on rain-fed agriculture, which spread to the west to Jabal Sinjar, and to the east into the Kirkuk plain.

The third environmental element is the Kurdish mountains. As a geographical unit, this third area belongs to the western boundary of the Iranian plateau.

In terms of the relationship of physical geography to community identity, it is clear that there have always been two basic regions, the northern and southern plains, of which the southern has a highly unusual character, which in ancient times was capable of generating

---

4 O. Aresvik, *The Agricultural Development of Jordan*, New York: Praeger, 1976, table 8.4.

exceptional agricultural wealth, but which has declined as an asset owing to increasing alluvial and salinisation problems.

Ancient civilisation and identity

It is a commonplace that the idea of 'ancient Mesopotamia' was much exploited by Saddam Hussein as a source of Iraqi identity.[5] He was commonly accused of having done so crudely: damaging archaeological remains by an order to build Babylon anew, comparing himself to Nebuchadnezzar,[6] and building a palace in Mesopotamian style at Babylon. The truth is both less and more than the accusations. There was a similar programme to promote the relationship with the Islamic past. For instance, Saddam Hussein built a palace in the Abbasid style close to the Baghdad airport. There was also a project to rebuild the archaeological site of the Abbasid capital at Samarra. However, that project did not go as far as the rebuilding of Babylon, probably because the excavations of Samarra are not so well published as those of Babylon, and the necessary information database (which exists for Babylon), did not exist for Samarra. Nevertheless, Saddam Hussein's activities were not very different from those of other countries. Israel powerfully exploits archaeology as a source of national identity. Uzbekistan has recently rebuilt the medieval Shah-i Zindeh necropolis at Samarkand in an equally insensitive fashion.

The fact that Saddam Hussein may have acted somewhat highhandedly in calling upon archaeology to play a political role in Iraqi identity does not negate the objective relationship of the past to the

---

5 M. Seymour, 'Ancient Mesopotamia and Modern Iraq in the British Press, 1980–2003', *Current Anthropology*, vol. 45, 2004, pp. 351–68; Z. Bahrani, 'Conjuring Mesopotamia: Imaginative Geography and a World Past', pp. 159–74 in Lynn Meskell (ed.), *Archaeology Under Fire: Nationalism, Politics and Heritage in the Eastern Mediterranean and Middle East*, London: Routledge, 1998; M.T. Bernhardsson, *Reclaiming a Plundered Past: Archaeology and Nation Building in Modern Iraq*, Austin: University of Texas Press, 2005.

6 The accusation that Saddam Hussein compared himself to Nebuchadnezzar was one of Western origin (Seymour, *Mesopotamia*, p. 358). In fact, there was at least one mural in Baghdad depicting Saddam face to face with Hammurabi.

present. The ancient past, often a more or less imagined one, has frequently been used to consolidate an identity, and does play a certain psychological role in as far as the average individual thinks about the past.[7] The reason that Baathist exploitation of the Mesopotamian past was depicted negatively in the West is that the West commonly appropriates Mesopotamia as part of its own past, through the Biblical heritage; the idea that modern-day Iraqis—and particularly a detested dictator—might also have a claim provokes resentment.[8] A re-evaluation of the position is certainly necessary.

The earliest civilisation of which written records survive was that of Sumer, on the southern Euphrates, the complex of city-states of the third millennium BC around the shores of the Gulf and the banks of the lower Euphrates, as they would have extended at that time. However the culture in its prehistoric phase goes back at least three thousand years more. In the second millennium BC, the Sumerian language—whose origins are unknown—was replaced by Semitic Akkadian in the Mesopotamian plain. From the early second millennium BC onwards, Babylon was the dominant state. In particular, the Akkadian language, with the Babylonian pantheon, spread throughout southern Iraq.

In the north, the old Assyrian period developed, with a culture based on Assur, south of Mosul, with the same Akkadian language, but a different dialect. The common language, not found elsewhere, provided a sense of unity in a period where there was little sense of contrast with the outsider.

At any rate, Babylonian fought with Assyrian, two cultural centres, until the Persian conquest by the Achaemenid Cyrus the Great in 539 BC. Babylon was established as one capital of a Persian empire which extended from the Mediterranean coast of Turkey to the In-

---

7 P. Gathercole and D. Lowenthal (eds), *The Politics of the Past*, London: Unwin Hyman, 1989; P.L. Kohl and C. Fawcett (eds), *Nationalism, Politics, and the Practice of Archaeology*, Cambridge: Cambridge University Press, 1995; M. Díaz-Andreu and T. Champion, *Nationalism and Archaeology in Europe*, London: University College London Press, 1996.

8 Seymour, *Mesopotamia*.

dus. The other capitals were Susa, Hamadan, and Persepolis in Iran. At this point, the danger for Iraq was exposed: the plains of Iraq are easy to conquer for warlike peoples, whether from the east or the west. Nevertheless, Mesopotamia remained stable until the arrival of Alexander the Great in 331 BC. However, Alexander had little success, and perhaps little interest, in the administration of his massive empire—a feature that was also true of later great conquerors. In consequence, these conquests were often ephemeral. The Hellenistic states in the east were organised by the successors of Alexander; in the case of Mesopotamia, the Seleucids. A number of Greek cities were founded, including Seleucia on the Tigris, the first time that the area around modern-day Baghdad was chosen for the capital.

Nevertheless, the Greek population was slight, limited to the cities, and Mesopotamian culture was resistant. The Babylonian dialect of Akkadian written in cuneiform had been used along with Old Persian—and placed first before the Persian—in the trilingual inscription celebrating the achievements of Darius the Great at Behistun in Iran circa 515 BC. Cuneiform script on clay tablets, a very impractical writing system, survived into the second century BC, and the last cuneiform tablet dates from AD 75.

The Greeks were succeeded by the Iranians as the foreign conquerors, apart from two brief moments when the Romans attempted to set up a province: the Parthians (140 BC–AD 226), an Iranian tribal dynasty from what is today Turkmenistan, and the Sassanians (AD 226–637), a family of landowners from the province of Fars in southern Iran. The two empires were increasingly Iranian-dominated—Hellenism was slowly abandoned. This was particularly true of the Sassanians, who instituted Zoroastrianism as a state religion. Nevertheless, it is remarkable that both dynasties sited their major capital in Iraq at Ctesiphon, facing Seleucia across the Tigris. Both dynasties had had early capitals in their home provinces: the Parthians at Nysa near Ashkabad in Turkmenistan, and the Sassanians at Firuzabad and Bishapur in Fars, but these were later abandoned. It is paradoxical that these two dynasties, with a strong Iranian identity, nevertheless sited their capital outside Iran, in a territory where there was not more than an immigrant Iranian elite. How can the attraction of Iraq to these peoples be explained? There are two sorts of answer to this question: one is the power of the Mesopotamian culture, which retained its reputation even after many centuries of outside domination, and secondly the wealth of the Mesopotamian economy. By this time, Mesopotamia already had 3,000 years of recorded history, while Iran did not write much before the Islamic period, as far as one can detect. At any rate little survives in Middle Persian. But the fact that Mesopotamia was the economic powerhouse of the state and the source of tax revenues was an important issue in a world where transferring tax revenues from one province to another meant literally a train of donkeys with sacks of coins. The economic motor was the multiplication factor of irrigation agriculture in a hot climate, for, like many ancient states, government revenue depended on land tax from agricultural production.

In any case, it is clear that the Sassanians invested in a massive expansion of irrigation agriculture in the alluvial plain. A network of canals has been identified, among which two systems are each 225 kilometres long.[9] Some questions remain as to the effectiveness of this development, but Islamic sources report high tax revenues for the late Sassanian period in the sixth century—a peak of 340 million dirhams per year, as against 100–120 million under the Abbasid Caliph Harun al-Rashid at the end of the eighth century.[10] The lack of economic information does not really permit an understanding what happened, but it is possible that one can apply the model of the modern Soviet experience with irrigated cotton agriculture in the

9 R.M. Adams, *Land Behind Baghdad*, Chicago: University of Chicago Press, 1965; idem, *Heartland of Cities*, Chicago: University of Chicago Press, 1981, pp. 104–5.

10 Qudama b. Ja'far, *Kitab al-kharaj*, excerpts in Ibn Khurdadhbih, 'Ubaydallah b. 'Abdallah, *Kitab al-masalik wa-al-mamalik*, ed. de Goeje, (Bibliotheca Geographorum Arabicorum 6), Leiden: Brill, 1889; Adams, *Land Behind Baghdad*, p. 84. The figure for the Sassanian period can be described as legendary, but a large expansion in the number of settled sites can be seen on the ground.

Central Asian republics. There, massive quantities of water derived from the Amu Darya and the Syr Darya were applied to the land; yields were high, but within a number of decades, there were problems with salinisation, and production declined precipitately. At any rate, in Iraq the benefits continued into early Islam, and the wealth of the late Sassanian dynasty, and that of the Abbasid caliphate in Baghdad, depended on them.

In the late Sassanian period also, the composition of the population became more complex: Aramaic-speaking descendants of the Assyrians and Babylonians, a greatly expanded Jewish community, Iranian aristocrats and military, Arabs on the desert frontier, Kurds, and Indians. At the same time Christianity saw a rapid development in the sixth century, alongside Judaism and the official religion of Zoroastrianism.[11]

Islam and the Abbasid caliphate

After the battle of Qadisiyya in 637 and the Islamic conquest of Iraq, there was an additional inflow of Arabs from the east of the Arabian Peninsula, who were settled in the two new garrison cities (*amsar*) of Kufa and Basra. Initially, in numbers, this was not a great addition to the population, though slowly over the centuries, more Arabian tribes did move from the peninsula. However over the centuries following the conquest, there were significant cultural changes: there was slow conversion to Islam, and the Aramaic-speaking population began to speak the cognate language of Arabic. Today it is difficult to know how much DNA of ancient Babylonians and Assyrians remains, as the situation is not presently propitious for the kind of tests that have taken place in Europe to link modern-day populations with ancient ones. But the Arabian peninsula, being relatively lightly populated, is unlikely to have contributed a heavy load of new genes to the population, although there were continuing movements of tribes later. It

11 M.G. Morony, 'Continuity and Change in the Administrative Geography of Late Sassanian and Early Islamic al-'Iraq', *Iran*, vol. 20, 1982, pp. 1–50.

is quite common to see people in northern Iraq who look like the figures represented in Assyrian stone reliefs.[12]

After the first century of Islam under the Damascus-based Umayyad caliphate, resistance to domination from Syria increased in the eastern lands of the Islamic empire, and the revolution of 750 eventually brought the Abbasid family to the caliphate. The origins of the revolution lay in Iraqi opposition to the Umayyads, and it was not surprising that the Abbasids decided to stay in Iraq even though the decision was certainly also based on Iraq being the wealthiest territory of the caliphate. The choice was only confirmed by the foundation of Baghdad as capital by Abu Ja'far al-Mansur in the 760s. From 750 until the collapse of power under al-Muqtadir (908–932), the Abbasid caliphate can be described as one of the great powers of the world, controlling territory that extended from Tunisia to the lower Indus valley. The economic influence of the caliphate was felt as far as Britain, where Offa, the king of Mercia, minted imitations of Abbasid dirhams in the ninth century.

It is well recognised that Baghdad under the Abbasids became an intellectual and cultural centre for the Islamic world and beyond. Much of the classic theology of Islam was elaborated there. Many of the early chroniclers and poets wrote there. Greek philosophy and science were translated in the Dar al-Hikma of al-Ma'mun—the 'house of wisdom' which housed both scholars and a library. It is less appreciated how much of this cultural phenomenon was specifically Mesopotamian in character, and not Iranian, as is often suggested. The formulation of the royal court, with a harem and veiled women, goes back to Assyrian models. One could well describe the architecture of Baghdad and the second capital, Samarra, as the last manifestation of the Mesopotamian royal city.

In the ninth and tenth centuries the first systematic geographical descriptions of the Islamic world appeared in the works of the

---

12 The situation is comparable to Egypt, where the physical traits of ancient Egyptians, recovered from the ancient royal tombs, can be seen in the modern-day population, both Muslim and Copt.

so-called 'Arab geographers'—who wrote in Arabic, though many were ethnically Iranian. These works permit delineation of the imperial territories. As before Islam, the territory of modern-day Iraq is described as belonging to two areas: Iraq and Jazira.

Al–ʿiraq is a word probably of Arabic origin, meaning the low land along a river.[13] It was used by the geographers to mean a territory extending from Tikrit in the north to Abadan at the head of the Gulf in the south, and from al-Qadisiyya (close to Kufa) in the west to Hulwan (near the modern-day Iranian border) in the east. The graphic form of this arrangement is presented in a schema from the illustrated version of Ibn Hawqal's *Kitab Surat al-Ard*.

A secondary term is *al-sawad*. This term was also used for the alluvial Babylonian plain, meaning the black and thus fertile land.[14] One could speak of *sawad al-ʿiraq*, or more localised areas as *sawad al-kufa*, and *sawad wasit*. In principle Sawad should be a subset of the territory of Iraq. Yaqut distinguishes Sawad from Iraq in saying that Sawad is a *rustaq* (district) of Iraq, and extends from Hadithat al-Mawsil[15] to Abadan on the Gulf, and from Qadisiyya in the west to Hulwan in the east.[16] Curiously 'Iraq' is described by Yaqut as smaller than Sawad, extending only from al-Alth, south of Samarra, to the furthest limit of the province of Basra and the island of Abadan.

---

13 Yaqut b. ʿAbdallah al-Hamawi al-Rumi al-Baghdadi, *Kitab muʿjam al-buldan*, 6 vols., ed. Wüstenfeld, Leipzig, 1866–73, vol. 4, p. 107 (*s.v.* al-ʿIraq). Yaqut gives variant etymologies for the name, but these can be described more as word-plays than as explanations of real origins. According to Hans Heinrich Schaeder, 'Iraq' is a loan word from the Middle Persian *erag*, low land; *Encyclopaedia of Islam*, second edition (EI²), Leiden: Brill, 1954–2003, *s.v.* Sawad. However, the initial *ʿayn* of the root *ʿayn-raʾ-qaf* is only found in Semitic languages, and forms a very distinctive feature of them. Accordingly, it may be unsuitable to look for an origin in an Iranian language, where *ʿayn* does not occur, other than in Arabic loan-words.

14 EI² *s.v.* Sawad.

15 Haditha of Mosul is distinguished from the better-known Haditha on the Euphrates. It was located south of Mosul. Haditha on the Euphrates could be referred to as *hadithat ʿana*, if necessary, to distinguish it (Northedge et al., *ʿAna*).

16 Yaqut, *Muʿjam*, *s.v.* al-Sawad.

Some think that 'Sawad' was an older Arabic term for the Mesopotamian plain than 'Iraq', as it is the appellation commonly used in the texts describing the Islamic conquests, though the expression 'Iraq' is also found in those works.[17]

At a later date a defining adjective was added to the name 'Iraq': *al-'iraq al-'arabi*. This addition was made to contrast with a new appellation: *'iraq al-'ajam* ('Persian Iraq').[18] This latter expression was used to refer to western Iran, the Zagros mountains and the ancient Media. That region had been called 'Jibal' at the beginning of Islam. The change seems to have occurred in the Mongol period; it was current when the Moroccan traveller Ibn Battuta passed through in 1327, but had been unknown a century earlier.[19]

Al-jazira is used to describe the northern area between the Tigris and the Euphrates, as far south as Tikrit and Anbar, which as an ancient city was located close to Falluja.[20] However Jazira also extended west into Syria as far as the bend of the Euphrates east of Aleppo, and today the eastern province of Syria continues to be called Jazira. In addition the Jazira extended some distance into the mountains of southern Turkey. Diyarbakir was counted the northern limit of Jazira. The major city of eastern Jazira was Mosul, and according to various sources, the plains east of Mosul also counted as part of the province. The two poles of political power in medieval Jazira were Mosul and Aleppo, although technically speaking the latter lies outside the province. Whereas there were periods in which the same power ruled in both Aleppo and Mosul (for example Imad al-Din Zengi who ruled from 1127 to 1146, and his successors in Aleppo until 1183 and in

---

17 EI[2] *s.v.* Sawad.

18 *'Ajam* means a non-Arabic speaker of any type, but was specifically used of Iranians (EI[2] *s.v. 'Adjam*).

19 Ibn Battuta, Muhammad b. 'Abdallah, *Tuhfat al-nazzar fi ghara'ib al-amsar wa-'aja'ib al-asfar*, published as *Rihlat ibn battuta*, Beirut: Dar Sadir, 1960, p. 191; Yaqut, *Mu'jam, s.v.* al-'iraq.

20 EI[2] *s.v.* al-Djazira. The name 'Aqur' is employed by al-Muqaddasi in the tenth century; this seems to be a variant of 'Assur' (Assyria), based on the Islamic name for the city of Assur (Yaqut, *Mu'jam, s.v.* Aqur).

161

Mosul until 1233), political power was normally separated, and Mosul fell under the orbit of the Mongols.[21]

Although early geographical texts were written descriptions, a tradition of map-drawing also developed in the tenth century, beginning with the work of al-Balkhi (d. 934). The German Orientalist Konrad Miller called the eastern tradition of al-Balkhi the 'Islam-Atlas'; it appears in various versions based on a now lost world map of the caliph al-Ma'mun (called *al-Sura al-Ma'muniyya*), in which Iraq was placed in the centre of the world.[22] The clearest presentation for Iraq is the provincial maps represented in Ibn Hawqal's *Kitab Surat al-Ard* (completed between 967 and 988). In the map of Iraq, a line is drawn around the territory from the Gulf to Tikrit, and labelled *hadd al-'iraq* ('boundary of Iraq'). The Tigris is represented as a straight line, lined by the cities on its banks, and with Baghdad in the centre. The Euphrates plays only a small role, disappearing into the marshes south of Kufa. In the map of Jazira, the Tigris is again represented as a straight line extending from Diyarbakir as far as Baghdad. The Euphrates is represented as a semi-circle extending from Manbij (on the modern Turco-Syrian border) as far as Kufa in the south. As Baghdad had to be included, the words *hadd al-'iraq* are placed between Anbar and Tikrit.

It is not surprising to find Abbasid geographers placing Iraq in the centre of the world map, and Baghdad in the centre of Iraq. Al-Ya'qubi was a Baghdadi, and begins his geography (circa 891) with this statement:

---

21 After the decline of the Abbasid caliphate, Mosul and Aleppo were first united under the Hamdanids in the mid-tenth century, then under the Zengids, but from the taking of Aleppo by the Ayyubids in 1183, the two remained separate until the Ottoman conquest.

22 K. Miller, *Mappae Arabicae*, ed. H. Gaube, Wiesbaden: Reichert, 1986, vol. 1, p. 12; A. Miquel, *La géographie humaine du monde musulman jusqu'au milieu du XIe siècle*, Paris: Mouton, 1967; *EI*² s.v. *kharita, djughrafiya*.

I begin with Iraq because it is the middle of the world and the navel of the earth, and I mention Baghdad because it is the middle of Iraq and the greatest city that has no equal in the east of the earth or the west of it...[23]

By contrast, his contemporary, Ibn Khurdadhbih—who was an Iranian from Hamadan who wrote in Arabic—begins his *Kitab al-Masalik wa-al-Mamalik* (editions dated 844 and 886) thus:

I begin with the mention of al-Sawad, which the kings of the Persians called Dil Iranshahr (Persian: 'the heart of the land of Iran'), that is, the heart of al-Iraq.[24]

The paradox that Ibn Khurdadhbih calls Iraq the heart of Iran in Persian (at a time when there was in fact only a relatively slight Iranian population) symbolises the importance of Iraq for the Sassanian empire and its Iranian descendants.

Medieval Iraq

The economic and intellectual activity of the Abbasids created a cultural image of Iraq, based on Baghdad, which has lasted to this day. The architecture and art of later pre-modern Iraq were directly derived from the Abbasid models. This was not such a strong graphic image as that of the Umayyad caliphate, with its Umayyad mosque in Damascus, and the Dome of the Rock in Jerusalem. The materials of Iraqi architecture were less durable, and only the spiral minaret of Samarra (al-Malwiyya), and the castle of Ukhaydir survived to be printed on twentieth-century Iraqi banknotes. Also, Islam is a universal religion, and the Abbasid caliphate was multi-ethnic. The poetry, the theology, the science and the philosophy, were the heritage of all Muslims and Arabs.

Nevertheless, the cultural identity of Iraq would have continued to strengthen over the centuries, had it not been for the economic

---

23 Ahmad b. Abi Ya'qub b. Wadih al-Ya'qubi, *Kitab al-buldan*, ed. de Goeje (Bibliotheca Geographorum Arabicorum 7), Leiden: Brill, 1892, p. 7.

24 'Ubaydallah b. 'Abdallah Ibn Khurdadhbih, *Kitab al-masalik wa-al-mamalik*, ed. de Goeje, (Bibliotheca Geographorum Arabicorum 6), Leiden: Brill, 1889. p. 5.

and political decline which led many scholars and poets to seek their living elsewhere. The historian and geographer al-Mas'udi (d. 956), who left Baghdad for Egypt, explained that 'the most central of the climes is the one in which I was born, albeit Fortune has taken it from me, set it at a great distance from me, and filled me with longing for it, since it is my home and birthplace, that is to say, the clime of Babylon,' and then adding, 'the noblest portion thereof is the City of Peace [the classic epithet of Baghdad], and I deplore the destiny that compelled me to leave it.'[25]

It is striking that, while Iraq was by far the wealthiest territory of the Islamic world under the early Abbasid caliphate, from the late tenth century onwards, Iran, Egypt and Spain overtook it. The comparative decline continued, and no upswing occurred before modern times. Contemporary chroniclers bewailed the decline of the caliphate, and attributed the problem to mismanagement and conflicts.[26] Ibn Ra'iq breached the great Nahrawan canal in 937, to protect Baghdad from a rival, and it took twenty years to repair it. Yaqut (d. 1226), brought up in Baghdad, generalises:

None of these sultans was interested in construction and building, their only aim was to collect taxes and consume them. It was also on the route of their armies, so the population left their lands, and it continued to go to ruin.[27]

The economic problems of Iraq, however, may have been more long-term than could be understood by medieval authors, or resolved by medieval rulers. The alluvial plain of Iraq is a very unusual environment for human life: a natural desert dependent on lengthy irrigation canals for cultivation. If the canal was cut or for some reason ceased to flow, the population was forced to move. According to modern-

---

25 Abu al-Hasan 'Ali b. al-Husayn al-Mas'udi, *Muruj al-dhahab wa-ma'adin al-jawahir*, vol. 2, pp. 65-6, quoted in M. Cooperson, 'Baghdad in Rhetoric and Narrative', *Muqarnas*, vol. 13, 1996, p. 101.

26 Notably Ahmad b. Muhammad Miskawayh, *Tajarib al-umam wa-ta'aqib al-himam*, ed. de Goeje, Leiden 1871, and Hilal al-Sabi'. Miskawayh was an Iranian.

27 Yaqut, *Mu'jam*, vol. 1, p. 252.

day standards, in early historic times canals may have been short,[28] but, by the Sassanian period, there were several canal systems more than 100 kilometres in length, with consequent problems of silting. There was an attendant requirement for a centralised government to maintain and renew the canals, for no canal lasted more than a few centuries. Egypt and Iran are different; in Egypt, the canals from the Nile are only a few kilometres long, in Iran the underground *qanat*s somewhat longer. However, with the decline of the centralised caliphate, Islam became 'medievalised', that is, political power was local, and resources small, within a larger commonwealth of Islam, no different from medieval Europe. Replacing the Sassanian canals was beyond government resources, and so it was never undertaken. By the Ottoman period, the vision had disappeared, and new extensive irrigation schemes were not undertaken until the twentieth century. In consequence, Iraq remained poorer than its flourishing neighbours, where irrigation could be maintained on a local basis.

Nevertheless, Baghdad retained an identity born under the Abbasid caliphate. In early Abbasid times it had been one of the largest cities on Earth, with an area said to have been as much as 70 square kilometres in the ninth century, and it had dominated Iraq.[29] By the thirteenth century it was much smaller, with areas of open land between the inhabited quarters.[30] The taking of Baghdad by the Mongol Il-Khan Hulagu in 1258 was only one of many destructions, but it showed well the problem of the city's geographical situation. The junction of roads from Iran, Syria and the Gulf, the site was well located for trade, but it was also an obvious target for invaders from Iran or from areas west. As a consequence, Baghdad was increasingly diminished in status, while retaining its mythic glory. Mosul and

---

28 Adams, *Heartland of Cities*.

29 Adams, *Land Behind Baghdad*, p. 89; J. Lassner, *The Topography of Baghdad in the Early Middle Ages*, Detroit: Wayne State University Press, 1970. The true area of Abbasid Baghdad cannot be detected under the modern city. Samarra in Abbasid times was 58 square kilometres of built-up area, and suggests what early Baghdad may have looked like.

30 Adams, *Land Behind Baghdad*, pp. 89–90.

Jazira did not suffer from the economic problems of irrigation, and this fact perhaps explains why Mosul became more significant in medieval times and later. It was certainly the decline of Baghdad which put Mosul and later Basra on a level with Baghdad, and periodically led the Ottomans to govern Iraq and Jazira as three *vilayet*s rather than as a single charge.

Following loosening of ties with Istanbul in the early eighteenth century, Baghdad regained autonomy—as well as pre-eminence in a regional world that was to correspond quite closely with the modern state of Iraq. Hasan Pasha, appointed in 1704, revived Baghdad, and led to the Mamluk pashas (1747–1831). In this period, security improved, and in 1774 Baghdad was described as a 'grand mart for the produce of India and Persia, Constantinople, Aleppo and Damascus'.[31] At the same time, economic activity in the countryside of the south redeveloped, independent of the pashas of Baghdad, based on the tribal confederacy of the Muntafiq and others, with tribal forts constructed along the flowing waterways of the lower Euphrates.[32] These twin developments, independent of Istanbul, set the scene for the social structure of Iraq in the late nineteenth and twentieth centuries.

---

31 EI², *s.v.* Baghdad

32 Adams, *Heartland of Cities.*

8

BORDERS, REGIONS AND TIME: DEFINING THE IRAQI TERRITORIAL STATE

Richard Schofield

The precise territorial definition of the modern Iraqi state was the product of a series of discrete regional episodes in which Britain was centrally involved, both before and after an independent Mesopotamian state had even been imagined. As such, nearly every one of its territorial limits was the product of a different set of strategic and regional calculations and considerations. In many of these episodes the Iraq region was itself at the edge of the big imperial issues of the day, and this was reflected in the ultimate basis of territorial settlement. The imperial strategic imperative of maintaining the Persian Gulf as a British lake in the years before World War I was the governing consideration in squeezing the Ottoman Empire from Gulf waters and in defining a narrow sovereign land corridor that was later inherited by Iraq. The remarkably ambitious and ultimately tortuous nineteenth-century Anglo-Russian project to narrow the traditional Anglo-Persian frontier along the spine of the Zagros mountains was to intervene in an area that had often been beyond the reach of surrounding central authority.

Deciding upon the exact territorial extent and form of the future Iraqi territorial state during and immediately after World War I would be the difficult outcome of imperial schemes and negotiations and regional accommodations, though the ultimate shape of things to come had been closely anticipated by Britain's de Bunsen Com-

167

mittee report of 1915, certainly in terms of the rump area that would ultimately comprise the new state. However, if Britain's blueprint for the future location of Iraq's northern boundary with Turkey had been articulated as early as 1915, this should not disguise the huge effort that was required to make this a reality a decade later. After seemingly endless negotiations and various changes of strategy and direction, Britain and France opted for a very basic (and arbitrary) boundary allocation to separate Iraq and Syria, on the basis that this was all that was required at the time. To the south and south-west, a different set of territorial challenges was present in the shape of a small but highly mobile desert population and the perceived need to set limits to the northwards expansion of the Wahhabis under Ibn Saud. After all of the preceding decades of procrastination narrowing the Perso-Ottoman frontier, no one, least of all Britain, had the stomach for revisiting territorial definition at the head of the Gulf or further north.

This chapter covers each of these episodes, highlighting both regional and imperial determinants in the modern territorial definition of Iraq. It raises many questions, many of which remain relevant or even unanswered today, about the manner in which an Iraqi state emerged with a recognisable shape and agreed international boundaries by the mid-1920s.

Prejudicing the Iraqi territorial state: the eastern frontier towards Persia

Of all Iraq's contemporary borderlands, only that to the east with Iran functioned historically as a traditional frontier, a phenomenon that dated back to pre-Islamic times. The Zagros mountains and the eastern Mesopotamian plain comprised a fluctuating, conflict-prone zone to which competing central (or imperial) authority was never extended on a permanent basis. Ancient Persia and the Byzantines fought out the battle to extend territorial control here by proxy, hiring the Arab Ghassanid and Lakhmid groups for this very purpose. The Zagros themselves provided a barrier that the original Arab expansions of the seventh century could not cross, though it would be almost a millennium later before the mountain range (with its margins) could be regarded as having attained the status of a political frontier. For the Perso-Ottoman attempt to define and regulate their borderlands through treaty began with the 1555 Treaty of Amasya— a crude codification of a post-war balance of power that allocated a border of sorts along the spine of the Zagros from Georgia and Armenia southwards to the Persian Gulf.[1] It continued with the May 1639 'Treaty of peace and demarcation of frontiers' of Zuhab; nominally, at least, one of the oldest boundary demarcation agreements signed at state level. Despite its name, this treaty was—like all successor Perso-Ottoman agreements culminating in the first Treaty of Erzurum (1823)—merely another ratification of the immediate territorial spoils of war. Yet the Zuhab agreement would have the effect of introducing a modicum of shape and stability to the frontier: gone were the wild fluctuations in territorial fortunes witnessed in previous centuries. Nonetheless, though each of the Zuhab, Hamadan (1727), Kerden (1746) and Erzurum (1823) treaties introduced lines of momentary control, their combined effect was to shade what was still a fairly wide strip of territory in which the authority of Ottoman sultan and Persian shah was weak, invariably transitory and disputed. As such the nominal allegiance of the borderland zone at a generic level would shift eastwards and westwards over the two-century period, in a manner roughly analogous to Europe's historical tribulations of a Polish state trapped between Germany and Russia.

This is not to say that within a general picture of sovereign fluidity, boundaries—as visible lines of militarised control—were not a feature at certain points of time along various stretches of the borderlands. Fixed border transit posts for pilgrims and merchants crossing the mountains operated with precision, particularly those near Mandali on the hugely important Kirmanshah–Baghdad route. Persian Sa-

---

1   Keith McLachlan, 'Boundaries with the Ottoman Empire', in Ehsan Yarshater (ed.), *Encyclopaedia Iranica*, New York: Routledge and Kegan Paul, 1989, vol. 4, fascicle 4, p. 401.

favid sources also allude fairly consistently to a generally militarised Ottoman border that separated the alien lands and people to the west.[2] For these reasons, Matthee argues that the 'Ottoman-Safavid border area ... was a political border as much as a frontier'.[3] Yet, for most of its length, this borderland always resembled a frontier zone more than it did a linear boundary, certainly over anything beyond the decades following the conclusion of those early Perso-Ottoman territorial treaties. The implicit element of the unknown represented by the frontier was discernible in the attitudes maintained by surrounding central authority. To Persia, the borderlands separated the aliens to the west; as far as the Ottomans were concerned, they constituted remote and unfamiliar terrain. To everyone, from the malarial marshlands of the south to the remote valleys and mountains further north, the borderlands seemed inhospitable and inaccessible. Albeit within an unstable context, this at least provided borderlanders with the opportunity for localised political autonomy and relative freedom of socio-economic movement. They had to be flexible and adaptive however, for as imperial fortunes fluctuated and temporary territorial limits changed, then so necessarily would their loyalties.[4] Realising that these could never really be relied upon, distant central authority developed a pragmatic frontier policy of alliance-building beyond the usual fleeting lines of territorial control or notional sovereign limits. Not only was this a tried and tested imperial consolidation strategy employed by the Romans in previous millennia but there was often localised commercial advantage to be found in a loosely-arranged border zone. As McLachlan comments: '...the Ottomans hesitated to

---

2   Rudi Matthee, 'The Safavid–Ottoman frontier: Iraq i-Arab as Seen by the Safavids,' *International Journal of Turkish Studies*, vol. 9, nos. 1–2, 2003, p. 165.

3   Ibid. Firoozeh Kashani-Sabet convincingly makes the same point in her *Frontier Fictions: Shaping the Iranian Nation, 1804-1946*, Princeton: Princeton University Press, 1999, p.30.

4   Richard Schofield, 'Narrowing the Frontier: Mid-Nineteenth Century Efforts to Delimit and Map the Perso-Ottoman Boundary', in Roxanne Farmanfarmaian (ed.), *War and Peace in Qajar Persia*, London: Routledge, 2007 (forthcoming).

define the boundary too precisely because of the potential loss of large revenues collected from client tribes in the area.'⁵ Such practices reinforced the zonal function of the frontier, a situation that seemed to confer benefits to both borderlanders and surrounding governments. Perhaps surprised by the effectiveness of a concerted European stance in cutting Mehmet Ali Pasha down to size at the turn of the 1840s and realising more pragmatically that such commonality of purpose was rare, Britain and Russia went on to busily seek agreement on a raft of Middle Eastern questions, most of them concerned with clarifying the spatial frame of their Great Game in these parts. Seizing the opportunity to put their names (along with that of the Ottoman Empire) to conventions aimed at pacifying the Levant and establishing a regime for the Turkish Straits, Britain and Russia then set about narrowing the Perso-Ottoman frontier, a remarkably ambitious project but a determinedly prioritised one. Russia wanted greater stability for its recently-acquired Caucasian provinces, while Britain feared that its fast developing commercial interests at the head of the Persian Gulf would be severely impacted by another bout of serious Perso-Ottoman hostilities—a real possibility following the Ottoman sacking of Muhammara (in Persian territory vis-à-vis Basra, today known as Khorramshahr) in 1837. So, a full seven and a half decades before the form of a future Mesopotamian state began to seriously exercise British minds, the process of delimiting its territorial limits was set in motion when Britain and Russia joined a quadripartite boundary commission in the late spring of 1843.⁶ Its expressed purpose of narrowing the frontier into a mappable line was largely doomed from the beginning.

First, Britain was not fully empowered to take control of the exercise it was leading. As mediating powers, Britain and Russia could try to bring the disputants closer together, but it was the Ottoman

---

5 McLachlan, 'Boundaries'.

6 Richard Schofield, 'Old boundaries for a New State: The Creation of Iraq's Eastern Question,' *The SAIS Review of International Affairs*, vol. 26, no. 1, 2006, pp. 27–40.

Empire and Persia who still held the reins in negotiating the territorial dispute. Second, in most respects, Persia was the weaker of the two local powers, and the tortuous record of intermittent negotiations throughout the nineteenth century reflected the reality that, on many occasions, Constantinople was locking horns with London and St. Petersburg as representatives and defenders of Persia's position. So, from an early stage, in attempting to fix limits to territory, they were dealing with the art of the possible. The early years of the four-party commission's activities were spent thrashing out the basis of a territorial settlement. Mediating Persian and Ottoman claims based upon the vague and brittle treaty settlements of the previous two centuries, Britain and Russia then tried to superimpose their own understanding of where the contemporary territorial balance of power lay along the frontier—referred subsequently as 'the *status quo* of 1843'.[7] The fact that they could never do this satisfactorily within an established traditional frontier was predictable, yet the attempt to freeze situations in time would soon become the recognised basis for drawing boundaries throughout the colonial world, often in a far more obviously arbitrary manner than was discernible here.

If narrowing the Perso-Ottoman frontier was not a sufficiently daunting prospect in itself, then the decision to place its southernmost reaches along the Shatt al-Arab river considerably added to the difficulties faced by the commission. For, once Britain and Russia had concluded that Muhammara had greater (if only very recently established) links with Persia, an international river boundary had been effectively prescribed. While rivers as boundaries had their adherents around this time (and remained popular throughout the century, with the pronounced vogue for the adoption of 'natural' boundaries), history retrospectively suggests that their nomination has created more problems than it has solved. Around the shorelines of the Persian Gulf a large degree of political autonomy was the norm, and in previous centuries the Bani Ka'ab Arabs had maintained control of the deltaic flats either side of the Shatt al-Arab river

---

7 Schofield, 'Narrowing the frontier'.

by developing an irrigated agricultural economy and defending it by playing off competing (though distant) central authority, as well as through adroit use of their own small navy. Based largely on the eastern banks of the Shatt, the sheikh of Muhammara himself continued this tradition of pragmatically allying with either Constantinople or Tehran as the situation demanded into the nineteenth century, just as borderland tribes to the north along the land frontier had always done. To the south, too, along the eastern (Persian) littoral of the Persian Gulf, it was usual for most of the major ports to be effectively run by semi-autonomous Arab groups.

Most river boundaries that had eventuated in state practice before this time tended to be drawn along banks—a ratification of the results of conflict that left the waters to the victor. In the Shatt al-Arab, Britain and Russia had intervened in part to avert further conflict, yet the quadripartite 1847 treaty that resulted from their efforts and that nominated a boundary along the Shatt for the first time would do exactly the same. Britain knew by this stage that if the river was navigable and of value to both states then its waters really ought to be shared, with no less a figure than Foreign Minister Lord Palmerston admitting as much just two months before the 1847 treaty was signed.[8] In other words, if a river boundary really had to be nominated, then at least one ought to make sure it was fair. Yet the reality at the time was that a settlement leaving the waters of the Shatt entirely to themselves was as much as the Ottoman Empire was prepared to concede and even then, only very reluctantly. The price for gaining the assent of the local powers to the 1847 treaty was a deliberate vagueness, which saw a river boundary introduced without specifically mentioning one.

While this temporarily bought treaty signatures, it effectively scuppered any chances a new mini-commission formed by the same treaty had of laying down the prescribed territorial settlement on the ground a few years later. This was supposed to specify a boundary from Muhammara in the south to Mount Ararat in the north based

---

8   Schofield, 'Old Boundaries', p. 33.

upon the governing delimitation principles of the 1847 Erzurum Treaty. Yet, while the mediating powers sought to lay down a line on the basis of what they had intended to introduce during the 1850–52 period,[9] the local disputants manipulated its hazy wording to advance wholly irreconcilable territorial claims, not just in the Shatt region but in other stretches of the borderlands covered specifically by the 1847 settlement: most notably Zuhab, supposedly partitioned into western Ottoman lowlands and eastern Persian highlands. As the ambitions of the chastened mediating powers were consequently relegated to surveying and mapping the Perso-Ottoman borderlands, a much more pragmatic Palmerston conceded that 'the boundary between Turkey and Persia can never be finally settled except by an arbitrary decision on the part of Great Britain and Persia'.[10] Prescient words, though Britain and Russia would not gain such powers until the eve of World War I.

Even the relegated mission of mapping the frontier was a protracted tale of woe. The revised idea had been for the local powers to plot their claimed lines on a detailed, large-scale Anglo-Russian map, yet this was not ready for presentation in Constantinople and Tehran until the 1870s. By this time, the prized window of European co-operation that had enabled the project to be dreamt of in the first instance had long misted over, with, ironically, almost everyone but the two local powers themselves having been engaged in conflict at one point or another. If this had delayed things, then perhaps more fundamentally so had the loss of most of the records and recommendations maintained by the 1850–52 commission to the muddy Thames at Gravesend on the return voyage of the British delegation in early 1853. Gone was their documented reconciliation of the 1843 territorial *status quo* with features on the ground, and also the vast majority of their mapping data. While it looked good,

---

9   Richard Schofield, 'Laying It Down in Stone: Delimiting and Demarcating Iraq's Boundaries by Mixed International Commission', *Journal of Historical Geography*, 2007, forthcoming.

10   Schofield, 'Old Boundaries', p. 31.

the huge joint Anglo-Russian map that resulted was therefore an error-strewn mess and quickly identified as such by the local powers. Although uncompromising Anglo-Russian diplomacy would result in Constantinople and Tehran penning their claim lines (in gold and silver respectively) on a heavily revised but still deeply compromised version half a decade or so later, the Serbian uprising against the Ottomans and the subsequent Russo-Turkish War (1877–78) broke out to draw a line under things for the nineteenth century. Privately Britain would admit that it faced enormous difficulties in reconciling the claims lines and even finding a basis for doing so. Reviewing the supporting Ottoman and Persian memoranda from the 1870s that were contradictory, inaccurate and inconsistent, Britain realised why the frontier had always escaped the projection of more rigid control from surrounding central authority.[11] Despite all their determined efforts, Britain and Russia naturally knew even less of the social geography of the borderlands. Nonetheless, once they had been granted those all-important arbitrating powers in 1913, the imperial powers decisively picked up where they had left off in the mid-1870s.

The discovery of oil in the central and southern stretches of the borderlands in the early years of the twentieth century increased the incentives for imperial intervention in the frontier question. So, after thirty years away, Britain and Russia returned to the fray to finish off an essentially mid-nineteenth century episode. At a local level at least, there had been some interesting territorial developments. Probably unaware of the ineffectual 1847 treaty settlement, the local authorities on either side of the Shatt had arrived at an eminently fair and sustainable arrangement where the mid-channel was respected as the working river boundary alongside Muhammara and elsewhere. While Britain would generally subjugate regional realities to the bigger picture of its relations with the Ottomans in a new 1913–14 boundary settlement (and in this instance stuck to the governing criteria of the 1847 settlement specifying the Shatt as an Ottoman river), it would nonetheless broker a deal whereby the river

---

11   Schofield, 'Narrowing the Frontier'.

boundary was extended to the midstream for a few miles opposite Muhammara. Well aware that Muhammara needed new anchorage facilities on the Shatt to export newly-discovered oil from the Zagros mountains, and that only a midstream delimitation could accommodate such a development, Britain decided to point to the reality of the locally recognised boundary in this particular case. Along the land frontier further north, the dealmaker had proved to be virtual capitulation to Ottoman demands over Zuhab, involving the actual transfer of Persian oil installations to the Ottoman Empire and the future designation of the surrounding localities as 'transferred territories'. In return, and under some pressure from a determined Russia, Constantinople vacated all of the (presumably Persian) territory it had occupied in the northern borderlands since the turn of the century. Another four-power treaty, the Constantinople Protocol of November 1913, would bundle together all the territorial deals to enshrine and articulate the guiding principles for a comprehensive boundary settlement. In truth, it was the document the 1847 treaty might have been. The British and Russian delegations on the commission set up by the protocol to work out the final details of delimitation (and demarcation) on the ground would now be accorded the powers to arbitrate in any remaining disputes. The emphatic result was that this time they completed their job in ten months flat.[12]

By this stage an inexorable weariness had set in on all sides and there was a grim determination to draw a line under things and let sleeping dogs lie, further explaining the rapid progress. Despite its mini-success over Zuhab, the Ottoman Empire was ailing and about to disintegrate. The long-overdue territorial settlement was clearly out of kilter with times of great dynamism in the region. Nowhere was this more evident than in the imperial demarcation effort of 1914 itself, where the eventual culmination of an elusive international quest seemed strangely irrelevant in many ways, even visually: here the baronial splendour of the four delegations contrasted with the bemusement of generally impoverished borderlanders who would tear

---

12 Schofield, 'Laying it Down in Stone'.

down ninety percent of the pillars laid down to demarcate the Perso-Ottoman boundary within hours of them being emplaced and would openly boast in advance of their intention of doing so.[13] While it may have seemed an outdated exercise, even irrelevant in regional terms, the delimitation decisions reached during the 1914 demarcation continue, for the most part, to regulate the Iran–Iraq boundary today. Its juridical significance was obviously of much greater consequence for the surrounding states than for the borderlanders themselves.

Very few official records of territorial definition explain the basis of decisions reached, and scant information was available until the individuals involved in the 1914 demarcation exercise published their recollections.[14] Hubbard (1916) reckoned that the Perso-Ottoman boundary as defined before World War I 'supplie[d] instances of practically every principle of delimitation known to the science'.[15] Unlike Iraq's contemporary international boundaries to the south and west, there were plenty of physical features to utilise, and given the prevailing wisdom that territorial limits based upon such phenomena were somehow superior, they were always going to be referenced in the boundary-drawing process. This would have occurred with any colonial boundary drawn at this time, irrespective of its location. Accordingly, the frequent employment in the official demarcation record of such terms as 'line of low tide', *medium filum aquae*, 'crest line', 'watershed' and 'foot of the hills' was fairly common.[16] In was also usual when nominating a boundary through mountainous terrain to confer strategic parity by balancing control of and access to the major passes and routes, and this was also done here in the case of the

---

13   C.H.D. Ryder, 'The Demarcation of the Turco-Persian Boundary in 1913–14', *The Geographical Journal*, vol. 6, 1925, pp. 227–42.

14   In addition to the article of Ryder (above), G.E. Hubbard's *From the Gulf to Ararat*, Edinburgh: William Blackwood, 1916, provides a particularly entertaining account of proceedings.

15   Ibid., p. 19.

16   Official *proces-verbaux* reproduced in Richard Schofield (ed.), *The Iran-Iraq Border, 1840–1958*, Farnham Common: Archive Edns, vol. 6, 1989, section 6.03.

Zagros. More interesting, perhaps, was the way in which the specific human geography of these borderlands was accommodated. Any talk of nationality here would have been a non-starter, for the populations of the border zone knew they were marginal to distant central authority and had long seen themselves primarily as borderlanders (as had central authority itself). Moving north from the Shatt (where the boundary was based solely on the location of the river), Hubbard reckoned that the 1914 boundary delimitation generally separated Lur from Arab along fairly clear ethno-linguistic lines, then its middle sections used more subtle and less obvious linguistic (even dialectical) distinctions, while in the mountains of Kurdistan the border reflected more fully tribal and religious (Sunni/Shiite) divides.[17]

It is fair to say that the attitudes of the Ottoman and Persian governments changed considerably towards both their mutual borders and international boundaries more generally during the seven decades of the European-led project. Originally, the Ottoman government saw the better chances for territorial stability promised by European intervention as a chance not only to improve its knowledge of the remote border regions but actually to physically extend its control to them. In fact, the proceedings of the 1850–52 demarcation commission were held up by the Ottoman delegation stopping off at various borderland localities en route to their first session at Muhammara, even going so far as to officially annex one of them—Qotur, in Kurdish territory. The delegation's charismatic head, Dervish Pasha, had (unbeknown to his European and Persian colleagues) the official dual function of participating in the commission's activities and bringing frontier lands under the firmer control of his government.[18] A different form of pragmatism governed Persian thinking. Mindful of its humiliating losses to Russia in the Caucasus early in the nineteenth century, Persia considered that it would ultimately gain more with Russia and Britain doing its bidding than by confronting the Ottoman Empire itself. Confronting Britain and its territorial

17 Hubbard, *From the Gulf*, p. 20.
18 Schofield, 'Narrowing the frontier'.

claims in the Persian Gulf had also forced Tehran into accepting the international rules of the game to an increasing degree. It is as well to remember that at the time the four-party commission was embarking upon the project to narrow the Perso-Ottoman frontier, the Persian foreign minister was restating his country's universal claim to all the waters and islands of the Gulf on the basis that ownership should follow nomenclature. Within a few decades, however, Persia had evidently been persuaded of the need to present arguments and evidence for the territory it was claiming. It would increasingly differentiate between the contemporary political boundaries it was having negotiate to the east and west, and imperial Persian territorial limits of the past. Buying quickly into the popular territorial vocabulary of the day, some writers even portrayed the latter as Persia's 'natural' boundaries. According to Mirza Hussein Khan, these ran something like this: '[I]n the south to the Persian Gulf and the Indian Ocean, in the east to the Sind River, in the north to the wilderness of Turan and the Caspian Sea, and in the west to the Euphrates'.[19] Yet the underlying reality was that Qajar Persia was increasingly determined to police and defend its diminished state territory by the century end. This would soon develop into a project to Persianise its better defined margins in the next.[20] Such pragmatism had been illustrated in its much more concerted attempts to forcibly wield authority over its Persian Gulf coastline, a process that began with the abolition of semi-autonomous Arab rule in Linga at the turn of the 1880s and ended with Reza Shah's subjugation of the sheikh of Muhammara in the mid-1920s. The new-found territorial pragmatism also found its way into the classroom, with published regional maps depicting

---

19 As quoted from *Tarbiyat* (August 1898) in Firoozeh Kashani-Sabet, 'Picturing the Homeland: Geography and National Identity in Late Nineteenth-Century and Early-Twentieth Century Iran', *Journal of Historical Geography*, October 1998.

20 Kashani-Sabet, *Frontier Fictions*.

cartographic reality rather than the traditional cosmographic visions of the past.[21]

An obvious consequence of the project to narrow a traditional frontier into a mappable line was a much greater determination to project state authority up to whatever limits were being negotiated. Whereas in the past distant central authority had been generally content to turn a blind eye to what happened in a remote, inaccessible and, above all, socially complex zone—and found periodic advantage in doing so—the expected consolidation of state control proved difficult and confusing for both neighbouring governments and the populations of the borderlands. Customary movements within and across the old border zone would increasingly be viewed by Constantinople and Tehran as unwarranted infringements of sovereign territory, and with no one really any the wiser as to where the frontier had narrowed, border incidents would increase in number. While the Ottoman Empire and Persia would embrace the logic of European linear boundary drawing, buying into concepts such as the 'natural boundary' surprisingly quickly, they understandably found it difficult to physically extend such logic to the ground, to complex traditional borderlands. It must be remembered that local borderland tribes not only saw the 1914 demarcation operation as an unwanted irrelevance; they physically removed the markers of state control laid down during that exercise. For the European imperial powers, the project to narrow the traditional frontier proved, in Hubbard's immortal words, '[a] phenomenon of procrastination unparalleled even in the chronicles of Oriental diplomacy'.[22] Yet is as well to note that Kaikobad has suggested that not just the borderland populations but the modern states of Iran and Iraq have always had a problem reconciling themselves to the presence of a linear international boundary in place of the old traditional frontier.[23]

---

21 Schofield, 'Old Boundaries', p. 32.

22 Hubbard, *From the Gulf*.

23 Kaiyan Kaikobad, *The Shatt al-Arab: A Legal Reappraisal*, Oxford: Clarendon Press, 1988.

Squeezing the Ottomans from Persian Gulf waters: the morphogenesis of Kuwait

Lying only a few miles away from the Iran–Iraq international boundary, the Kuwait–Iraq borderlands historically never functioned as such. The network of water channels and mudflats in the northwestern Gulf could best be described as a no-man's-land at the turn of the twentieth century. While Britain in its project to narrow the Perso-Ottoman frontier had been deeply immersed in discussions over this boundary line here and that line there, a lack of concern for such detail was clearly discernible when it came to the nineteenth-century territorial organisation of the western Gulf littoral. Until Sheikh Mubarak of Kuwait and the competing European imperial powers of Germany and Russia made London think differently in the 1890s, that is. Until this time Kuwait's status had not been a priority, reflected in the fact that Britain had variously and carelessly recognised the sovereignty, jurisdiction and dominion of the Ottomans there during the last quarter of the nineteenth century.[24] This is not to deny Kuwait's long-established independent character and its role as an autonomous actor in Gulf affairs.[25] Kuwait, in contrast to Ottoman Basra, was also a *de facto* free port, possessing real attractions for the extensive but essentially small-scale maritime operations that proliferated in these parts. Links between Kuwait and Basra were numerous and varied on a human level, while the ruler of Kuwait would continue to own in private deed extensive tracts of date gardens on the western bank of the Shatt al-Arab. From the early days right up until the middle of 1990 there was always a functional logic to co-operation between Kuwait and Iraq, a history that tended to get masked by the parallel but more prominent record of tension, mistrust and dispute.[26]

---

24 Schofield, 'Old Boundaries', p. 35.

25 Ben J. Slot, *The Origins of Kuwait*, Leiden: E.J.Brill, 1993; Richard Schofield, *Kuwait and Iraq: Historical Claims and Territorial Disputes*, London: Royal Institute of International Affairs, 1993 [second edn], pp. 1–23.

26 See Gerd Nonneman, 'The (Geo)Political Economy of Iraqi-Kuwaiti

The enterprising Mubarak's greatest achievement was to make Britain care about Kuwait's status.[27] It did so by successfully playing off the international players in the region against one another. Keen at the turn of the century to maintain the Persian Gulf as a 'British lake' and a forward defence line for British India, Britain had reacted nervously to Russo-German proposals to extend a railway down through Mesopotamia to its shoreline. Britain ultimately decided that entering into a protectorate-style treaty with the ruler of Kuwait was the best means of denying its European imperial rivals a foothold on the Persian Gulf. So after twice having his overtures rejected in London, Mubarak signed a secret bond in January 1899 to effectively cement Kuwait's place as an international player. The second part of the strategy to keep the Gulf British was, once in Kuwait, to minimise the Ottoman shoreline in the region in such a manner that there would be no suitable site for a railway terminus. This would ultimately dictate the choice of territorial limits Britain was prepared to defend for Kuwait in the period before World War I. So the reasons for Britain getting into Kuwait had very little to do with what was there at the time, rather than the recognised potential of its geographical position. As a senior India Office official commented at the time the 1899 treaty was signed: '...we don't want Kuwait, but we don't want anyone else to have it.'[28]

The logic of keeping the 1899 bond with Mubarak always seemed questionable. So Britain was first there, but if no one else knew, the fact could not act as much of a deterrent. Back in 1899 Whitehall had not wanted to alienate Berlin and Constantinople at a time

Relations', *Geopolitics and International Boundaries*, vol. 1, no. 2, autumn 1996, pp. 178–223.

27   See Briton Cooper Busch, 'Britain and the Status of Kuwait, 1896–1899', *The Middle East Journal*, vol. 21, no. 2, 1967. Busch's subsequent *Britain and the Persian Gulf, 1896-1914*, Berkeley: University of California Press, 1968, remains the classic account of the international emergence of Kuwait.

28   Comments of Sir Arthur Godley, permanent undersecretary at the India Office, January 1899, quoted in Busch, 'Britain and the Status of Kuwait', p. 196.

when their co-operation was needed elsewhere over much larger international questions. Once the cat was out of the bag, however, Britain drew up a much more explicit bargain with Constantinople that directly tackled its security concerns. A *status quo* convention struck up during the autumn of 1901 held that the Ottoman Empire would not intervene militarily in Kuwait so long as Britain did not materially enhance its position there. If ever Kuwait's international status was confused it was now. Despite its nominal position as an Ottoman *qada* (district) of the *vilayet* (province) of Basra, the bay area was now an effective Ottoman exclusion zone. When Britain then enforced the bargain by turning back Ottoman steamers from the bay, Constantinople probably realised that it would no longer exercise much clout in Kuwait. Suddenly the Kuwait question was about what boundaries Britain was prepared to defend for it.[29] Constantinople cottoned on to this quickly and accordingly changed strategy, calculating that by moving its southern garrisons through the no-man's-land that was the north-western corner of the Gulf south to Kuwait Bay, it would soon discover the territorial extent Britain recognised for Kuwait. Wrong-footed by a canny Constantinople, the Foreign Office and the Indian government then argued about what Kuwait comprised. The former reckoned that the mere existence of its commitment to defend Kuwait's ruler would dissuade imperial competitors, but Indian Viceroy Lord Curzon was adamant that physical control of territory was the key here, and that the recent stationing of Ottoman troops at Umm Qasr, Safwan and on the eastern tip of Bubiyan island was threatening to whittle the 1901 *status quo* out of existence.[30] Curzon's frantic representations won the day and further Ottoman encroachment north of Kuwait Bay was checked. Whitehall had been moved from British Foreign Secretary Lord Lansdowne's original view that Kuwaiti territory extended no

---

29 Richard Schofield, 'Britain and Kuwait's Borders, 1902–23', in Ben J. Slot (ed.), *Kuwait: The Growth of a Historic Identity*, London: Arabian Publishing, 2003, pp. 58–94.

30 Ibid., pp. 69-70.

further than the shores of the bay of that name but the precise question remained: how much further?

Mubarak now felt encouraged to claim a northern boundary for Kuwait that minimised Ottoman possibilities. During the Foreign Office–Government of India debate, Lansdowne had commented of the Kuwaiti ruler, '…no one knows where his possessions begin and end, and our obligations towards him are as ill-defined as the boundaries of his Principality.'[31] As the nature of his links to the north was investigated and the basis of territorial claims formulated, Britain moved to secure the territories under discussion when signing a lease agreement with Mubarak in October 1907. This gave them pre-emption rights over Kazima Bay, Warba Island and any territory over which he might (in future) exercise jurisdiction. Meanwhile, resident Government of India historian J.G. Lorimer elaborated on Lansdowne's view that the boundaries of Kuwait were not easy to characterise when explaining that allegiances to its ruler were forged more on a communal than a territorial basis: '[t]he boundaries of Kuwait principality are for the most part fluctuating and undefined: they are, at any given time, the limits of the tribes which then, voluntarily or under compulsion, owe allegiance to the Shaikh of Kuwait.'[32] Giving a shape to boundary claims based squarely upon communal allegiance is far from easy. Nonetheless, Lorimer dutifully suggested a diamond-shaped area of predominantly Kuwaiti influence that was eventually incorporated into British Foreign Secretary Sir Edward Grey's proposal to Constantinople for a settlement of the Kuwait and other outstanding Persian Gulf questions during the summer of 1912.[33] This had been proposed irrespective of the prevailing realities of surrounding spatial control but would be adjusted to reflect both these and Britain's strategic desiderata over the next year. The idea of a two-tone autonomous Kuwait was now hit upon in one of colonialism's most bizarre territorial schemes.

---

31 Ibid., p. 71.

32 J.G. Lorimer, *Gazetteer of the Persian Gulf, 'Oman and Central Arabia*, vol. 2, Calcutta: Superintendent Government Printing, 1908, p. 1059.

33 Depicted in Schofield, *Kuwait and Iraq*, p. 41.

For with the May 1913 Anglo-Ottoman convention Kuwait was defined as comprising an inner and outer zone of diminishing sheikhly authority. While the Kuwaiti islands of Warba and Bubiyan would both be circumscribed within the inner (red line) limit—supposedly territory within which Mubarak's control was not in dispute—Kuwait's northern terrestrial limits to its west were marked by an outer green line, designed to enclose territory where his authority may not have been absolute but was probably greater than anyone else's. Extraordinarily, the northern portion of the green line survived with virtually no changes to define Iraq's international boundaries with Kuwait and, even more surprisingly, to comprise the delimitation formula for the United Nations Iraq–Kuwait Boundary Demarcation Commission (UNIKBDC) during its operation between 1991 and 1993. It was defined as follows:

From the intersection of the Wadi el-Audja with the Batin and thence northwards along the Batin to a point just south of Safwan; thence eastwards passing south of Safwan wells, Jebal Sanam and Umm Qasr leaving them to Iraq and so on to the junction of the Khor Zobeir with the Khor Abdullah. The islands of Warbah, Bubiyan, Maskan [or Mashjan], Failakah, Kubbar, Qaru and Umm-el-Maradim appertain to Kuwait.[34]

In this classic imperial fudge, Constantinople was denied any presence within the newly defined two-tone Kuwait despite the fact that nominally, it belonged to it. The principality had been formally re-established within the convention's text as an autonomous *qada* of the Ottoman *vilayet* of Basra, and Mubarak recognised as *qaimmaqam* (provincial sub-governor) with the Ottoman flag flying over his palace. In this sense the Ottomans got what they wanted, but the victory was little more than symbolic. Constantinople was deeply worried about being squeezed out territorially from the Persian Gulf and its admission of Kuwaiti rights over the islands of Warba and Bubiyan had been the last substantive concession wrought by Britain before the May 1913 convention was signed. The same agreement also recorded provisional Anglo-Ottoman concurrence on the definition of the southern Perso-

---

34 Ibid., p. 152.

Ottoman boundary (including the Shatt al-Arab), the text of which would later be incorporated in the Constantinople Protocol signed half a year later. It would also draw a Blue Line through the middle of Arabia to separate a British sphere of influence in the south and east from nominal Ottoman territory to the north and west. Yet by this stage Ottoman control south of Kuwait and in Arabia more generally was notional at best and non-existent by any other name. As such the reality was that the convention had successfully limited Ottoman access to the Persian Gulf. Although squeezing Constantinople hard on Kuwait may have been balanced by effectively safeguarding the Shatt as an Ottoman river, the ailing empire was left with a very narrow and largely undevelopable sovereign land corridor in the shape of the Fao peninsula. This would be inherited by Iraq.[35]

Shaping the Iraqi rump: the inclusion of Mosul

Reconciling the contradictory commitments made by Britain during World War I to the Hashemites, the French and the Zionists concerning northern Arabia and the eastern Mediterranean would prove a predictably impossible task in the following decades, and

---

35 It might have been even worse. Back in 1912, as the British government discussed the boundaries of Kuwait, Captain W. Shakespear, an official of the Indian government, had noted strong Kuwaiti contacts with Umm Qasr and Safwan. Since Britain had already effectively recognised an Ottoman presence there, no further action was taken when shaping the two-tone Kuwait. Yet, in return for siding against the Ottomans in World War I, the ruler of Kuwait was 'guaranteed ... against all consequences of your attack against Safwan, Umm Kasr and Bubiyan'. While it is not clear that he led any attacks on these localities, the fact remains that following the Mudros Armistice of October 1918, the sites of the former Ottoman garrisons were no longer in Ottoman hands. A Foreign Office memorandum penned around this time intriguingly concludes that 'our assurance [of 1914] practically commits us to recognising Sheik Salim's sovereignty over Safwan and Umm Qasr as well as Bubiyan'. In the end, the observation was never communicated to Kuwait and if such an opportunity existed, it was not recognised by Salim. Within half a decade, the outer green line of the 1913 Anglo-Ottoman convention would be set as the boundary between Iraq and Kuwait. See Schofield, 'Britain and Kuwait's Borders', pp. 88–90.

some would argue that the consequences are still felt very acutely to this day. And, to a degree, Britain realised at the time that its actions would not bear close scrutiny, with Foreign Secretary Arthur James Balfour himself famously commenting on the eve of his retirement, 'in short, …the Powers have made no statement of fact which is not admittedly wrong, and no declaration of policy which, at least in the letter, they have not always intended to violate'.[36]

Once World War I had commenced, Sir Maurice de Bunsen was instructed to preside over a series of British interdepartmental committees that would consider the possible responses to Ottoman disintegration in the Middle East. His final report on 'Asiatic Turkey', completed in June 1915, broadly envisaged four scenarios: partition and the restriction of an Ottoman or Ottoman successor state to Anatolia; maintenance of the Ottoman Empire under effective European control; with a few territorial exceptions, perpetuation of the *status quo* and, lastly; survival of the Ottoman Empire but in an even more decentralised form.[37] Since the first scheme would most closely anticipate the events to follow, it is worth looking at some of the prevailing thinking. Starting at the head of the Persian Gulf, both the ruler of Kuwait and sheikh of Muhammara had been promised that they would never again be subject to Ottoman control, while the inhabitants of Basra had been promised a more benign rule than experienced hereto. On the basis of these pledges, therefore, Britain seemed 'committed to some sort of permanent control and occupation of Basra port and of the country from Basra to the mouth of the Shatt-el-Arab'.[38] Yet it was realised that limiting annexation to

---

36 Quoted in J.C. Hurewitz, 'Preface' in Patricia L. Toye (ed.), *Palestine Boundaries, 1833–1947*, Farnham Common: Archive Edns, 1989, vol. 1, p. vii. Admittedly, this comment was made about Palestine but its applicability could be extended to the surrounding area.

37 'Report of the Committee on Asiatic Turkey', 30 June 1915, in Richard Schofield (ed.) *Arabian Boundary Disputes*, Farnham Common: Archive Edns, 1992, vol. 8, pp. 3–48.

38 Ibid., p. 13.

this restricted territorial extent was a practical impossibility, for both traditional imperial strategic reasons and newer commercial ones.

The established strategic mentality of maintaining the Persian Gulf as a British lake loomed large. As did the attractions of strong defensible boundaries based upon natural features. It was realised that by placing itself just in Basra, France or Russia might take up the effective reins of control to the immediate north. In such circumstances, the de Bunsen Committee foresaw the day arriving 'when the real master of Baghdad and owner of Mesopotamia will be France or Russia, and once more the direct menace of a rival European Power will challenge our supremacy in the Persian Gulf'.[39] Arguments from the Indian government that Britain might acquire sovereign rights in the Basra region and establish a less hard and fast protectorate over Baghdad along the lines of its existing arrangements in Aden and the Aden Protectorate would be frowned upon since it was held that 'Basra by itself is untenable and that Baghdad commands it'.[40] However, it was also considered that no combination of Baghdad and Basra could be easily defended from the north. So inclusion of the old Mosul province in any area of extended control would automatically come onto the agenda—even though the search for a suitable natural boundary would cause eyes to be cast even further to the north:

We cannot maintain permanently in Mesopotamia a force of such size as could successfully cope with an invasion from the north. We require, therefore, a frontier where a enemy's advance can be delayed until the arrival of reinforcements, and, in spite of the reluctance which the Committee understand is felt by the Commander-in-Chief in India to the inclusion of Mosul in the British sphere, they think that such a frontier can only be found along the ranges of hills to the north of the Mosul vilayet. Further, the possession of Mosul would meet two important requisites of a military occupation of the Baghdad and Basra vilayets.[41]

---

39 Ibid.
40 Ibid.
41 Ibid.

On a strategic level therefore, the merits of cementing together the three former Ottoman *vilayet*s under some form of unitary control had been recognised by the middle of 1915.

Yet there were inherent liabilities and responsibilities in such thinking that were considered problematic. Britain wanted to avoid a situation where its future areas of control would directly border Russian ones, so it hit upon the idea of possibly defining a wedge of indirectly controlled French territory stretching eastwards from the Mediterranean coast, through the northern reaches of the old Mosul *vilayet* to Lake Urmia in the northern reaches of the recently demarcated Perso-Ottoman borderlands to act as a buffer. This might be labelled as compensation to France since it had missionary interests in the Assyrian/Nestorian regions here, and was also likely to be completely denied any future role in Palestine.[42] Such considerations would largely manifest themselves in the Sykes–Picot arrangements negotiated during the following year, although Britain would revert to its original defining logic for claiming a mountain boundary line north of the Ottoman province of Mosul following the 1917 Russian revolution and the end of World War I.

Generally, the de Bunsen Committee concluded that more recently established economic incentives supported the strategic arguments to block together control of the former Ottoman provinces of Basra, Baghdad and Mosul. Basra was regarded as the gate to Mesopotamia but Baghdad as its distributing centre and control of the latter commanded not only Mesopotamian trade but links, for instance, to the east with north-west Persia. The committee was adamant that Basra needed Baghdad: 'with Baghdad and Basra both in our possession, Basra may develop at the expense of Baghdad, but if those places are held by different Powers it will inevitably be Basra that declines'.[43] Integrating control of all but the upper courses of the Tigris–Euphrates river system by extending Mosul province into the equation and thereby capturing most of the area that would

42 Ibid., p. 17.
43 Ibid., p. 15.

come under irrigation was seen as vital if full advantage was to be taken of the '…opportunity to create a granary which should ensure and ample and unhindered supply of corn…' for the region.[44] Safeguarding the security of Britain's fast-developing oil interests along the Perso-Ottoman boundary was seen as an additional incentive for integrating control of the old Basra and Baghdad *vilayets* and here, too, the logic extended to including Mosul, at least partially: '[a]nd oil again makes it commercially desirable for us to carry our control on to Mosul, in the vicinity of which place there are valuable wells possession of which by another Power would be prejudicial to our interests'.[45]

So most of the strategic and economic issues that would be thrashed out in creating the external framework of the Iraqi territorial state had been rehearsed by the middle of 1915. The committee concluded that, 'under a policy of partition, British desiderata would be adequately met by the annexation of the *vilayets* of Basra, Baghdad, and the greater part of Mosul, with a port on the Eastern Mediterranean, at Haifa, and British railway connection between this port and the Persian Gulf'.[46] This clearly clashed with the earlier provisions in the Sykes–Picot correspondence of a defensive French buffer being extended across the northern reaches of Mosul province. However, a series of Anglo-French conferences following the Mudros Armistice gradually clawed back from this undertaking and saw the planned extension of British control to the whole of Mosul province admitted in return for extending eastwards the area of French control in what would become Syria.[47] The effect of these territorial adjustments was

---

44 Ibid.

45 Ibid.

46 Ibid., p. 17. Ideally, Britain would have preferred the port of Alexandretta (Iskenderun) but realised that this would have been squeezing the French too far.

47 Britain would also offer the additional sweetener of granting France a 25 per cent stake in the future exploitation of oil in Mosul province, a measure ultimately extended in an agreement of 24 April 1920 between the two states, reproduced in J.C. Hurewitz (ed.), *Diplomacy in the Near and Middle East: A*

to hastily allocate a boundary between the future mandated territories of Syria and Iraq.[48]

The Syria–Iraq borderlands allocated as a result of Anglo-French consultations has no historical or objective basis. Inspection of successive Ottoman official calendars (*salname*) suggests provincial boundaries were generally fleeting, ambiguous and never marked on the ground and, even then, the new borderlands being contemplated corresponded to nothing on the record. When quizzed by the India Office about the question of a notional Anglo-French separation line during the autumn of 1918, Iraq's chief imperial architects, Arnold Wilson and Gertrude Bell, admitted as much, concluding that the future mandates might respectively police the caravan routes east and west of a point arbitrarily drawn along 39 degrees of longitude. There might be supervision of these routes and some control over the traffic but none extended, as such, over the new, projected borderlands, for 'no government will exercise effective control over Syrian desert. Governments are concerned only with the administration of settled districts, and the relations of tribes to borders of cultivated land'.[49] These realities were understood in London and Paris, to the degree that when the Anglo-French convention of December 1920 was signed to allocate an Iraq–Syria boundary, it was recognised as such, as little more than a vaguely worded imperial sphere of influence.[50] The issue of properly delimiting the boundary would only really eventuate during the preparations for Iraq's admission to the League of

---

Documentary Record, New York: Van Nostrand, 1956, vol. 2, pp. 75–7.

48 Schofield, 'Laying It Down in Stone'.

49 Comments quoted in note by India Office entitled: 'Settlement of Turkey and Arabian Peninsula', 30 November 1918, in Schofield (ed.), *Arabian Boundary Disputes*, vol. 8, p. 355.

50 With this agreement, an Anglo-French line of sorts was prescribed in less than six lines of treaty text, though since it was realised that this was purely a European office creation, the convention also contained the promise that in the future a joint commission would take the prevailing social and spatial organisation of borderlanders into account by plotting a line out on the ground. See Schofield, 'Laying It Down in Stone'.

Nations as an independent state in 1932. The 1920 allocation would then be described as little more than a sketch map that could only be taken as the general intention of its framers.[51]

In the very same (almost valedictory) memorandum of August 1919 in which he had been so candid about the confusion caused by the Great Powers, Balfour had also called for the nomination of new boundaries in the Middle East that practically addressed newly-emergent regional realities, e.g., economic and ethnographic considerations, rather than reflecting the imperial strategic mindsets of old. Recommending that a British zone in Mesopotamia extend at least up to Mosul, he recognised that precise issues of territorial delimitation might be difficult. Concluding, perhaps a little optimistically, that there was no real disagreement about where the rumps of Syria, Mesopotamia and Palestine basically lay, he concluded that Britain and France's principal challenge was '…to make such international arrangements, economic and territorial, as will enable each region to develop itself to the best advantage without giving occasion for jealousies or disputes'.[52]

Trimming the Iraqi rump: agreements with the Saudis and with Turkey

Though Persia would revive many old territorial claims to broadcast the view that it no longer felt intimidated by its western neighbours at Versailles in 1919 following the Ottoman wartime collapse, not even they—after all the preceding decades of procrastination— really had the stomach to seriously re-examine definition of the Perso-Ottoman boundary. Britain certainly did not! Britain would take the predictable though in many ways unsatisfactory step of getting its representatives in Baghdad and Kuwait to affirm the outer green line of the 1913 Anglo-Ottoman convention as the Kuwait boundary by

---

51 Ibid.

52 'Memorandum by Mr. Balfour respecting Syria, Palestine and Mesopotamia, dated August 11, 1919' in Schofield (ed.), *Arabian Boundary Disputes*, vol. 8, pp. 460–4.

an exchange of letters in 1923, effectively confirming Iraq's narrow sovereign corridor to Gulf waters. To the west with Syria and Transjordan, territorial disputes would just about be held in check by the vague Anglo-French territorial allocation of December 1920, with its promise of later elaboration. This left the difficult issue of drawing lines in the south to lend recognition to the communal allegiances of a mobile, sparse and transitory desert population and, to the north, the vexed question of persuading modern Turkey to drop its claims to Mosul.

From an early stage following Iraq's formal inception as a modern state in 1920, Sir Percy Cox, Britain's high commissioner in Baghdad, was determined to stabilise shifting tribal allegiances in north-eastern Arabia by fixing limits to territory—a task far easier to do on paper than in practice. One of the crucial strategic priorities itemised in the June 1915 de Bunsen Committee report had been to protect the integrity of the Mediterranean–Persian Gulf overland route, though plans for a connecting railway were soon dropped. With the allocation of mandates at the San Remo conference in April 1920, Britain obtained control of the strategic land corridor through discharge of its responsibilities as mandatary in Palestine, Transjordan and Iraq. Early in 1922, however, the Saud dynasty's defeat of the Rashidis, their long-time rivals for supremacy in the north-eastern Arabian peninsula (who had previously been greatly reliant on Ottoman Basra in maintaining their regional position), was seen to have altered Arabian geopolitics with the new *ikhwan* threat of radical Islamic warriors emanating from the Saudi south seen as a genuine security concern.[53] This was treated by Cox in two conferences convened during 1922 that successively aimed to tackle tribal allegiance and territorial definition. A first summit during May resulted in Cox and Abd al-Aziz Ibn Saud signing the Treaty of Muhammara, an instrument that basically established the nomadic Muntafiq, Dhafir and Amarat as Iraqi tribes and the Shammar Najd as belonging to Najd. Provisions were made in the treaty's six articles for establishing

---

53 Schofield, *Iraq and Kuwait*, pp. 56–8.

ownership over wells and pasture in what was, at this stage, a very loosely defined borderland. [54]

When the same two figures added their signatures to the Uqayr protocol on 2 December 1922, a crudely defined delimitation was established to constitute the Iraq–Najd boundary from Jabal Anayza in the west to the Batin in the east, with a rhomboid-shaped Neutral Zone at its eastern extremity—a demilitarised area where both sides supposedly enjoyed equal rights of access to water and pasture.[55] Cox's *diktat* had been accepted only reluctantly by Ibn Saud, who argued throughout that a system of linear boundaries was unsuitable for the Arabian desert.[56] Furthermore, if arbitrary territorial limits were to be established, he suggested they should be based upon tribal access to wells and *dira*s (grazing grounds), extending the territorial definition of Najd in his opinion right the way up to the Euphrates. Reportedly, Ibn Saud was partially reassured by the protocol's specification that wells and oases close to the newly drawn boundary could not be used for military purposes, and that Najdi tribes would be guaranteed safe passage to traditional watering holes now defined as lying within Iraq.[57] It is deeply ironic that today, in 2007, the Saudi authorities are building an elaborate and costly system of defences along their Iraq boundary so as to guard against the chaos of an imploded state spreading south. In the early 1920s, the situation had been the opposite: Cox's determination to fix territorial limits had been guided by the motive of better organising a response to

---

54 Ibid., p. 56.

55 The 1922 delimitation would survive for a full half-century before Saudi Arabia and Iraq partitioned the Neutral Zone with an agreement of 1975, then smoothed out the course of the whole boundary with a further 1981 treaty revision. See Richard Schofield, 'Borders and Territoriality in the Gulf and Arabian Peninsula During the Twentieth Century' in Richard Schofield (ed.), *Territorial Foundations of the Gulf States*, London: UCL Press, 1994, p. 27.

56 True, Cox was accompanied at the Uqayr conference by Sabih Bey, an official representative of King Faysal, who articulated an Iraqi territorial claim to the northern Arabian desert and signed the resultant protocol. There is little doubt, however, that Cox called the shots. For a fuller account, see H.R.P. Dickson, *Kuwait and Her Neighbours*, London: Allen and Unwin, 1956.

57 Ibid.

threatening tribal movement from the south. The boundary he introduced could never really serve as a barrier, however, and would never be truly securitised until the time of Desert Shield in the autumn of 1990 when defensive measures against possible Iraqi military operations beyond Kuwait were put in place. In fact, the zonal arrangements for tribal movement, watering and pasturing prescribed in the text of the protocol reflected the reality that at the time of the early 1920s, the boundary was something of a legal and statist abstract. The British authorities in Iraq possessed neither the resources nor inclination to effectively police a long desert boundary drawn through sparsely populated desert. Yet the menace perceived from the *ikhwan* to the south would persuade Britain that another accommodation needed to be reached with Ibn Saud to combat tribal raiding; the 1925 Treaty of Bahra with its more detailed mechanisms for dealing with trans-border issues represented a step in this direction.

As for Mosul, having bought French clearance for incorporation into the Iraqi state with a promise of 25 per cent of the proceedings from any oil sales and territorial compensations along the Syrian frontier, Britain was surprised at the determination with which Kemalist Turkey maintained Ottoman claims to Mosul province in the early 1920s. Modern Turkish claims rested principally on two points. First, Mosul had been occupied by Britain following the October 1918 Mudros Armistice. Secondly, the Turkish National Pact of January 1920 had claimed that all territories occupied by 'Ottoman Muslim' majorities should form the Turkish homeland. Whereas Arabs were implicitly excluded, the Kurds were regarded as part and parcel of the 'Ottoman Turkish nation' and were believed to form a majority of the population of the province.[58] When, in the July 1923 Treaty of Lausanne, Ankara renounced all claims to former Ottoman territories outside Anatolia except for Mosul, Britain probably realised the seriousness of Atatürk's intent.

---

58 See Foreign Office Research Department memorandum on 'Turkey's frontiers and interests beyond them', 15 January 1946, reproduced in Richard Schofield (ed.), *Arabian Boundary Disputes*, vol. 9, pp. 677–85.

The Mosul question was referred to a League of Nations commission of enquiry in September 1924, but with each side viewing the dispute under consideration quite differently. For Turkey it was all about the sovereign fate of the former Ottoman province, for Britain seemingly the location of the boundary between an Iraqi Mosul province and Turkish territory to the north. If Britain was concerned about the findings going in favour of Ankara, it certainly did not show in the government records of the time and this was some years before the League would commonly be viewed as an Anglo-French club. Yet, for the vast majority of its operation, the Mosul Commission had been involved in a full investigation to ascertain the wishes and presumed identity of some 800,000 people centred on the territory of the old Ottoman province. The text of its final report suggested that the verdict had been a close call. The promises made by Britain of special status and protection within an Iraqi state for the religious and ethnic minorities, along with what was portrayed as an overriding case for fuller economic integration with the south seemingly swung the balance.[59] The commission would admit that Turkey's legitimate legal claims were being subjugated to arguments about Mosul's greater geographical and economic connections with the south, basically the same arguments that had led the de Bunsen Committee to conclude almost a decade earlier that the Mesopotamian area to be annexed by Britain should include not just the former Ottoman provinces of Basra and Baghdad but Mosul too: 'Iraq has no legal right or right of conquest... The Iraq state did not exist at the termination of hostilities... Nevertheless, it is morally entitled to ask that, since it has been created, it should be given frontiers which will allow it to live, both politically and economically'.[60]

---

59 League of Nations, 'Question of the Frontier between Turkey and Iraq: Report Submitted to the Council by the Commission Instituted by the Council Resolution of September 30th', in Schofield (ed.), *Arabian Boundary Disputes*, vol. 9, 1992, pp. 163–328.

60 Ibid., p. 248.

Once it had decreed that Mosul was Iraqi—however close the call may or may not have been—the task of delimiting a northern boundary also fell upon the commission. Back in 1915, the de Bunsen Committee had eyed a mountainous, 'natural' boundary running to the north of the old Ottoman provincial boundary. Evidently the traditional strategic imperatives that had dictated such thinking had not completely vanished with the disappearance of imperial Russia and the collapse of the Ottoman Empire, despite Balfour's (and the Foreign Office's) call of 1919 for the adoption of more regionally suited and practical territorial limits. For Britain would aim for a delimitation in the early 1920s that would supposedly serve both a security and extended ethnographic function. Sir Percy Cox pushed, as had the de Bunsen Committee before him, for a boundary that ran north of the old Ottoman limit, ostensibly so as not to separate a temporarily displaced Christian (Assyrian/Nestorian) population from its traditional homeland in the Turkish Hakkari further north, thereby seeking 'a frontier which, while fulfilling the recognized requirements of a good treaty frontier, will at the same time admit of the establishment of the Assyrians as a compact community within the limits of the territory.'[61] The Mosul Commission did not give Britain all it was claiming for a northern boundary, deciding in the end on a delimitation that recognised instead the extent of the regional Assyrian base that had been recaptured with British assistance from Turkish control in the period since 1921. This was a ruling that left the Hakkari truncated. Ultimately, with an Anglo-Turkish treaty of June 1926, all remaining territorial loose ends would be sorted with the Mosul Commission's recommendation for a boundary adjusted in places for ease of local use and administration, and a new border regime introduced whereby a frontier zone was introduced to extend from the newly introduced delimitation for 45 miles in either direction. A permanent joint frontier commission established by the same treaty was given the principal task of demarcating the

61 Schofield, 'Laying It Down in Stone'.

boundary, a task it completed by the end of the following year.[62] As the result of its huge international prioritisation, the Turkey–Iraq boundary had thereby been conceived, delimited and demarcated in the space of a decade—even if residual disputes were always likely to concern the status of adjoining territory rather than any precise boundary delimitations themselves.

Aftermath

Following the Anglo-Turkish treaty of June 1926, Iraq had basically emerged in its current shape. There was considerable variation in the rigour with which its respective territorial limits had been introduced. Some had been the outcome of determined international action and negotiation (yet even here there was little comparative basis to be found, with the prioritised European project to narrow the traditional Perso-Ottoman frontier taking ten times as long as it took an equally determined but better equipped international community to 'sort' the Mosul question in the years following World War I). Other boundaries were poorly defined and regulated; some—like Iraq/Syria—on the basis that they would do for the time being, others—like the Transjordan boundary to the south—because they were seen as not mattering. Amid great self-congratulation, France and Britain beefed up the threadbare definition of the Iraq–Syria boundary with a showcase League of Nations territorial settlement in advance of Iraq joining the League of Nations as an independent state in the autumn of 1932. With no imperial issues at stake, the mandatory powers treated the challenge as a purely technical issue, proclaiming the result an 'equitable and practical frontier' that, with its improved detail and several regional adjustments, far better served the needs of local borderlanders and reflected existing circulation patterns. Yet the reality remained that the defining basis of the boundary had,

---

62 Great Britain, 'Iraq-Turkey: Treaty between United Kingdom and Iraq and Turkey Regarding Settlement of Frontier between Turkey and Iraq, together with Notes Exchanged, Angora, June 5, 1926', reproduced in Schofield (ed.), *Arabian Boundary Disputes*, vol. 9, 1992, pp. 255–70.

in the shape of its original 1920 allocation, been entirely arbitrary. While Britain had seen fit to sort the Syrian boundary in definitional terms in the early 1930s, it considered that the Iraq–Kuwait boundary—defined in equally ambiguous and misleading terms—could continue to be regulated by its original Anglo-Ottoman specification, confirmed by yet another exchange of notes during the summer of 1932. Perhaps history will judge this as a mistake and that Britain might have done more to find a more satisfactory territorial *modus vivendi* while it was in charge of the foreign affairs of both states.

Perhaps no state has had more trouble adjusting to its shape and size historically than Iraq. At the risk of sounding deterministic, it could be argued that the legacy of Anglo-Ottoman territorial arrangements it inherited at the head of the Persian Gulf bequeathed to the Iraqi state an 'eastern question' (or, to be more accurate, a south-eastern question) of its own. The introduction of linear international boundaries, not just within a traditional frontier zone, but also to divide a unitary river system, created an unstable territorial legacy for Iran, Iraq and Kuwait. The states have been engaged in continuous disputes since the late 1930s over both the positioning and the status of their international boundaries, while the wars Iraq launched against its neighbours in 1980 and 1990 clearly possessed nominal territorial roots.

A profound geopolitical restlessness has characterised the self-view of successive Iraqi governments—with respect to neighbouring states generally, but above all in regard to the question of access to Persian Gulf waters. This has been reflected in a history of struggling efforts to find a consistent regional voice and role, and in the way territorial questions have been used to symbolise wider inter-state tensions, particularly with Syria, Iran and Kuwait. The Syrian boundary had been used as a political football between the hard men of Damascus and Baghdad for decades before the allied invasion of 2003, whereby the major border crossings and trans-boundary pipelines were always shut or closed down at the first signs of a political spat. Unlike now, the closure of the boundary was purely symbolic but, all the same, immensely disruptive to already weak regional trade networks. Ever since the Iraqi revolution of July 1958, the dispute over the Shatt al-Arab has served as the physical expression of rivalries with Iran to the east. Historically, too, whenever Iran has held the upper hand in the Shatt dispute, Iraq has looked at Kuwait to compensate for its strategic misfortune.

Amid the chaos of an imploded Iraqi state in the early spring of 2007, considerable conjecture concerns its future operative shape. While the Iraqi state's operative capacity has shrunk significantly in spatial terms since the allied invasion of 2003—with coalition forces still struggling to make safe the seven kilometres of road from Baghdad's airport to the Green Zone—securing its sovereign territorial limits has been a prioritised project for the Iraqi government, the United States and Britain at least since the autumn of 2005. Just as the end of the Cold War briefly witnessed hopes that boundaries as barriers were a thing of the past, the early twenty-first century has seen a return to the traditions of fence building in many areas of enduring conflict. As the international community's security concerns have passed from a more static preoccupation with pivotal states and regions to dealing with critical trans-boundary flows as part of the 'War on Terror', sophisticated demands are being asked of international boundaries. Even as many Iraqi borderlands demonstrably remain beyond the reach of central authority, the country's boundaries are being expected to acts as filters that can distinguish between benign and hostile movement—a difficult task even in far easier circumstances. This is a two-way process which Iraq's six neighbouring states have been forced to address according to the individual dynamics at their borders. Saudi Arabia plans to spend billions of dollars fortifying its boundary with Iraq in an attempt to seal itself off the chaos to the north. The regime in Syria, for its part, has been under massive amounts of international pressure to prevent fighters entering Iraq across its eastern borders. As a result of its effort to play ball, the boundary is acting as more of a barrier than before (particularly in its more settled northern reaches), and the heavily truncated trans-boundary population of the Jazira is potentially more cut off than ever.

A contemporary *tour d'horizon* of Iraq's international boundaries and borderlands uncovers a complex interplay of new realities and old concerns. To the north, Iraq's boundary with Turkey (with the borderlands to its immediate south) has become more heavily militarised than ever before, a reflection of Ankara's nervousness in the face of an increasingly confident, autonomous and assertive Kurdistan Regional Government in immediately adjoining Iraqi sovereign territory. More heavily militarised that is than the Syria–Turkey boundary to its west, unthinkable even half a decade ago. To the east and south-east, the old Zagros frontier predictably has changed least of all. The latest efforts to securitise this limit have really fared no better than the many attempts made historically over the centuries. Certain stretches of the borderlands might be brought under strict(er) control, but never the whole, and never for very long. Instead, the established small-scale network of cross-border interactions and transactions is proving typically resilient. The constantly juxtaposed themes of conflict and opportunity remain as evident as ever—best witnessed in the desolate, partially abandoned marshlands of the south, a vivid testimony to the futility of the 1980–1988 war. Here a barren and damaged borderscape overlies massive reserves of oil in the shape of the enormous Majnun–Azadegan trans-boundary field. In a Gulf region to which conflict has often seemed endemic, states—whatever their rivalries—have in fact been surprisingly pragmatic when securing access to disputed reserves of oil and gas: the devices developed in the Persian Gulf region have, for instance, served as the blueprint for subsequent maritime resource development elsewhere in the world, as attested to by such cases as the 1958 continental shelf boundary agreement between Saudi Arabia and Bahrain, and even the bizarre 1971 memorandum of understanding between Iran and Sharjah (United Arab Emirates) over the Abu Musa island and shared revenue from the associated Mubarak oilfield. This sort of pragmatic approach could be of relevance to Iraq's southern and western borders, where Iraq and Kuwait share a huge hydrocarbons reserve in the shape of the Rumayla oilfield. The underlying logic of functional co-operation that has never grabbed the headlines in Iraq–Kuwait relations may yet see their borderlands developed beneficially by both sides, perhaps even with a symbolic joint port of Umm Qasr at some point in the future? Historical memories are still very raw in the short-term, however, and there continue to be small-scale problems and incidents at what is still a very heavily fortified and practically impassable border. The fortified Iraq–Kuwait boundary is about to be joined (literally) to its immediate west by another barrier that the Saudis are currently constructing to supposedly guard their northern borderlands. While heavy state sedentarisation of the kingdom's northern tribes (as well as a rapidly growing poverty gap between north and south) has meant that there is less and less incentive to criss-cross the international boundary with the customary movements of old, border fortification is bound to have a deleterious effect upon the diminished trans-boundary traffic that remains.

The Shatt dispute itself is worthy of greater comment. Navigational incidents over the last few years have highlighted the fact that no one is sure where the main channel (*thalweg*) of the river lies, since nature has gradually changed its position after it was defined as the international boundary by a package of Iran–Iraq territorial agreements in 1975. While the renewed consideration of the definition of its outer margins might not be an obvious priority for a beleaguered Iraqi government right now, it can be argued that recommitting to the eminently sensible and sustainable territorial arrangements introduced for the Shatt al-Arab back in 1975 is a medium-term measure that would best serve the interests of the interested parties and, in particular, the reconstruction and regeneration of the northern Gulf in the coming decades. That sort of approach should not be read as backing for contemporary Iranian claims and desiderata (though it should be admitted that recommitting to the 1975 package is one of very few strategic carrots that Iraq might have to offer its eastern neighbour at present). There is in fact a certain truth to the standard

Arab nationalist line that the 1975 settlement was imposed on Iraq when it had little alternative but to accede. Instead, this argument is ultimately based on the general truism that a mid-channel boundary line is the most suitable delimitation for a navigable river boundary. The vexed history of this territorial limit also strongly suggests the *thalweg*'s appropriateness. For the status of the Shatt as a predominantly Iraqi (and previously Ottoman) sovereign river in the 130-year period before 1975 provided endless opportunities for intrigue. Iran and Iraq's inability to agree upon workable arrangements for the maintenance and conservancy of the river channels and the administration of the major ports of Abadan, Basra, Khorramshahr and their approaches allowed for all manner of functional disputes in the latter part of this period. Tellingly, as the major architect of the territorial structures of these parts, Britain had been aware from the start that a mid-channel boundary was most appropriate from the viewpoint of local socio-economic considerations and international law more generally. Diplomatic niceties and political expediency would ultimately trump such logic.[63]

Beyond the historical psychoses of the Iraqi state engendered by its territorial definition and consequent self-view, one should not forget the trials and tribulations of Iraq's immensely varied borderland populations. Traditionally, to the east, borderlanders saw themselves as just that, but were left with a zone in which to function, relatively untouched by the projection of surrounding central authority. Adjusting to the presence of fixed lines was every bit as hard for them as it was confusing for the governments of Iran and Iraq and their imperial forbears. Other territorial limits, such as the desert boundaries to the south and west with Jordan and Saudi Arabia, were lines on maps but traditionally of little relevance at the local level for sparse, mobile borderland populations that needed to cross them on a routine basis. It is bizarre that these are now being developed as

---

63 Richard Schofield, 'Back to 1975 and All That: Iran, Iraq and the Shatt al-Arab', unpublished paper delivered to the University of Exeter's *Global Gulf* conference, July 2006.

barriers. Given loaded historical memories on all sides, the success with which will be met the dual (but almost contradictory) challenge of preserving the economic vitality of border regions while guarding against trans-boundary security threats remains to be seen.

9

THE NON-ETHNIC REGIONAL
MODEL OF FEDERALISM: SOME
COMPARATIVE PERSPECTIVES

Liam Anderson

The end of the Cold War and the attendant collapse of the complex bipolar security architecture has shifted the locus of violence in world politics from the international to the domestic level of analysis. Interstate wars, and Great Power wars in particular, have become largely extinct as a species. In their place have emerged bloody, seemingly intractable intrastate wars, often fuelled by intense ethnopolitical hatreds. With the international community seemingly unwilling or unable to mount a coherent and consistent response to the problem of intrastate ethnic conflict, attention has shifted to the domestic arena. The question, simply put, is whether domestic political institutions can be crafted in such a way as to prevent or ameliorate conflict in deeply divided societies, and if so, how? The various 'waves' of democratisation that have swept the globe over the last twenty years have provided a living laboratory for scholars of comparative constitutional design to perfect their art, and there has been no shortage of comparativists willing to offer 'lessons' for newly democratising countries—often based, it should be noted, on the empirical study of stable and highly developed democracies. The adoption of a federal system of government, whereby power is constitutionally divided among different levels of government, is among the most frequently advocated 'solutions' to the problem of managing conflict in divided societies.

Within this sub-field, however, there is little in the way of consensus on how to structure a federation to achieve this goal. A debate that has aroused considerable controversy, especially in the context of Iraq, is how to define geographically the sub-units of a federation. Should boundary lines be drawn to create ethnically homogenous sub-units (often referred to as 'ethnic', or 'plurinational' federalism), or should they be deliberately crafted to ensure ethnic heterogeneity (variously termed, 'administrative', or 'territorial' federalism)? Or, is a compromise possible between these two extremes—a 'middle-way' that avoids the problems associated with both? The following chapter provides a comparative assessment of three possible models of federal system—ethnic, territorial, and regional—each of which offers a different perspective on the issue of sub-unit boundary delineation.

Ethnic conflict: managing the unmanageable?

Ethnicity is a notoriously slippery concept. To avoid an interminable debate over definitions, the following discussion will rely on Vernon Van Dyke's definition of 'ethnic community' as 'a group of persons, predominantly of common descent, who think of themselves as collectively possessing a separate identity based on race or shared cultural characteristics, usually language or religion'.[1] This basic but plausible working definition hints at some of the reasons why ethnicity is, perhaps, the most difficult of societal divisions for democracy to manage. Ethnic conflicts are inherently less amenable to compromise than, say, conflicts over the distribution of material resources. Distributive conflicts, the basic issues of 'who gets what, when, and how' are normally susceptible to a multitude of possible bargaining outcomes. There are many ways to divide up the economic pie to the satisfaction of all. Ethnic conflicts are intrinsically less malleable. As one expert observes, 'ethnicity taps cultural and symbolic issues—basic notions of identity and the self, of individual and group worth

---

1   Vernon Van Dyke, 'The Individual, The State, and Ethnic Communities in Political Theory', *World Politics*, vol. 29, no. 3, April 1977, p. 344.

and entitlement'.[2] At heart, because 'ethnic conflicts revolve around exclusive symbols and conceptions of legitimacy, they are characterised by competing demands that cannot be easily broken down into bargainable increments'.[3] Put another way, 'How does a policymaker divide up the "glorification" of the national language?'[4] Divisions of ethnicity also tend to be deeper and more permanent that other social cleavages. Unlike other divisions, of social class, for example, individuals cannot easily change their ethnic attributes. There are consequently no 'in-between' groups, or 'floating voters' to bridge ethnic divides. Democratic elections under standard majoritarian rules may therefore 'take on the character of a "census" and constitute a zero-sum game'.[5] The losers, presumably the demographic minority, may legitimately fear the risk of permanent exclusion from access to power. Democracy as a mechanism to resolve conflicts peacefully is only accepted as legitimate to the extent that today's losers stand some chance of being tomorrow's winners. Losers have few incentives to participate in a democratic system if permanent exclusion is the only plausible outcome.

The problem then is not just about resolving ethnic conflict—this can be achieved through a variety of mechanisms, from the forcible suppression of ethnicity to the elimination of entire ethnic groups— the problem is how to do this within a peaceful democratic framework. More precisely, the challenge for political scientists is how to craft democratic political institutions that can alleviate rather than exacerbate ethnic divisions. Many scholars flatly reject the possibility that stable democratic institutions are compatible with deep ethnic divisions. Rabushka and Shepsle, for example, state with admirable bluntness, 'democracy... is simply not viable in an environment of

2 Larry Diamond, and Marc F. Plattner (eds), *Nationalism, Ethnic Conflict, and Democracy*, Baltimore: Johns Hopkins University Press, 1994, p. xviii.

3 Ibid., p. xviii.

4 Donald Horowitz, *Ethnic Groups in Conflict*, Berkeley: University of California Press, 1985, p. 224.

5 Diamond and Plattner, *Nationalism*, p. xviii.

intense ethnic preferences'.[6] Others have emphasised the role of national identity as an indispensable pre-condition for the emergence of stable democracy. More often than not, ethnically divided societies come into conflict precisely over the issue of national versus group identity. Even Daniel Elazar, an otherwise staunch advocate of federal systems as a means of transcending social cleavages, has concluded that federalism may have little to offer in terms of a solution to the problem of ethnic divisions. According to Elazar, 'Ethnic nationalism is the most ego-centric of all nationalisms, and the most difficult basis on which to erect a system of constitutionalised power-sharing; the essence of federalism.'[7] Hence his conclusion, 'ethnic nationalism is probably the strongest force against federalism'. Unfortunately, therefore, in precisely those contexts in which federalism is most needed, it is also all but impossible to sustain. In the face of such pessimism, it is important to remember that while democratic solutions to ethnic conflicts are undoubtedly difficult to engineer, the non-democratic alternatives (forced assimilation, or genocide, for example) are almost always far worse.

Federalism

Federalism, as Elazar notes, 'is a genus that includes several species',[8] and federations are, by some distance, the most common species of the genus. Most definitions of the term 'federation' share common features—at least two levels of government (federal and regional), with separate powers or competencies allocated to each level via a written constitution (though powers may also be shared between levels). In meaningful federations the constitutional division of powers between levels cannot be altered unilaterally by either level of

---

6 Alvin Rabushka and Kenneth Shepsle, *Politics in Plural Societies: A Theory of Democratic Instability*, Columbus, OH: Charles E. Merrill Publishing Company, 1972.

7 Daniel J. Elazar, 'International and Comparative Federalism', *PS: Political Science and Politics*, vol. 26, no. 2, June 1993, p. 194.

8 Ibid., p. 190.

government and the consent of both levels is required, usually via constitutional amendment. Beyond this, there is little consensus regarding specifics; indeed almost every aspect of federalism is a topic of controversy.[9] One of the most controversial issues concerns the effectiveness of federations as mechanisms for alleviating conflict in divided societies. Most of the world's durably successful democratic federations—the United States, Germany, and Australia, for example—have highly homogenous societies, dominated by a *Staatsvolk*.[10] In these societies, federal systems may be desirable for any number of reasons, but they are not *necessary* as a means of holding the state together. By contrast, in societies with long histories of inter-ethnic tensions and powerful secessionist sentiments, a federation may be the *only* way to sustain democracy while maintaining the territorial integrity of the state. Precisely *how* a federation should be organised to achieve this goal is, however, a matter of debate.

9　The literature on various elements of federalism is extensive. Among the most important works are: Daniel J. Elazar, *Exploring Federalism*, Tuscaloosa, AL: The University of Alabama Press, 1987; Ronald L. Watts, *Comparing Federal Systems*, Montreal and Kingston: School of Policy Studies, Queen's University, 1999; Preston King, *Federalism and Federation*, Baltimore, MD: The Johns Hopkins University Press, 1982; Mikhail Filipov, Peter C. Ordeshook, and Olga Shetsova, *Designing Federalism: A Theory of Self-Sustainable Federal Institutions*, Cambridge: Cambridge University Press, 2004; Thomas Franck, *Why Federations Fail: An Inquiry into the Requisites for a Successful Federation*, New York: New York University Press, 1966; Valerie Earle, *Federalism: Infinite Variety in Theory and Practice*, Itasca, IL: F.E. Peacock, 1968; Ivo Duchacek, *Comparative Federalism: The Territorial Dimensions of Politics*, New York: Holt, Rinehart and Winston, 1970; William H. Riker, *Federalism: Origin, Operation, Significance*, Boston: Little, Brown, 1964. For a useful summary article of the state of the discipline, see Daniel J. Elazar, 'International and Comparative Federalism', *PS: Political Science and Politics* vol. 26, no. 2, June 1993.

10　A *Staatsvolk* can be defined as a single national (or ethnic) people that dominates a state demographically and electorally. On the significance of a *Staatsvolk* for the stability and success of federations, see Brendan O'Leary, 'An Iron Law of Nationalism and Federation?: A (Neo-Diceyian) Theory of the Necessity of a Federal *Staatsvolk*, and of Consociational Rescue', *Nations and Nationalism*, vol. 7, no. 3, 2001, pp. 273–96.

Despite a voluminous extant literature on federalism, issues relating to the character of sub-units in federal systems—such as the implications of having fewer rather than more sub-units—have been relatively neglected.[11] The geography of boundary delimitation in ethnically divided societies has been studied in greater detail, and from this body of work, it is possible to synthesise two basic theoretical approaches to this issue. One approach, 'administrative', or 'territorial' federalism, is based on the logic of pluralism, and involves drawing boundary lines with the specific intent to divide up territorial concentrations of ethnic groups. The main alternative is 'ethnic' or 'plurinational' federalism, in which the boundaries of sub-units are defined by the geographic distribution of ethnicities. In its purest form, ethnic federalism involves allocating a separate sub-unit to each ethnic group, such that the number of sub-units equals the number of ethnicities within the state. A third possibility, to be considered in greater detail below, is regional federalism. As a means of addressing conflict in divided societies, regional federalism remains understudied and theoretically underspecified, yet it merits serious consideration as an approach because it offers a plausible 'middleway' between the two other extremes.

Ethnic federalism and the consociational tradition

Ethnic federalism, whereby sub-unit boundary lines are drawn to coincide with the geographic distribution of ethnicities, provides a popular, though controversial solution to the problem of governing ethnically divided states. The theoretical rationale underlying the argument for ethnic federalism shares much in common with the theory of consociational democracy. The concept of consociational democracy, associated primary with the work of eminent Dutch political scientist Arend Lijphart, emerged in the 1960s as a direct challenge to the then prevailing wisdom about the merits of pluralism.

---

11 On the importance of the character of sub-units, see Ronald Watts, *Multicultural Societies and Federalism*, Ottawa: Royal Commission on Bilingualism and Biculturalism, 1970.

The puzzle for Lijphart is why countries such as Austria, Switzerland, and the Low Countries should exhibit a high level of stability and effectiveness despite having subcultures divided by deep, mutually reinforcing cleavages. Accounting for stability in the absence of the cross-cutting cleavage pattern deemed necessary for stability by theorists of pluralism leads Lijphart to the concept of consociational democracy. Lijphart subsequently identifies four defining features of consociations—elite accommodation (expressed as grand coalitions, or 'government by elite cartel'), segmental autonomy, proportionality, and minority veto.[12] Of these, it is clear that the first two are the most significant for Lijphart's theory. In early formulations of the concept, Lijphart maintains, 'The essential characteristic of consociational democracy is not so much any particular institutional arrangement as the deliberate joint effort by the elites to stabilise the system.'[13] This requires that elites understand the dangers of political fragmentation, that they are committed to preserving the system, that they have the ability to transcend cleavages to co-operate with elites of other subcultures, and that they can adequately represent the interests of their respective subcultures. The segmental autonomy element provides the clearest conceptual link between consociationalism and ethnic federalism.

Though Lijphart does not use the actual term 'ethnic federalism', it is clear that this is essentially synonymous with his concept of segmental autonomy. In fact, it appears vital to the effective functioning of consociational democracy that ethnic groups (or 'subcultures', as Lijphart terms them) be kept as separate as possible. Groups interact via their elites at the national level, but otherwise remain entirely segregated at the mass level. The reason, according to Lijphart, is that 'subcultures with widely divergent outlooks and interests may

---

12 Standard early statements of Lijphart's theory are included in Arend Lijphart, 'Consociational Democracy', *World Politics*, vol. 21, 1969, pp. 207–25; and idem, *The Politics of Accommodation: Pluralism and Democracy in the Netherlands*, Berkeley: University of California Press, 1968.

13 Lijphart, 'Consociational Democracy', p. 213.

coexist without necessarily being in conflict; conflict arises only when they are in contact with each other'.[14] Hence, Lijphart's contention is that 'good social fences may make good political neighbours', and that, 'a kind of voluntary apartheid policy' is the 'best solution for a divided society'.[15] Underlying this argument is a theory of political conflict that views interaction among heterogeneous groups as likely to increase mutual tension rather than generating norms of compromise and consensus. This is precisely the logic used to justify the idea of ethnic federalism. Lijphart himself explicitly recognises the strong 'conceptual and empirical links' between consociationalism and (ethnic) federalism. After noting that 'territorial segmental autonomy means, in practically all cases, a federal arrangement',[16] he proceeds to specify that type of federal arrangement that is most consistent with consociationalism. Among the elements identified are that 'the segments of the plural society must be *geographically concentrated*', and that 'the *boundaries between the component units* of the federation *must follow the segmental boundaries* as much as possible', such that the component units of the federation will be highly homogenous as far as their segmental composition is concerned'.[17] This is, in essence, the definition of ethnic federalism.

In contexts such as those examined by Lijphart, where subcultures have a history of mutual tension and remain deeply divided by reinforcing cleavages, ethnic federalism may be the only viable way to ensure that overall political stability can be maintained and potential conflict minimised. In this sense, ethnic federalism is primarily a mechanism for the avoidance of conflict rather than the active promotion of consensus and co-operation. This may be especially relevant in the aftermath of ethnic wars, where segregating ethnicities

---

14 Ibid., p. 219.

15 Ibid., p. 219.

16 Arend Lijphart, 'Consociation and Federation: Conceptual and Empirical Links', *Canadian Journal of Political Science*, vol. 12, no. 3, September 1979, p. 505.

17 Ibid., p. 505.

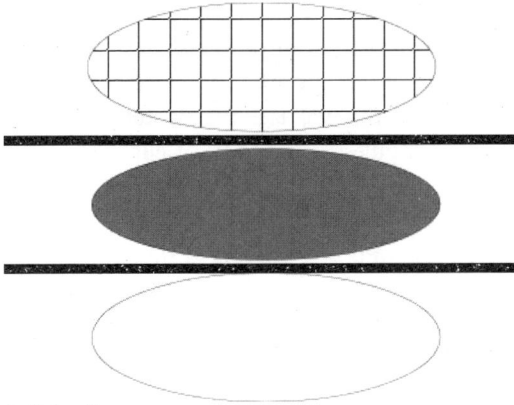

Fig. 1: Ethnic federalism

territorially may be the only plausible way to prevent secession or the resumption of violence. Kaufmann, for example, makes a powerful case that ethnic civil wars can end only when 'opposing groups are demographically separated into defensible enclaves'.[18] According to Kaufmann, during ethnic wars, 'hypernationalist rhetoric and real atrocities harden ethnic identities to the point that cross-ethnic appeals are unlikely to be made and even less likely to be heard'.[19] Institutional devices that seek to foster cross-cutting cleavages, such as territorial federalism, are simply ineffective in this environment of intense hatred. Similarly, leaving ethnic populations intermingled creates 'real security dilemmas that intensify violence, motivate ethnic "cleansing", and prevent de-escalation unless the groups are separated'.[20] In contexts of intense ethnic hatred, therefore, ethnic federalism may be necessary for the very survival of the state itself, and, perhaps, the survival of entire ethnic populations within it.

The goal of ethnic federalism, then, is to preserve the territorial integrity of the state by segregating its component ethnicities into

---

18 Chaim Kaufmann, 'Possible and Impossible Solutions to Ethnic Civil Wars', *International Security*, vol. 20, no. 4, spring 1996, p. 137.

19 Ibid., p. 137.

20 Ibid., p. 137.

autonomous physical enclaves. To keep the whole together almost inevitably requires some form of power-sharing arrangement at the centre. Unless minority groups are guaranteed participation in decision-making structures they will lack the institutional means to defend their autonomy, and unless some form of elite-level co-operation is institutionalised at the centre, it is difficult to see how the whole can hold together. In this respect, ethnic federalism is umbilically linked to the broader notion of power-sharing at the centre. Hence, there is a strong affinity between ethnic federalism and consociational democracy. Proportional representation in the important institutions of state and veto power over key decisions enable minorities to protect their autonomy, while elite accommodation at the centre prevents the whole from splintering into its constituent pieces. Conceptually, therefore, ethnic federalism needs to be nested in a broader web of power-sharing institutions and cannot be considered separable from these.

The ethnic model of federalism is inherently defensive in nature. The goal is stability rather than the transformation of the political space. To function as intended it requires little in the way of heroic assumptions about the capacity of people to transcend ethnic differences, or of institutions to transform identities. Though often left unspoken, the basic underlying assumption is that there is a permanence to ethnic identity that cannot be easily engineered out of existence. In deeply divided societies, where cross-cutting cleavages that transcend ethnicity cannot simply be created, system stability can best be obtained by minimising contact among groups, giving them the institutional means to protect their autonomy, and relying on elites to co-operate at the centre.

Ethnic federalism in practice

While many multiethnic states continue to survive and prosper, federal states that have used ethnicity as the basis for the definition of sub-units have an 'abysmal track record' of survival.[21] Ethnic fed-

---

21 John McGarry, 'Can Federalism Help To Manage Ethnic and National Diversity?' *Federations*, vol. 4, no. 1, March 2004, p. 3.

erations have failed in post-communist Eastern Europe (the Soviet Union, Czechoslovakia, and Yugoslavia), Africa (the East African Federation and Ethiopia–Eritrea), and Asia (Pakistan and Malaya– Singapore). Conversely, successful examples of ethnic federations are relatively few and far between. Within the developed world, Switzerland, Belgium and Canada are obvious counter-examples, though none is an ethnic federation in its purest form. Among developing countries, India stands out as the exception to the rule. Ethiopia's bold experiment with ethnic federalism is, perhaps, the purest form of the genus in existence today, but definitive judgment on Ethiopia's success (whether as a democracy or as an ethnic federation) must await the further passage of time. This catalogue of failure has led many to question the wisdom of adopting ethnic federalism as a means of governing ethnically divided states.

Generally, criticisms of ethnic federalism fall into one of three basic categories: the problems associated with drawing boundary lines to separate out ethnicities, the dysfunctional operations of ethnic federal systems and their attendant consociational mechanisms, and the tendency of such federations toward ultimate fragmentation. Among the problems associated with defining the geography of subunits in an ethnic federation, one of the most serious concerns the basic cartographical problem of drawing boundary lines that separate out concentrations of ethnic groups such that each group occupies a coherent and contiguous piece of territory. To draw a boundary line along sectarian lines to separate out Iraq's Sunni and Shiite populations, for example, would leave a sizeable population of each in the territory of the other regardless of where the line was drawn. Much the same problem would have confronted efforts to separate Hutu from Tutsi in Rwanda in 1994. Conversely, where ethnicities are highly concentrated geographically, as in Belgium, establishing the boundaries for a viable ethnic federation may be much easier; but the fact remains, that very few multiethnic states have such clearly defined concentrations of ethnicities.[22]

This territorial dispersion of ethnicities created a major problem for efforts to partition a country like Bosnia-Herzegovina. Bosnia's population includes roughly 45 per cent Muslims, 35 per cent Serbs, and 17 per cent Croats, but their distribution across the territory of Bosnia is such that drawing coherent boundary lines to separate them has proven extremely problematic. Bosnia has been described as 'ethnically a leopard's skin' in which concentrations of ethnicities exist (Serbs in the west and east, Croats in the south and centre, and Muslims almost everywhere) but not on contiguous pieces of land. Efforts by the European Community (EC) to resolve the tense ethnic stand-off in Bosnia before the 1992 referendum on independence and the onset of war proposed dividing the country up into twelve non-contiguous ethnic cantons—two Muslim, six Serb, and four Croat. The EC's version of the reality of Bosnia's ethnic distribution was immediately challenged by all three sides. Each produced a map that offered widely differing interpretations of reality. The Croats claimed that the EC map would condemn nearly 60 per cent of Bosnian Croats to living as minorities in another group's canton. They also proposed drawing cantonal borders using 1961 census figures rather than those of 1991—a stratagem to bring the city of Mostar under Croat control.[23] Ultimately, all three sides rejected the map. Even if all three sides had agreed in principle on the idea of ethnic cantons—which they did not in 1992—their widely differing interpretations of what constituted 'their' territory would have been sufficient to scupper the agreement. Where inter-ethnic tensions are especially acute, the drawing of lines on a map becomes an intensely political act that is as likely to create animosity as it is to diminish

---

22 Of course, Belgium has the capital Brussels located in Flanders but with a Francophone majority that complicates the ethnic division.

23 On this see Steven L. Burg and Paul S. Shoup, *The War in Bosnia Herzegovina: Ethnic Conflict and International Intervention*, Armonk, NY: M.E. Sharpe, 2000.

it. Where sub-units comprise nationalities, borders acquire added significance and issues such as the defensibility of terrain, control of symbolically important territory, access to trade routes, and the location of key resources (water or oil, for example) are perceived as matters of life or death. In the presence of these sorts of concerns, border demarcation to separate ethnic groups becomes a source of conflict rather than a means to end it.

Ultimately, the EC mediation effort in Bosnia merely served to reinforce the perception on all sides that the territorial claims of the three groups were incompatible. The example also highlights a more general problem with drawing boundary lines to encapsulate ethnicities. If, as is normally the case, it proves impossible to create entirely homogenous sub-units, the alternative is to draw boundaries that capture the majority of a given ethnicity, and to accept that, unless peaceful population transfers are feasible, minorities will inevitably be 'trapped' inside its borders. This creates a different set of problems, however. Firstly, if ethnic federalism is implemented in the aftermath of inter-ethnic conflict, trapped minorities are essentially caught 'behind enemy lines' and vulnerable to violent reprisals. Such has been the fate of Serbs left behind in Kosovo following the termination of conflict in 1999. Secondly, if the state's ultimate division into ethnic enclaves is anticipated in advance, this anticipation provides incentives to warring ethnicities to maximise territorial gains before peace breaks out and to cleanse this territory of rival ethnicities. Though all sides were guilty of this during the Bosnian conflict, the best known examples are of Bosnian Serb forces ethnically cleansing Muslim enclaves at Zepa and Srebrenica as part of a broader strategy of carving out ethnically 'pure' territory in eastern Bosnia from which to create a Serbian Republic. Overall, by the end of the war it was estimated that nearly 50 per cent of the entire population of Bosnia had been displaced, many involuntarily.

A second cluster of problems associated with ethnic federations concerns how such systems function after the boundary lines have been determined. Perhaps the most taxing of these is whether the

217

power-sharing mechanisms that inevitably accompany the partition of a state into ethnic enclaves can produce a stable, functioning polity, or whether they instead provoke gridlock, thereby exacerbating ethnic tensions. Though consociational devices, such as the minority veto, are not a defining element of ethnic federalism, in practice, they are often unavoidable. In Bosnia, the partition of the country into three 'nations' and two entities—The Federation of Bosnia-Herzegovina (mainly Muslim and Croat) and Republika Srpska (mainly Serb) was accompanied by a complex network of institutional devices designed to ensure protection for each ethnic group. A three-person collegial presidency guarantees that each ethnic group achieves executive representation, and ethnic quotas determine the membership of the two chambers of the federal parliament. Of the fifteen delegates to the upper chamber (known as the 'House of Peoples'), five are reserved for each group, and there is a quorum requirement of nine delegates with a minimum of three delegates in attendance from each group, meaning that three delegates of any ethnicity can effectively paralyse the chamber. A similar, though more limited veto provision applies in the first chamber of the Bosnian parliament. Ultimately, any proposed law can be rejected by a two-thirds majority in either of the parliaments of the two entities and there is no provision for overriding this veto. Though less extreme than Bosnia, ethnic federations like Belgium and India (according to Lijphart) have similarly elaborate consociational mechanisms to ensure representation on the basis of ethnicity and to allow minority groups to defend the status quo.[24]

The problem with these arrangements is that they elevate ethnic identity to a position of primacy in the political life of the state. Ethnic divisions are frozen institutionally. Political parties organised around ethnicity become the key players as the political space fragments along ethnic lines, and parties that appeal across ethnic

---

24 On the dubious claim that India is an example of consociationalism, see Arend Lijphart, 'The Puzzle of Indian Democracy: A Consociational Interpretation', *The American Political Science Review*, vol. 90, June 1996.

lines—on the basis of economic ideology, for example—become increasingly marginalised. Moderate parties also tend to disappear in an escalating process of 'ethnic outbidding', in which parties of the same ethnicity attempt to outmanoeuvre each other by adopting more extreme positions on the all-encompassing 'ethnic question'. There is a possibility, therefore, that once ethnic federalism is reinforced by power-sharing arrangements at the centre, the political life of the state gets caught up in a vicious cycle whereby those attributes that are essential to the effective sharing of power (moderation and a willingness to compromise on the part of elites) are precisely those qualities that are in the shortest supply. The result, as post-war Bosnia amply demonstrates, is intense ethnic polarisation and political gridlock. The three extremist parties that led the country to war in the first place—the Bosniak Party of Democratic Action (SDA), the Serbian Democratic Party (SDS), and the Croatian Democratic Union (HDZ)—still dominate the political life of the country today. In the absence of moderation and compromise on the part of these three pre-eminent parties, Bosnia survives as a unified territorial entity, but barely. Without the presence of a sizeable contingent of NATO and later EU troops, and the dictatorial powers vested in the Office of the High Representative (an ad hoc international body charged with implementing the civilian aspect of the Bosnian peace accord), it is doubtful that Bosnia would function at all. This highlights what is probably the central flaw at the heart of the consociational idea. The core of the theory relies on the willingness of elites to transcend ethnic divisions and make compromises in order to safeguard the integrity of the state. But this assumes that the problem is with the masses, and that elites are the solution. In the case of Bosnia, as with many other ethnic wars, the conflict was mostly inspired and sustained by warring political elites. Of course if elites are the real source of the problem, then it is not clear that Lijphart's idea of 'elite accommodation' can provide the solution to anything.

A final critique of ethnic federalism, and in some ways the most serious, is that federations ordered along ethnic lines have a very poor track record of survival. As noted at the beginning of this section, the list of ethnic federations that have come apart at the seams is extensive, and, with the recent demise of Serbia–Montenegro (if indeed 'Montenegrin' can be considered an ethnicity), still growing. The basic argument is that ethnic federalism fuels secessionist tendencies by reinforcing, or even creating, ethnic identities, and by providing ethnicities with access to the resources necessary to mount a secession bid. Much of the empirical evidence underlying this argument comes from the experiences of the Eastern Europe and the Soviet Union since the collapse of communism, and in particular, the straightforward observation that the three states that fragmented during the 1990s— the Soviet Union, Yugoslavia and Czechoslovakia—were all federations, and all organised around 'nationalities'. Against the obvious point that ethnic diversity, rather than federalism provides a better explanation for the break-up of these specific states, Bunce (2004) maintains that 'national federalism, not the mere presence of minority populations, even if they are geographically concentrated, is critical for generating secessionist demands on the state'[25]. According to Bunce, the status as nations of ethnic groups within each of the three provided access to the necessary 'institutional resources' without which 'groups cannot take advantage of any expanded opportunities for change that present themselves'.[26] Hence, while ethnicities with their own constituent units led the charge for independence in all three federal states, no such demands were made by ethnic minorities among the unitary socialist states. A similar argument has been made in the case of Canada. As a stable, democratic and prosperous multiethnic society, Canada is generally considered a successful example of ethnic federalism. Simeon, however, questions this interpretation, noting that the autonomy conferred by Canada's federal structure

25 Valerie Bunce, 'Federalism, Nationalism and Secession: The Communist and Post-Communist Experience', in Ugo M. Amoretti, and Nancy Bermeo (eds), *Federalism and Territorial Cleavages*, Baltimore: The Johns Hopkins University Press, 2004, p. 433.
26 Ibid.

'helped reshape Francophone identities, from the original *Canadiens*, the first white settlers of what is now Canada, to *French-Canadians*, defined primarily by language and religion, and eventually to the contemporary *Quebecois*, a national identity centred on the Quebec state'.[27] Not only did ethnic federalism have the effect of 'opening the institutional space from which Francophones could pursue self-government', but it reconstituted Canada's French–English cleavage 'almost entirely as a Canada–Quebec conflict, a conflict between two "nations"'.[28] In a 1995 referendum, Quebec came within a whisker of seceding from Canada.

If the defects associated with ethnic federalism are so readily apparent, what can be said in its defence? The most obvious defence is that while ethnic federalism may not ever be the ideal solution, it is often the *only* possible solution short of continued violence or secession. The example of Bosnia is again instructive. The first serious effort on the part of the international community to negotiate an end to hostilities culminated in 1993 in the so-called Vance–Owen Plan.[29] Along with an outline of proposed power-sharing political institutions, the plan included a map that divided Bosnia into ten provinces. Of the ten, Muslims constituted a majority in three, Serbs in two and Croats in one. The remaining four provinces were ethnically divided. Because ethnicity was only one of the factors considered in the delineation of the boundaries, this proposal represented a hybrid ethnic/territorial federation. The map was partly an attempt to satisfy demands for local autonomy, but the primary purpose was to make Bosnian Serb secession all but impossible by parcelling the Serbs out into non-contiguous patches of territory. This ensured that the map would be unacceptable to the Serbs. Bosnian Muslims also

---

27   Richard Simeon, 'Canada: Federalism, Language, and Regional Conflict', in Amoretti and Bermeo, *Federalism*, p. 96.

28   Ibid., p. 96.

29   For details of the inside story of the Vance–Owen Plan, see David Owen, *Balkan Odyssey*, New York: Harcourt Brace, 1995; and Burg and Shoup, *The War in Bosnia*, Chapter 5.

opposed (but on the basis of a more general aversion against decen-tralisation as a principle), leaving only the Bosnian Croats willing to accept its provisions.[30] Thus the Vance–Owen map, like those that preceded it and most of those that came after, proved unacceptable to one or other of the warring parties. The only map that gener-ated the minimum of consensus necessary to make the deal stick was the map produced as part of the Dayton peace plan (1995), and this was the map that partitioned Bosnia along ethnic lines and gave the country its current state structure. The partition of Bosnia was clearly not an ideal solution, but it was the *only* remaining solution after all others had been tried and failed. Especially in the aftermath of ethnic conflict, therefore, ethnic federalism may be the least bad of the op-tions available. Viewed form this perspective, a high failure rate for ethnic federations is to be expected because it is often an option of last resort in the absence of viable alternatives.

Much the same defence can be mounted against critics of power-sharing arrangements. Devices such as the minority veto allow ethnic minorities to thwart the will of the majority and defend the status quo. Obviously, this does little to enhance the efficiency of the leg-islative process, but the alternative to gridlock in ethnically polarised states may be far worse. Veto power for each of three groups in Bos-nia was an indispensable prerequisite for an agreement at Dayton, so gridlock and political frustration was the inevitable cost of ending a ruinous war with Bosnia's borders still intact. Likewise the argument that ethnic federalism and power-sharing schemes institutionalise ethnicity as the defining feature of politics requires qualification. The intense ethnic polarisation of Bosnian society began long before the Dayton Accord codified ethnic identity institutionally. During Bos-nia's first freely contested elections in 1990, for example, the former communists were routed and the three ethno-nationalist parties won over 75 per cent of the seats in parliament between them. These same

---

30 Bosnian Muslims were opposed to the Vance–Owen map because at this stage in the conflict they still entertained hopes of dominating politically a unitary state and were, therefore, opposed to any effort to decentralise.

parties then mobilised their respective ethnic support bases and embarked on a vicious three year ethnic war that had already partitioned Bosnia along ethnic lines by the time of the Dayton Accord. In this respect, Dayton did no more than recognise an existing reality on the ground. It certainly did not create a new reality. Most of the pathologies associated with ethnic federations and consociationalism—extremism, ethnic outbidding, and so on—may indeed be products of the institutions, but it is equally plausible that they are the products of heightened ethnic tensions or ethnic conflict that often precede a decision to federalise along ethnic lines. To determine the direction of the causal arrows at work here requires demonstrating that the institutions preceded ethnic tensions, rather than the other way round. This makes little sense, however, because ethnic federalism is invariably a *response* to pre-existing ethnic tensions. There is also reasonable doubt as to whether ethnically homogenous sub-units really do harden ethnic identity and generate more extreme politics. For example, a detailed study of voting behaviour in municipal elections in Bosnia across two elections (1997 and 2000) found that the percentage of votes obtained by nationalist parties was significantly higher in heterogeneous municipalities (defined as those in which the largest group constitutes less than 66 per cent) than in homogenous municipalities.[31] According to the author of that study, the results indicate that 'heterogeneous municipalities fostered support for nationalist parties rather than moderation', from which she concludes, 'integrative structures especially foster instability following an intense war'.[32] The corollary of this, of course, is that homogenous units (i.e. ethnic federalism) foster stability and moderation.

---

31 Nina Caspersen, 'Good Fences Make Good Neighbours? A Comparison of Conflict-Regulation Strategies in Postwar Bosnia', *Journal of Peace Research*, vol. 41, no. 5, 2004, pp. 569–88. For a similar argument, see Roberto Belloni, 'Peacebuilding and Consociational Electoral Engineering in Bosnia and Herzegovina', *International Peacekeeping*, vol. 11, no. 2, summer 2004, pp. 334–53.

32 Caspersen, 'Good Fences', p. 580.

Finally, on the issue of the dangers of secession associated with ethnic federations, there are several points to be made. The positive relationship between ethnic federations and secessions appears to apply only to non-democratic federations. No truly democratic federation has suffered from this problem, though both the United States and Canada have clearly come close. Moreover, the intense violence that has sometimes accompanied the breakdown of ethnic federations has normally been the result of the insufficient homogeneity of the sub-units. During the disintegration of Yugoslavia, for example, conflicts were fought over the presence of 300,000 Serbs in Croatia and the ethnic mosaic of Bosnia. Ethnically homogenous Slovenia broke free without violence. At a minimum, if secession is inevitable, then ethnic federalism increases the prospect that this option can be accomplished peacefully by defining ethnic borders in advance.

Territorial federalism: manufacturing pluralism

Territorial federalism involves the delineation of sub-unit boundary lines with the deliberate intent to divide up, or 'crack' otherwise ethnically homogenous territorial concentrations. There are two basic versions of territorial federalism, termed here 'pure' and 'modified'. The two versions differ somewhat in the manner in which they seek to divide up ethnic concentrations, but at heart, the theoretical rationale underlying both draws heavily on the logic of pluralism. The term pluralism, much like federalism, has been defined in a variety of ways, but in essence all definitions equate the term with the fragmentation and dispersal of political power. All societies are divided to some extent, but the significance of these divisions for political stability vary according to their number, their depth, and the degree to which divisions are cross-cutting or mutually reinforcing. Mutually reinforcing cleavages will tend to produce a small number of segregated, monolithic groups, whereas multiple, cross-cutting cleavages result in a 'fine partition of society into a large number of relatively small preference clusters'.[33] According to theorists of pluralism, the former pattern of cleavage distribution is dangerously destabilising to the political system, while the latter is conducive to stability.

A number of explanations for why multiple cross-cutting cleavages should generate political stability have been advanced by advocates of pluralism. Firstly, pluralism causes moderation. In a pluralist society, individuals must inevitably interact across groups and interact with different groups at different times depending on the issue at stake. As Bailey notes, 'those who are enemies in one situation are sometimes required to act as allies in another situation. With an eye on future co-operation, they restrain their behaviour in present competition.'[34] The prospect that today's enemy could become tomorrow's ally, therefore, provides incentives for moderating political interactions. A second, related explanation is that where there is a multiplicity of lines of conflict, none is likely to develop into the kind of deep, intense cleavage that endangers the stability of the entire system. Conversely, where cleavages are mutually reinforcing, every single issue risks intensifying the divisions that separate groups. Every political battle becomes existential. Pluralism, therefore, helps to 'de-intensify' existing divisions. Finally, and most significantly, pluralism helps avoid the problem of permanent exclusion. Across a range of issues, no one group is likely to be permanently included in the winning majority, but for the same reason, no group must face the prospect of permanent exclusion. Knowing this, losers have incentives to continue to abide by the democratic rules of the game rather than seek redress in more violent, extra-constitutional ways. It is precisely the fluidity and instability of coalition politics in pluralist societies that constitute its strength as a source of underlying systemic stability.

---

33 Nicholas R. Miller, 'Pluralism and Social Choice', *The American Political Science Review*, vol. 77, 1983, p. 735.

34 F.G. Bailey, *Stratagems and Spoils: A Social Anthropology of Politics*, Oxford: Basil Blackwell, 1970.

Fig. 2: Pure territorial federalism

In the context of federalism, much the same logic that drives plu-ralist theory underpins the 'territorial' approach to defining constitu-ent units. Under territorial federalism boundary lines are drawn de-liberately to avoid creating a small number of ethnically homogenous units. The goal is to break down otherwise monolithic ethnic groups into smaller fragments, at which point pluralist dynamics can take hold. In essence, therefore, territorial federalism seeks to create cross-cutting cleavages through the geography of boundary delineation. The pure form of territorial federalism involves crafting boundaries that intentionally cut across concentrations of ethnic groups in order to create ethnically heterogeneous sub-units in which, ideally, no one ethnic group can command an absolute majority. In such a unit, no single ethnicity can govern alone, and each needs the support of at least one other group in order to govern. To participate in govern-ment, each group must moderate its positions in order to make itself more appealing as a coalition partner. Moreover, the very process of negotiating coalition formation and reformation should foster norms of compromise and consensus among group elites. Over time, so the argument goes, groups can build up reservoirs of mutual respect and trust that enable politics to transcend the zero-sum dynamics of eth-nic conflict. Presumably, improved inter-ethnic relations at the unit

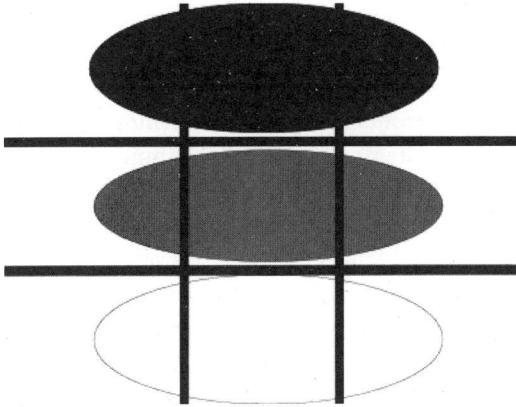

Fig. 3: Modified territorial federalism

level will at some point percolate up to the national level. System stability and nation building are, therefore, the ultimate goals of territorial federalism. Clearly, this version of territorial federalism cannot accommodate situations in which only two ethnic groups are present. In a bi-ethnic state, it is virtually impossible to draw boundary lines to avoid creating numerical majorities of one or other group.

Modified territorial federalism relies on a variant on this same basic logic, but focuses on intra-ethnic competition rather than on inter-ethnic co-operation. The number of sub-units is more important than the ethnic composition of their respective populations. The goal is not to create sub-units with equal populations of each ethnicity, but to ensure that the territory occupied by each community is divided into multiple sub-units. Similar to the pure form, the intention of the modified variant to use boundary lines to create cleavages that cut across ethnic groups. The focus, however, is more on the deliberate fragmentation of monolithic ethnic blocs in order to manufacture potentially competitive sub-ethnic identities. More broadly, the goal is to shift the locus and intensity of conflict. Rather than large ethnic blocs clashing at the national level—clashes that will inevitably involve issues of intense symbolic and material importance—it is better, according to this line of reasoning, to displace conflict to

227

the regional level. Moreover, disputes at the regional level will take place *within* rather than *across* ethnic groups. The basic assumptions underlying this argument are that disputes involving issues of local or regional concern are inherently less threatening to the stability of the overall political system, and that intra-ethnic disputes are more manageable than those between ethnicities.[35]

This approach has nation-building potential. By creating new lines of cleavage within ethnic groups, or by exploiting existing ones, territorial federalism can stimulate new coalitions of interests at the national level *across* ethnic lines. Temporary coalitions that attract support from portions of all ethnic groups may emerge for instance along lines of economic interest, or based on an urban/rural split. These coalitions are likely to be formed issue by issue, and are also likely to be unstable and, therefore, temporary. But this kind of fluid, unstable, issue by issue coalition dynamic is precisely the environment in which the benefits associated with pluralism—moderation, lower preference intensity, and non-exclusion—are most strongly evident. In this sense, modified territorial federalism uses the geographical definition of sub-units in an attempt to replicate the cross-cutting cleavages required for pluralism to function.

Both visions of territorial federalism are optimistic about the capacity of political institutions to help transcend ethnic divides. Both are pro-active strategies that rest on (mostly) unspoken assumptions about the motivations of actors—namely that the desire to access political power and resources is sufficient to override inter-communal hostilities, or intra-communal coherence.

Territorial federalism in practice

The main problem with assessing the practical merits or otherwise of territorial federalism is locating unambiguous examples of the phenomenon on a map of the world. There would appear to be no obvious cases of pure territorial federalism, and but a few marginal

---

35 This logic of territorial federalism is most closely associated with the work of Horowitz, *Ethnic Conflict*, especially pp. 601–19.

cases of the modified variant. On paper at least, Malaysia exhibits some of the features of a territorial federation, but in practice, as many have noted, Malaysia remains politically dominated by ethnic Malays and most of the elaborate constitutional provisions, including those relating to federalism, are designed to perpetuate this dominance.[36] Nigeria is the clearest example of a federal system where the boundary lines of the sub-units have been redrawn (frequently) with the specific intent to divide up lager concentrations of ethnicities.[37] Though scarcely a model of democratic peace and harmony over the last forty-five years, Nigeria must be among the more difficult states on the planet to govern, and so its survival as a unified state may be considered something of an achievement in and of itself. How much of this is attributable to changes in its federal system over time remains an open question.

A brief overview of the evolution of Nigeria's federal system is useful because it enables a controlled comparison between the respective merits of ethnic and modified territorial federalism. Nigeria began independent life in 1960 as a (more or less) ethnic federation of three large regions. Though none of these was entirely ethnically homogenous, each was dominated numerically by one of Nigeria's three major ethnicities. The Northern Region, by far the largest of the three geographically and in terms of population, was dominated by the Muslim Hausa-Fulani; the Eastern Region by the predominantly Christian Ibo; and the Western Region by the bi-communal (Muslims and Christians) Yoruba. This design was based in part on the past administrative practices of the British, in part because of the approximate lines of demarcation provided by the Benue and Niger rivers, but primarily because of the perceived need to provide each of the country's dominant ethnic groups with its own

---

36 See Diane Mauzy, 'Malaysia: Malay Political Hegemony and Coercive Consociationalism', in John McGarry and Brendan O'Leary (eds), *The Politics of Ethnic Conflict Regulation*, London: Routledge, 1993, pp. 106–27.

37 On the rationale underlying the redrawing of boundary lines in Nigeria, see Rotimi T. Suberu, *Federalism and Ethnic Conflict in Nigeria*, Washington, DC: United States Institute of Peace Press, 2001.

region.[38] The most serious design flaw was the overpowering size of the northern federal unit, which contained over 55 per cent of the country's population. This enabled the north and its primary ethnic component, the Hausa-Fulani, to dominate political institutions at the federal level—first by 'decimating its rivals' at the regional level, then overpowering its ethnic opponents, the Yoruba-based Action Group (AG), and the Ibo-dominated National Council of Nigerian Citizens (NCNC) at the centre.[39] A second problem with this system was the exclusion of minority groups from access to political power. The denial of sub-unit status to ethnic minorities, such as the Tiv and the Ijaw, rendered them powerless in the political arena, and provoked violent protest in all three regions against the hegemony of the dominant ethnicity.[40] The small number of regions and their colossal size also created problems for the stability of the system as a whole. According to Suberu, 'Nigeria's regional federalism, built around a few large ethno-regional bastions, worked to abet, and not to moderate, disruptive centrifugal tendencies.' Indeed, many experts attribute Nigeria's descent into civil war (1967–1970), a war that cost over one million lives, to fatal flaws in the design of the federal system.

The solution to Nigeria's federal problem was deceptively simple: create more sub-units. The first adjustment occurred in 1963, when the Western Region was divided in two to create a new entity for non-Yoruba minorities, the Mid-Western Region. Subsequently, the number of sub-units increased to 12 in 1967, then to 19 in 1976, to 21 in 1987, 30 in 1991, and, finally, to 36 in 1996. This continuous process of unit sub-division has led one observer to liken Nigeria to a 'biological cell which sub-divides and sub-divides again, creating

38 On the background to the three region model, see Adiele E. Afigbo, 'Background to Nigerian Federalism: Federal Features in the Colonial State', *Publius*, vol. 21, no. 4, autumn 1991, pp. 13–29.
39 Rotimi T. Suberu, 'Nigeria: Dilemmas of Federalism', in Amoretti and Bermeo, *Federalism*, p. 330.
40 Ibid., p. 331.

more and more replicas of itself.[41] The end result of this process is that the original three regions are now carved up into multiple sub-units. The territory of the once monolithic Northern Region, for example, today comprises 19 states, many of which remain dominated by the Hausa-Fulani, but an almost equal number of which are ethnically mixed. Much the same pattern prevails in the other two original regions. The net result is that while the three major ethnic groups enjoy dominance in 18 states, the remaining 18 federal entities are either of mixed ethnicity, or dominated by a minority ethnic group. This process has, therefore, cracked the three major groups, provided new ethnic homes to several minorities, and created multiple ethnically heterogeneous sub-units. The scholarly consensus appears to be that these changes have not only allowed Nigeria to survive as a coherent territorial entity, but have also had a significant positive effect on Nigeria's overall political development. Hence, the exemplar case of Nigeria would appear to provide powerful empirical support for the claims of territorial federalism and against those of ethnic federalism. Moreover, the way in which politics has evolved in Nigeria as a consequence of the repeated redrawing of sub-unit boundary lines would appear to reflect the expectations of the theory underlying territorial federalism. Thus, there is some evidence that breaking up the monolithic three-region federal structure succeeded in fostering intra-ethnic competition in place of inter-ethnic conflicts. Particularly in the north, the net impact was to create a functioning multi-party system where previously, the Muslim-dominated Northern Peoples Congress (NPC) had ruled largely unchallenged.[42] A second, critical effect was to force the National Party of Nigeria (NPN), successor to the NPC, to broaden its electoral appeal to areas outside the north and *across* ethnic lines. The NPN thus became a 'consociational party embracing political figures from all ethnic groups and states of the

---

41 Martin Dent, 'Ethnicity and Territorial Politics in Nigeria, in Graham Smith (ed.), *Federalism: The Multiethnic Challenge*, London: Longman, 1995, p. 129.
42 Horowitz, *Ethnic Conflict*, p. 610.

country.'[43] Its status as a catch-all party enabled it to triumph decisively in federal and presidential elections in 1983, thus sending a
powerful message to other parties as to the merits of moderation and
breadth of programmatic appeal.

More broadly, the carve-up of Nigeria's three regions into 36
helped to dilute the hegemony of the north, and, thus, stabilise the
system as a whole. Suberu offers an apt summation: 'the fragmentation of the north into several states has made it more unlikely that
the entire region would fall under the control of a Hausa-Fulani-
based party, which could then project its regional dominance into
the federal arena.' In turn, this has 'mitigated southern apprehen-
sions of northern domination, while promoting previously foreclosed
opportunities for credible inter-ethnic political co-operation across
the north-south divide'. It is also arguable that Nigeria's experiment
with territorial federalism has helped to solidify national unity, and
thus has served a nation-building function. Opinion polls in 2000
and 2001 show that support for national unity ranges from under
60 per cent in Ibo-dominated regions, to nearly 90 per cent in the
northeast, and runs at approximately 75 per cent across Nigeria as
a whole. Apparently, support for the federation embraces 'a wide
cross-section of the political, traditional and religious leadership of
each of the six zones of the federation'.[44]

According to one expert, federalism remains 'the lifeblood of Nigeria's survival as a multiethnic country'.[45] But to generalise from the
single case of Nigeria about the broader merits of territorial federalism
is problematic. The federal system is only one among many devices that
provide the institutional 'glue' holding Nigeria together. Other mechanisms, such as a system of presidential election that requires candidates
to garner broad support across multiple regions, may (or may not) be
at least as responsible for political moderation and national unity as

43 Stephan O. Olugbemi, 'The Ethnic Numbers Game in Interelite Competition
for Political Hegemony in Nigeria', in William C. McCready (ed.), *Culture,
Ethnicity, and Identity: Current Issues in Research*, New York: Academic Press,
1983, p. 279.

44 Suberu, *Nigeria*, p. 350.

45 Ibid., p. 346.

the design of the federal system. The distribution of societal divisions in Nigeria also appears to be particularly well suited to the success of territorial federalism. Alongside Nigeria's three major ethnic groups (which were never entirely coherent in any case) reside a multitude of smaller ethnic minorities, and the whole is criss-crossed by divisions of tribe, religion and ideology. The initial, three-region model of ethnic federalism artificially stifled these latent divisions, whereas territorial federalism allowed them to express themselves. In Horowitz's words, 'the new federal structure thus facilitated the expression of Northern heterogeneity more accurately than the earlier regional structure had permitted'.[46] It is not clear from this how effective territorial federalism would be in situations where *all* cleavages fall along, rather than across ethnic lines, or where ethnic cleavages run so deep that all others fade into irrelevance. In this sense, Nigeria's experience demonstrates that pre-existing, latent divisions can be exploited via the redesign of sub-units to fragment the political space and, therefore, facilitate the emergence of pluralism—but not that such pluralism can be necessarily created where none existed previously. A further highly problematic issue is the extent to which Nigeria can be considered a 'successful' democracy. Nigeria has been democratic for a maximum of perhaps 18 of its 47 years of independent existence. Major unresolved stresses on the social fabric of the country include a violent insurgency in the oil-producing Niger Delta region, and major violence associated with the introduction of Sharia law in Kaduna state. Sharia law is now operative in 12 of the 36 northern states. Moreover, as even enthusiasts of the system have conceded, Nigeria's party system remains 'unstable, shallow, contested, chaotic and artificially deethnicised',[47] and most of the major parties remain 'ethnic-bound'. A positive assessment of Nigeria's success as a federal democracy is, therefore, somewhat contingent on the definition of the term 'success'.

---

46 Horowitz, *Ethnic Conflict*, p. 607.
47 Suberu, *Nigeria*, p. 345.

Nonetheless, the case of Nigeria yields some general insights regarding the strengths and potential pitfalls of territorial federalism. On the positive side of the ledger, there appears to be a scholarly consensus that territorial federalism has been good for Nigeria, or better at least, than what preceded it or what might have been. Likewise, the conduct of Nigerian politics—its increasing moderation and fragmentation of interests—has evolved in ways consistent with the theory underlying territorial federalism. In short, there is a reasonably accurate translation of theory into practice in the case of Nigeria. Moreover it should be recognised that Nigeria is not an easy case. By the time the number of states began to proliferate in the mid- to late-1960s, ethnicity had already become politicised and each of Nigeria's three major ethnic groups had coalesced into quite coherent political blocs. This suggests that territorial federalism may have the strength to deal with rather robust ethnic divisions. More generally, beyond Nigeria, modified territorial federalism offers a potential solution to the intractable problem of bi-ethnic states. Bi-ethnic polities appear to be particularly resistant to constitutional engineering, and most federal designs struggle to deal with the inherently zero-sum nature of interactions that characterise such societies. This is less of a problem for modified territorial federalism because the key is the *number* of sub-units created rather than their ethnic composition. Two large ethnic groups can be cracked as easily as three smaller ones.

The example of Nigeria also highlights some of the potential problems associated with territorial federalism. The most significant of these concerns the likelihood that ethnic groups will consent to having their territories subdivided in the way prescribed by the theoretical blueprint. After all, why should a dominant ethnic group agree voluntarily to a break up its own power base and risk diluting its influence at the state and federal levels? More broadly, in the midst of the ethnic security dilemma that frequently follows inter-ethnic conflict, would any group willingly countenance the disruption to inter-group cohesion that territorial federalism entails? Unfortunately, the theory of territorial federalism is not equipped to answer these questions. The case of Nigeria is instructive here. Of the various iterations of new state creation, only that of 1963 (which created the Mid-Western Region) was achieved under democratic conditions and according to specified constitutional processes. All other bouts of state-creation took place under military governments and were then *imposed* on the Nigerian people. Predictably, the expansion of 1967 was strongly opposed by the Hausa-Fulani-dominated NPC, then the dominant political force in the country, because it feared (legitimately, as it transpired) that the division of the north into multiple units would threaten its regional and national hegemony.[48] This exposes a serious flaw in the argument for territorial federalism, because it suggests that the initial division of sub-units may have to take place against the will of some or all of society's major groups.[49] Authoritarian control at the centre many be necessary in order to put the initial architecture of territorial federalism in place. But the problem is even deeper than this. Assuming that a dominant ethnic group has no incentive to accede to a form of federalism specifically designed to dilute its own power, then only if an authoritarian regime is in place that *does not* comprise the dominant group itself can the initial system be implemented. A cynical interpretation of modified territorial federalism is that it relies on much the same 'divide and conquer' logic used by imperial powers and dictators throughout history. Boundary lines are drawn in order to foster intra-ethnic conflict and preclude the emergence of coherent, unified ethnic blocs at the central level. Effective collective action is avoided by keeping each group internally divided. Advocates of territorial federalism have focused on its benefits once the system is already in place, but have largely ignored the dilemmas of creating territorial federalism in the first place. Once these are explored, the

---

48 Olugbemi, 'The Ethnic Numbers Game', p. 276.

49 In Nigeria, the serious opposition to the initial redesign of the federation was notably absent during subsequent redesigns; indeed, with the creation of an upper house (Senate) with equal state representation under the Second Republic, and the introduction of a formula for resource distribution that stressed equality among states, the problem became how to satisfy demands for new states from all parties. See Suberu, *Federalism*, especially Chapter 4, for details.

conditions under which it is reasonable to expect territorial federalism to emerge, especially within a democratic framework, are quite seriously restricted.

A second problem, less serious than the first, but of particular relevance to the case of Iraq, concerns changes to the balance of power between the federal government and the constituent units as the units multiply. In federal systems, the division of powers between federal and state levels is specified in the constitution, but this is not the only determinant of relative power. Economies that are heavily dependent on oil revenues invariably concentrate power in the hands of the level of government that controls natural resources, which is usually the federal level. As studies have indicated, such states are often highly centralised and prone to authoritarianism. Federalism is an important means of dispersing power away from the centre, thereby in the hope of making authoritarian rule from the centre more difficult. However, all else being equal, a federal system comprising a larger number of smaller states will have a stronger central government than one containing a smaller number of more populous states. As the number of constituent units proliferates, so collective action on the part of the units becomes more difficult to co-ordinate and encroachments on the part of the federal government against the prerogatives of the states become more difficult to resist. In this respect, modified territorial federalism works against the dispersal of power and in favour of concentration of power at the centre. This has been a growing problem for Nigeria as the number of constituent units has expanded.

Regional federalism: A flexible hybrid?

Although the volume of literature on 'regions' and 'regionalism' has increased exponentially over the last decade or so, most of it has been geographically concentrated (on Western Europe) and has focused on one of three phenomena: the rise of political parties promoting regional agendas (such as the Northern League in Italy); the broad trend towards devolution of power from centre to periphery, even in stubbornly unitary states like the UK and France; and the increasing importance of regional–EU relations in the context of European integration.[50] Notably absent from the available literature is any serious examination of regionalism as an alternative to the ethnic and territorial models of federalism discussed above. Instead the norm is to treat regionalism as located somewhere between unitary and federal states in terms of the power of the central government relative to the constituent units. Swenden, for example, defines 'regionalised states' as 'states that exemplify some form of 'regional devolution" but that stop short of a 'full-fledged federation'. The basic distinction between the two, according to Swenden, is that, 'unlike the regions of a federation, the regions in a regionalised state remain subordinate to the central government'.[51] On the whole, Keating concurs with this assessment, but contends that 'the distinction between federalism and the stronger forms of regionalism is becoming ever more difficult to make'. Rather than 'making sharp distinctions between federal and regional models of government', Keating prefers instead to locate them on a continuum, 'from the strongest, represented by the German federal system, to the weakest, represented by the administrative deconcentration of the central state'.[52]

According to this line of reasoning, the label 'regional federalism' is either contradictory (because each of the two terms implies something different about the division of powers between centre and

---

50 The many works on these subjects include: Barry Jones and Michael Keating (eds), *The European Union and the Regions*, Oxford: Clarendon Press, 1995; Charlie Jeffery, *The Regional Dimension of the European Union: Towards a Third Level in Europe?*, London: Frank Cass, 1997; Mark O. Rousseau and Raphael Zariski, *Regionalism and Regional Devolution in Comparative Perspective*, New York: Praeger, 1987; Lieven De Winter and Huri Tursan (eds), *Regionalist Parties in Western Europe*, London: Routledge, 1998; Wilfried Swenden, *Federalism and Regionalism in Western Europe: A Comparative and Thematic Analysis*, Basingstoke: Palgrave/Macmillan, 2006; Michael Keating, *The New Regionalism in Western Europe: Territorial Restructuring and Political Change*, Cheltenham: Edward Elgar, 1998.

51 Swenden, *Federalism and Regionalism*, p. 14.

52 Keating, *The New Regionalism*, p. 114.

periphery), or is a truism in that all federations comprise regional sub-units. It is important to clarify at the outset, therefore, that the term 'regional federalism' is used here to refer to the criteria by which the boundary lines of the sub-units are drawn. Whereas the boundaries of the sub-units in ethnic federations are drawn to reflect the geographic concentration of ethnicities, and those of a territorial federation are designed expressly to divide up ethnic concentrations, those of a regional federation are drawn to express regional diversity on a non-ethnic basis. Thus while the ethnic and territorial models are both defined by their relationship to the geographic distribution of ethnic groups, ethnicity is irrelevant to the design of regional federations. In this sense, regional federalism is the only true 'non-ethnic' model of federalism. One immediate problem is the absence of serious scholarship on regional federalism as an option in multiethnic contexts. Scholars working in the field invariably view the debate over sub-unit definition in bipolar (ethnic versus territorial) terms. The assumption, presumably, is that the existence of multiple ethnicities in a single state is the core of the problem, and so the institutional solution must in some way address this directly. Consequently, there is no established corpus of literature to draw upon, and no obvious theoretical framework on which to hang a discussion of regional federalism. However, this should not prevent a serious consideration of an alternative that may be flexible enough to avoid the problems associated with the other two models.

Using regions as the basis for the design of a federal system involves, firstly, establishing what constitutes a region. This is no easy task because a region is not by definition limited in terms of geographical scale. Italy, for example, is currently divided into a 20-region model of quasi-federalism, but there is no obvious reason why twenty regions makes more sense than three larger regions. Regions occupy the territorial space somewhere between the local level and the level of the nation-state, but precisely where depends on the criteria used to define region. An obvious way to define regions is according to geography. Wannop distinguishes between homogenous regions defined by fixed characteristics, such as topography and climate, and nodal regions that gravitate around a central point, usually a city. If geographical criteria arc used, they can be used in a variety of ways. Politically, rivers often form the boundary line that separates regions, while economically and functionally, rivers tend to unite rather than divide. A more functional definition of region would focus on metropolitan areas, based on the territory within the catchment area of the hub city. Ultimately, however, for a region to be something more than lines on a map, there must be some sense of shared identity among inhabitants. Regional identity may be based on any number of factors—shared history and culture, common language or dialect, culinary traditions, folklore, and so on. Keating identifies three elements likely to determine the strength of regional identity: *cognitively*, people must be aware of the existence of their region, where it begins and ends territorially, and how it differs from other regions; the *affective* element concerns 'how people feel about the region and the degree to which it provides a framework for common identity and solidarity'; finally, the *instrumental* element relates to whether the region forms the basis 'for mobilisation and collective action in pursuit of social, economic and political goals'.[53] Accordingly, some combination of the elements above helps to determine the degree to which region constitutes a meaningful source of collective and individual identity and, therefore, a viable foundation on which to construct the units of a federation.

In the absence of at least some minimal level of cognitive and affective commitment to regions, it is difficult to see how defining sub-units in terms of regions can be an effective strategy for dealing with ethnically divided states. However, if regions can be tapped as a meaningful source of identity, then a regional federation may offer a promising alternative to ethnic and territorial models. By using a criterion other than ethnicity to define the boundaries of sub-units, regional federalism avoids some of the more serious problems associated with the other two variants. Using ethnicity as the sole criterion

---

53 Keating, *The New Regionalism*, p. 86.

for drawing boundary lines may be the option of last resort that helps the state to survive, but because it reinforces existing lines of ethnic cleavage and usually requires complex power-sharing arrangements at the centre, politics is essentially frozen along ethnic lines and may be unable to evolve beyond this point. Ethnic federalism may be the only option that groups agree to after ethnic conflict, but it will tend to produce a dysfunctional political system. Meanwhile, drawing boundary lines for the express purpose of fragmenting ethnic concentrations and fostering intra-ethnic conflict may be an effective means of displacing conflict from the centre, but it is not clear that ethnic groups would voluntarily accede to being deliberately fragmented in this way. This kind of territorial federalism may result in a functional political system, but is likely to require involuntary imposition at the outset. As a third-way alternative, a federation based on regions clearly avoids the major defect of ethnic federalism, and may stand a greater chance of being voluntarily accepted by all groups both because it draws on a potentially positive and non-exclusive source of identity (region), thus avoiding the stigma traditionally associated with the divide and conquer strategies that are central to territorial federalism.

The way in which a regional federation divides up ethnic groups and functions in practice depends on the context. However, absent some implausible patterns of ethnic distribution, the most likely product is a hybrid federal system that includes some ethnically homogenous sub-units (but none that are large and overpowering), and some sub-units that are heterogeneous. Sub-unit homogeneity may result from either the break-up along regional lines of large territorial concentrations of ethnicities, or the allocation of sub-unit status to smaller, regionally concentrated ethnic groups. Ethnically heterogeneous sub-units will result wherever regional populations are ethnically diverse, such as is usually the case with major metropolitan areas. The most plausible outcome of drawing sub-unit lines to express regional differences, therefore, is a non-arbitrary, hybrid system that combines elements of both ethnic and territorial models.

Fig. 4: Regional federalism

This is promising because in practice, almost all of the world's most successful examples of democratic multiethnic federations are flexible hybrids in which ethnicity is not the only, or even the main criterion for defining the sub-units, but in which the possibility of creating ethnic units is not dogmatically resisted. India is an important example of this. Having inherited from the British a 'patchwork of political units' that were 'economically, administratively, and linguistically and culturally illogical',[54] India initially ruled out the reorganisation of sub-unit geography along ethno-linguistic lines. Indeed, in a 1948 report, the Linguistic Provinces Commission of the Constituent Assembly warned specifically that creating linguistic provinces would threaten Indian unity, a view shared by Prime Minister Nehru. However, as a consequence of riots and protests in Madras, that province was divided in 1953 along linguistic lines into Andhra Pradesh (for Telugu speakers), and Madras State (for Tamils), and a State Reorganisation Commission was established to examine the issue of redrawing boundary lines throughout India. The goal of the Commission was to make sub-units more linguisti-

---

54 Emma Mawdsley, 'Redrawing the Body Politic: Federalism, Regionalism and the Creation of New States in India', in Andrew Wyatt and John Zavos, *Decentring the Indian Nation*, London: Frank Cass, 2003, p. 39.

cally and culturally homogenous while 'preserving and strengthening the unity and security of India'. The 1956 States Reorganisation Act redrew the sub-unit boundary lines to create more linguistically homogenous states and reduced their total number from 27 to 14. Subsequently, several new states have been carved out of existing ones on a variety of grounds—linguistic (the division of bilingual Bombay in 1960), religious (the creation of Punjab in 1966), and ethnic (the creation of Meghalaya, Manipur and Tripura in the early 1970s) to bring the total number of sub-units to 28. Currently, therefore, India's hybrid federation permits ethnically homogenous units to coexist alongside pre-existing regional units, like Uttar Pradesh. While India has certainly not been spared ethnic unrest, its successful accommodation of extreme diversity within a democratic framework has been remarkable by any standards. Similarly, while Nigeria is a prime exemplar of territorial federalism, its federal system has evolved in a way that has managed to accommodate minority ethnic demands while simultaneously breaking up the political dominance of the three largest ethnic groups. Hybrid federations do not deal with the ethnic issue dogmatically. Ethnicity is neither the defining principle of the federation, but nor is it a force to be engineered out of existence at all costs through the design of sub-units. This raises an important issue, however. If both ethnicity and the denial of ethnicity are excluded as defining principles for the organisation of the sub-units, then some other criterion needs to dictate the logic of where the lines are drawn. Plausibly, organising units around regions and on the basis of regional identity can provide the logic.

Regional federations in practice

Identifying examples of federations in which the boundaries of sub-units are defined by region is not straightforward. The Spanish system of autonomous regions contains sub-units organised along purely regional lines, but it also contains at least three discernibly ethno-linguistic regions (Catalonia, the Basque Country, and Galicia). Italy's system of regional federalism is similar, with 15 'ordinary' regions and 5 regions that are recognised as 'special' on account of linguistic or cultural exceptionalism. Spain is probably the more studied of the two systems, but Italy is in many ways the more interesting.[55] Spain's regional federation was clearly introduced, first and foremost, as a way to placate demands for autonomy from the three 'historic' (and, largely, ethnically defined) regions. Each of these acquired its own territorial sub-unit and a fast track route (under article 151 of the constitution) to autonomous status. Further, the three regions have capitalised on the Spanish constitution's provision allowing each region to negotiate its own statute of autonomy, to press for a significantly higher degree of autonomy than the remaining regions across a range of issues. Both in intent and in operation, therefore, Spain is closer to an ethnic rather than a regional form of federation. Italy offers a purer model both because its 'special' regions are less clearly 'ethnic' than the historic regions of Spain, and because in practice, the powers and privileges afforded to special regions are only marginally different from those of ordinary regions. At the same time, because Italy as a whole is hardly 'multiethnic', it is clearly problematic to use it as an exemplar case of how regional federalism can alleviate tensions in ethnically divided states.

Nonetheless, the experiences of Italy and Spain are not irrelevant. Notably, each followed a different track with regard to the initial formation of regions—an inevitable problem faced by any federation designed around regions. Unlike ethnic systems in which boundaries are defined by the territorial concentration of ethnicities, the boundaries of regions may not be intuitively obvious. This is critical because drawing boundaries determines not just the geographical ex-

---

55 For analyses of the evolution of Spanish federalism, see Pablo Beramendi and Ramon Maiz, 'Spain: Unfulfilled Federalism (1978–1996)', in Amoretti and Bermeo, *Federalism*; Thomas D. Lancaster, 'Nationalism, Regionalism, and State Institutions: An Assessment of Opinions in Spain', *Publius*, vol. 27, no. 4, autumn 1997, pp. 115–33; Luis Moreno, 'Federalization and Ethnoterritorial Concurrence in Spain', *Publius*, vol. 27, no. 4, autumn 1997, pp. 65–84; Robert Agranoff, 'Federal Evolution in Spain', *International Political Science Review*, vol. 17, no. 4, 1996, pp. 385–401.

tent of regions, but also their *number*. For example, Umberto Bossi, the head of the Northern League in Italy has, at various times, proposed dividing the country into three mega-regions—north, central, and south. Bossi's alternative map of Italy is no less 'regional' than the existing one, but the implications for how Italy is governed are obviously immense. In fact, the boundaries of Italy's fifteen 'ordinary' regions were created in the 1930s for purely statistical purposes.[56] Though many of the names of the regions (Lombardy, Piedmont, and Veneto, for instance) have obvious historical referents, the spaces defined by the regional boundaries do not correspond with past patterns of governance. In regions such as Liguria and Veneto the existence of dominant cities provided a 'solid core' of regional identity 'corresponding to the territorial states of the past'.[57] In such cases, regionalism was a force 'radiating out from the capital city and diminishing in intensity as one moved away from it'. Other regions, such as Emilia, and most of the regions of the south, lacked even this. As one expert observes, 'in spite of the claims that could be made for regions, in terms of a shared political past, or of a dominant model of social relations, it would be hard to argue that they were the primary focus for identification, either at the popular level, or among the literate classes'.[58]

This illustrates a broader problem confronting the design of the sub-units in a regional federation. How does one define regions territorially in the face of weak or non-existent regional identity? Spain has largely evaded this problem by allowing a bottom–up process to shape the definition of regions.[59] Article 143 of the Spanish constitution allows 'provinces with a historical regional unity' to 'accede

---

56 Swenden, p. 14.

57 Adrian Lyttleton, 'Shifting Identities: Nation, Region and City', in Carl Levy (ed.), *Italian Regionalism*, Oxford: Berg, 1996, p. 33.

58 Ibid., p. 35.

59 There are, in fact, three different routes to becoming a region defined in the constitution, but all permit their formation through a bottom–up process rather than top–down imposition.

244

to self-government and constitute themselves into autonomous communities'. The successful formation of a region requires that two-thirds of the municipalities in each province vote in favour, so long as this represents a majority of each province's electorate. The beauty of this formulation is that regional boundaries do not have to be imposed on populations devoid of regional identity. Rather, the people themselves (in theory) determine the boundaries of their own region. Under the Spanish model, the boundaries of regions are (presumably) some organic expression of pre-existing regional identity. Spain has essentially divided *itself* along lines of regional identity. Certainly, most of the Spanish regions that emerged have tangible historical points of reference. Even fairly obscure regions, such as Asturias, turn out to have extremely long and vibrant historical traditions which provide ample scope for constructing (or reconstructing) 'myths' of regional identity.[60]

South Africa's federal system is also worthy of consideration as an example of regional federation. Unlike the cases of Italy and Spain, South Africa faced a process of constitutional design that was literally a matter of life and death for its population. Given its history of intense ethnic animosities, the decision over how to structure the country's federal system assumed an existential importance that was simply absent from the experiences of Italy and Spain. The ultimate selection of an avowedly non-ethnic (though not anti-ethnic).design for South Africa's federal system was made easier by the egregious use of ethnic federalism by the white minority to preserve the *apartheid* system. President F.W. de Klerk's stated belief that 'in multicultural societies the assurance of group security was the key to inter-group peace' and that 'offering a high degree of autonomy to the various population groups, was the best way to defuse the tremendous

---

60 The Asturias region, for example, can trace its history back the Kingdom of Asturias (with Oviedo as its capital city), established in the eight century. Indeed, since the fourteenth century, the heir to the Spanish throne has assumed the title 'Prince of Asturias.'

conflict potential in South Africa's society'[61] is in fact a blunt but accurate synopsis of the theoretical rationale for ethnic federalism. In the context of South Africa, it was manifest in the policy of creating ethnic homelands or 'Bantustans' to accommodate the country's culturally homogenous African 'nations'.

This thinly veiled attempt to use of ethnic federalism to divide and rule the African majority meant that there was strong opposition to the concept of using ethnicity to define sub-units when the design of the country's federal system was debated after the end of apartheid in the early 1990s. The Afrikaner Volksunie (AVU) and the Afrikaner Volksfront (AVF) emerged as strong proponents of a separate white state, or *volkstaat*, centred on Pretoria and extending through most of Eastern Transvaal. The AVF's proposal for demarcation across the country as a whole created six large 'homogenic' regions on the basis of ethnicity. Other supporters of ethnic federalism included Chief Buthelezi of the Inkatha movement, who demanded wide-ranging autonomy and recognition of the Zulu monarchy. Ultimately, none of these demands was met. The demarcation of South Africa's nine federal regions was initially based around the nine existing 'development regions' first demarcated in 1983. The criteria used by the Commission on the Demarcation/Delimitation of States, Provinces and Regions to delineate the final lines were, 'the reduction of territorial disparities in social and economic development . . . and the prevention of negative forms of competition between regions', especially with respect to 'ethnic and chauvinistic' forces. In this sense, the boundaries were designed deliberately to avoid using ethnicity as the defining criterion. At the same time, ethnic groups were not deliberately cracked into smaller units, even where they constituted a potential rival power base to the ruling ANC, such as in KwaZulu-Natal.

The nine regions that resulted were a mix of homogenous and heterogeneous units. The Eastern Cape is the most ethnically ho-

---

61 Quoted in Anthony Egan and Rupert Taylor, 'South Africa: The Failure of Ethnic Politics', in John Coakley (ed.), *The Territorial Management of Ethnic Conflict*, London: Frank Cass, 2003, p. 100.

mogenous of the new regions (84 per cent IsiXhosa), followed by KwaZulu-Natal (80 per cent IsiZulu), and Northern Cape (69 per cent Afrikaans). Other regions, such as Gauteng and Mpumulanga, are highly heterogeneous in terms of ethnic composition. Nonetheless, South Africa's understandably contentious process of boundary delimitation illustrates some of the problems associated with designing sub-units in an 'ethnically neutral' way. Most notably, while the congruence between regional boundaries and the distribution of ethnicities is by no means total, it is still high. Of the nine regions, only the two mentioned above do not contain a linguistic majority, and five of the nine contain a linguistic majority that is either close to, or above, two-thirds of the population. It is, therefore, something of an exaggeration to conclude that, 'the crude ethnoterritorial approach of the National Party . . . was swept away by the new provincial boundaries'.[62] To be more precise, the 'approach' or intent underlying the delimitation of the borders may have been neutral with respect to ethnicity without necessarily producing ethnicity-neutral regions as a result. This is because linguistic groups in South Africa are regionally concentrated, so unless a conscious and deliberate decision is made to break up linguistic groups, boundary lines can be entirely 'neutral' in their intent, but still produce sub-units with a relatively high degree of ethnic homogeneity as a result. This would appear to be a generic problem for any state in which ethnicities are regionally concentrated. Under these circumstances, the difference between ethnic and regional federalism rests on a fairly nuanced (but still important) distinction between intent and *de facto* result.

The process in South Africa also highlights how difficult it can be to prevent the intrusion of ethnicity as factor. As participants in the process readily concede, 'the final decisions on the regional map of South Africa were neither in the hands of the experts, nor the public, but in the hands of political parties behind closed doors'—an acknowledgement of considerable gerrymandering even if the map that served as starting point may have been considered politically

---

62 Ibid., p. 111.

'neutral'.[63] Where political parties are organised along ethnic lines, as is often the case in ethnically divided societies, concern over preserving a territorially concentrated power base is likely to impinge on the debate over sub-unit boundary delimitation.[64] Once again, the primary concern may be political power and winning elections rather than ethnicity *per se*, but the result may nonetheless be ethnically homogenous provinces.[65] This is a generic concern that applies in any context where political parties are organised primarily along ethnic lines, and where the process of boundary demarcation takes place within a consultative, democratic framework.

A final concern that is evident from the case of South Africa is the problem of creating regions in the absence of well-defined regional identities. None of the nine provinces had any history of existence prior to the 1980s, and so the division of the country was, in no sense, a natural division. Partly as a consequence of this, is has proven difficult to make the boundaries 'stick', and numerous changes—some quite significant—have subsequently been made to the original demarcation. For example, in December 2005, the twelfth amendment to the South African constitution made changes to the borders of seven of the nine provinces.[66] In November 2006, the ANC government strongly implied that further changes were on the way, and it

63 Yvonne Muthien and Meshack Khosa, 'Demarcating the New Provinces: A Critical Reflection on the Process', in Meshack Khosa and Yvonne Muthien (eds), *Regionalism in the New South Africa*, Aldershot: Ashgate, 1998, p. 53.

64 Some have indeed argued that party political concerns yielded fundamentally dysfunctional provinces in the case of South Africa. See, for example, Richard A. Griggs, 'The Security Costs of Party-Political Boundary Demarcations: The Case of South Africa', *African Security Review*, vol. 7, no. 2, 1998.

65 Depending on the situation, calculations of political power could also result in more heterogeneous regions. For example, an ethnically based political party may seek to divide its support base between two regions if it calculates that by doing so it can win elections in both regions. As the case of Nigeria demonstrates, material incentives can also prove effective in stimulating the division of sub-units.

66 Subsequently, Matatiele successfully protested its annexation from KwaZulu-Natal to the Eastern Cape to the constitutional court.

seems likely that the number of provinces will be reduced from nine to seven at some point in the near future.[67] Some flexibility in this respect is probably necessary, but if boundary lines are continually drawn and redrawn, it is difficult to see how a coherent sense of regional identity can evolve.

Ultimately, the core issue is whether regional federalism is equipped to deal with ethnic conflict. Spain is not an ideal example to answer this question, because with respect to the historic nations, the country operates more as an ethnic federation. While Italy is not multiethnic, a case can be made that during much of the Cold War, the country faced ideological cleavages (between secular communists and the more religious conservative right) as intense and as threatening to stability as ethnic divisions. Perhaps surprisingly, despite having little or no power for a long period after their creation, the regional governments appear to have had a significantly moderating influence over the conduct of politics in Italy. Putnam offers compelling evidence in support of this, concluding that 'the first two decades of the regional experiment witnessed a dramatic change in political climate and culture, a trend away from ideological conflict toward collaboration, from extremism toward moderation, [and] from dogmatism toward tolerance'.[68] Positing 'institutional socialisation' as the key independent variable, Putnam concludes, 'the new regional institution fostered a tolerant, collaborative pragmatism among its members'.[69] This is an important finding because it suggests that the institutions themselves provided an arena for elite interaction within which initially intense ideological divisions lessened in severity over time rather than intensifying. In other words, the creation of ideo-

---

67 In particular, the viability of Northern Cape seems to be in considerable doubt. See Wyndham Hartley, 'South Africa: Mufamadi Warns of New-Look Provinces', *Business Day*, 16 November 2006, see http://allafrica.com/stories/200611160073.html.

68 Robert Putnam, *Making Democracy Work: Civic Traditions in Modern Italy*, Princeton: Princeton University Press, 1993, p. 36.

69 Ibid., p. 38.

logically heterogeneous regional sub-units helped to alleviate conflict of considerable intensity.

It is still too early to judge the quality and durability of South Africa's emerging democracy definitively. However, the decision to resist pressure for ethnically defined regions appears to have yielded tangible dividends. Support for an Afrikaner *volkstaat* has almost evaporated and parties appealing on the basis of ethnicity have slowly but surely been losing ground at the polls. The results of the 2004 general and provincial elections demonstrate the virtual extinction of parties whose appeal is primarily ethnic (with the exception of the Inkatha Freedom Party). Likewise, the staunchly segregationist Freedom Front Plus has continued its decline, winning only four of the National Assembly's 400 seats. At the provincial level, the (New) National Party lost control of Western Cape to the ANC, as did Inkatha in KwaZulu-Natal. The ANC now controls the governments of all nine provinces and more than two-thirds of the seats in the Assembly. This dominance permits the ANC to amend the constitution unilaterally and, therefore, to make changes to provincial boundaries at will.

Regional federalism is more difficult to pin down than either ethnic or territorial models of federalism. This is partly because the definition of region is inherently elusive, but also because the practical effects of regional federalism are heavily contingent on context. A federation in which region defines the sub-units will (almost) inevitably result in some form of hybrid ethnic/territorial federation. The exact ratio of heterogeneous to homogenous sub-units will depend on the number of regions, and the territorial concentration of ethnicities. On the negative side, this makes the outcome somewhat unpredictable; on the positive, it means that unlike the alternatives, regional federations are inherently responsive to changes in context. More generally, hybrid models of federalism that combine heterogeneous and homogenous sub-unit elements have a strong track record of success. This suggests that any alternative to the pure forms of ethnic and territorial federalism merits serious consideration.

250

Regional federalism in Iraq: a flexible alternative?

Territorial and ethnic federalism occupy different ends of a continuum with respect to ethnicity. Both use ethnicity as the primary, or even sole, criterion for defining the boundaries of sub-units, but in very different ways. Ethnic federalism draws lines to unite ethnic concentrations; territorial federalism deliberately draws lines to divide them. Ethnicity remains the defining variable for both, and in this sense, neither can be considered 'non-ethnic'. Regional federalism occupies a point on the continuum between these two extremes. This point is not fixed, however, because, unlike the other two versions, regional federations are highly sensitive to context. If regions based on regional identity are the primary building blocks for a federation, then in practice, a regional federation will function more like the ethnic model in certain contexts, and more like a territorial version in others. Precisely which end of the continuum depends on a range of factors, the most important of which are the size, number, and concentration of ethnic groups. The key benefit this provides is flexibility in terms of both process (how sub-unit boundaries are determined) and outcome (the degree of ethnic heterogeneity/homogeneity of the resultant sub-units). This inherent flexibility offers promise in the context of Iraq, where the absence of even the most basic consensus on the nature of the federal system among the country's various ethnic groups makes the imposition of more rigid alternatives highly problematic.

Constitutionally, two of the sub-units in Iraq's federation have already been determined. The Kurdistan Region is not ethnically homogenous, but its final borders will be ethnically defined (because of the provisions relating to the status of Kirkuk in the 2005 Iraqi constitution) and, efforts to create a 'Kurdistani' identity notwithstanding, the region's 'Kurdishness' is undeniable. Baghdad, meanwhile, is constitutionally prohibited from being amalgamated with other governorates to form a larger region and will, therefore, constitute its own, ethnically heterogeneous region (or remain as a standard governorate). According to article 115 (later renumbered 117) of the constitution, each of the remaining fourteen of the country's eighteen governorates has the right either to form its own region, to join with others to form a larger region, or to maintain its status as a governorate. There are, of course, a multitude of possible permutations that could result from this provision, but the constitutional reality of a Kurdistan Region effectively precludes the implementation of a territorial federation. Any attempt to divide up the Kurdistan Region territorially would certainly be forcibly resisted by the Kurds and it is not clear that any player in Iraq (other than the United States, perhaps) has the power or the will to force the Kurds to accept this solution. Nor is it clear how this sort of divide and conquer approach could be implemented in the south. Among Iraq's Shiite population, opinion is divided on the merits of federalism. SCIRI's Abd al-Aziz al-Hakim has expressed support for the emergence of a nine-province mega-region in the south, but other prominent Shiite political figures—Muqtada al-Sadr, for example—are openly hostile to any form of federation that threatens the unity of Iraq. Overall, however, the desire to maintain Shiite unity is likely to prove decisive, and this effectively rules out any federal system that is designed for the express purpose of fostering inter-ethnic competition and conflict in the Shiite areas. As was evident in the case of Nigeria, the problem with territorial federalism lies not with its theoretical logic, but with its initial implementation. Deliberately drawing sub-unit boundary lines in order to break up ethnicities is an extra-constitutional option under military dictatorship, but it is not a realistic option within the democratic constitutional framework currently (more or less) operative in Iraq.

The establishment of a nine-governorate region in southern Iraq would create an approximation of an ethnic federation, consisting of two reasonably ethnically homogenous regions (a Kurdish north and a Shiite south). It is not clear what would emerge in the centre except that, presumably, Baghdad would retain its status as a separate entity. This is a problematic scenario because while Iraq's Sunni Arabs probably oppose any form of federation for Iraq, the 'ethnic option' is undoubtedly their least preferred outcome and it is difficult to see how this form of federation will encourage the sorts of political compromises necessary to end sectarian conflict. It would also not be a clean division because certain of the remaining governorates, most notably Diyala and Baghdad itself, have highly heterogeneous populations. Perhaps the most troubling aspect of a *de facto* ethnic federation, however, is that it would almost certainly exacerbate rather than alleviate the ethno-sectarian nature of politics in Iraq. Ethnicity is already the defining feature of Iraq's political life, with political parties organised around ethnic groups, electorates that vote almost exclusively for ethnic parties, and positions of power in the central government allocated on the basis of ethnic quotas. An ethnic federation will obviously not create these divisions, but it will certainly reinforce them and make them extremely difficult to transcend in the future.

Ideally, unless or until the time comes when no options other than an ethnic federation are feasible, Iraq's federal system should be designed to help to break down rather than crystallise ethnic divisions. If a territorial federation is not practical for political and constitutional reasons, a regional federation offers a compromise position that would permit an ethnic Kurdish region in the north while, potentially at least, avoiding the emergence of a large, monolithic Shiite region in the south. Critically, a regional federation would allow the Iraqis themselves to determine the nature of their own federation. Article 115 (117) of the Iraqi constitution allows regions to form through a 'bottom–up' process, initiated by either one-third of governorate council members, or one-tenth of voters, and then voted on by the populations of the governorates concerned. This process is similar to that used to create Spain's autonomous regions and should help to avoid the possibility that Iraq's sub-units are defined by political elites behind closed doors and then imposed on unwilling citizens. Simply put, the Iraqi people themselves will determine whether Iraq's federation is defined by ethnicity or regional identity. On the basis of the evidence presented in Chapter 2 of this book, it appears plausible that at least two regions—Basra and the Middle Euphrates—will emerge in the south, defined not by ethnicity but on the basis of distinct historical and cultural identities. In terms of population, both these sub-units will be dominated by Shiite Arabs, but, critically, ethnicity will not be their defining feature. Under this scenario, Iraq evolves naturally and organically into a hybrid federation defined by a mix of ethnically heterogeneous and homogenous sub-units. Obviously, this will not automatically resolve the problem of Sunni areas, but it offers a more promising foundation on which to build a political consensus. Notably, it avoids the problems associated with ethnic federalism while offering some of the benefits of a territorial federation.

While a detailed analysis of the division of powers between the regions and the central government is beyond the scope of this chapter, it is worth noting that the hybrid form of federation that is likely to result from a regional approach to defining sub-units naturally inclines towards asymmetry in terms of the distribution of powers. An asymmetric federation in one in which the same powers are not invested uniformly across all sub-units. Once again, the Spanish example is useful. Rather than allocating equal powers to all regions, the Spanish constitution allows each region to negotiate its own statute of autonomy with the central government. This enables each region to choose its own level of autonomy in those areas deemed most important (language and education, for example) and permits each to enjoy its own particular power relationship with the central government. This is a highly flexible way to avoid many of the political pitfalls associated with the division of powers in a federal system. An asymmetric federation is a system that can accommodate variation in the intensity of preferences for autonomy among different groups. This seems appropriate in the case of Iraq because the Kurdistan Region is clearly able and willing to cope with a high level of autonomy, whereas there may be other regions that lack either the desire or the institutional infrastructure to exercise extensive powers. This system avoids the 'highest common denominator' problem whereby all regions are required to adopt the same degree of autonomy demanded by the Kurds, and it does so without treating the Kurds as a special case. All regions, after all, have the same rights, it is just that in practice, some may choose not to exercise these rights.

Ultimately, the Iraqi constitution allows the Iraqis themselves to shape their own federal system. This is as it should be, and any insights on the part of Western scholars into the optimum design of Iraq's federation are likely to be peripheral to the outcome. Having said this, there is clearly a need to broaden the debate beyond the dichotomy (ethnic versus territorial) that has so far dominated. Regional federalism, combined with an asymmetric distribution of powers offers a more flexible, fluid option than either of the other two alternatives and, particularly where there is fundamental lack of consensus on almost every aspect of the design of Iraq's federal system, it deserves to be entertained as a serious option.

10

CONCLUSION

Gareth Stansfield

Is the subject focused upon in this book—that is, regionalism and debates about Iraq's future political structure—important? When the news from Iraq is unremittingly terrible, to the extent that even the most atrocious acts of violence, killing and mutilation now have to be of such immense magnitude—in terms of numbers killed or maimed—to make the news headlines beyond a cursory 'suicide bomb rocks Baghdad'-type headline, how can analyses of regionalism and federalism, and the interplay of the two, be considered anything other than the maybe interesting musings of academics?

While the book only at times delves into the issue of violence in Iraq, the subject of identity, how it is constructed, and how its political manifestations could be managed exists at a level of abstraction higher than direct mechanisms of conflict management currently being promoted by Western politicians (such as the further sending of troops to Baghdad and the targeting of persons associated with regional powers) is fundamentally more important to get right if the intention is indeed to preserve the integrity of Iraq and find a structure through which the situation can become more normal, if not actually fully normalised. The editors of this book would therefore consider the subject matter to be at least one of, if not the, most critical in Iraq today, and the issues raised to be of perhaps unparalleled importance for those involved in Iraq's political affairs—whether members of Iraqi political parties, regional powers, or international actors.

There is also a further, practical, reason why a focus on 'an Iraq of its regions' could be ultimately prescient. By focusing on regionalism, we have explicitly placed the notion of 'constitutionality' at the centre of our analyses. The political process in Iraq is, still, that enshrined in the constitution of Iraq and, until it becomes apparent that the constitution has lost its relevance (and this may indeed happen if the civil wars develop further), then regions formed from the building blocks of the extant non-communally defined governorates—rather than areas deemed 'Sunni' or 'Shiite' or 'Kurdish'—are likely to coalesce. The constitutional process therefore promotes 'regionalism', and as long as the constitution is adhered to, knowledge of Iraqi regions will remain fundamentally important. The questions to ask now are (a) how this constitutional process will develop, and (b) whether we can expect the constitutional framework to continue to dictate the contours of Iraq's internal political structures in future years.

How will regions emerge?

Any attempt to predict what will happen in Iraq by extrapolating from its history is now a highly questionable enterprise as social and political structures from the most broad, in spatial terms, through to the inter-personal, have become transformed by the accumulative effects of fear, violence, occupation, and aspirations for the future. Yet, it is a necessary task to conclude this book with at least an attempt to chart out how 'an Iraq of its regions' may emerge, and the problems that may become manifest—however tentatively and proviso-loaded any such scenario-building by its nature has to be.

If we return to the process outlined in the constitution of Iraq, the procedure by which regions in Iraq will be formed is straightforward. Section five of the constitution (powers of the regions) required the passing of a law for the formation of regions, which was duly done on 11 October 2006 by a slim majority. The adoption of the law should not be considered as being uncontroversial, however. With the boycotting of the vote by the (Sunni) Iraqi Accord Front, in addition to several (Shiite) Sadrists and Fadila party members, the law was in effect passed by some Shiites in alliance with Kurdish representatives keen to push the federal arrangements onto Iraq at the earliest opportunity. However, even with the law in place, a previous agreement reached between Sunni and Shiite representatives over when federalism would be implemented and referenda held means that no region (other than Kurdistan, which was approbated by the constitution) will appear before April 2008 at the earliest.[1]

The procedure for forming regions now exists. But there are significant potential hurdles, including whether the Sunni–Shiite agreement holds, and how Kirkuk is handled by the Iraqi government and KRG. It is this latter issue that is fundamentally important. The discussions that are ongoing between KRG and Iraqi government negotiators may see this most sensitive of situations resolved (a) in a manner that does not damage the integrity of the constitutional provisions (with both sides appealing to the agreements already reached under the terms of the constitution), or (b) by the threatening and using of force that would divest the constitutional process of any relevance (with the KRG ordering the annexation of Kirkuk because the December 2007 deadline for a referendum on its status expires). In charting out the process by which regions will form in Iraq, therefore, the first indicator of it happening will be the management of the situation in Kirkuk at the end of 2007. The governorate may be incorporated into Kurdistan by the process outlined in article 140 of the constitution (with the KRG proclaiming its 'Kurdistani' regionalist credentials); it may be delayed by agreement reached in Baghdad between negotiators; or it may be resolved by the declaration of a Kurdish *fait accompli*.

---

1 How this ties in with the 'normalisation' of Kirkuk is unclear, particularly as the constitution of Iraq dictates that this should occur by the end of 2007 and culminate with a referendum that will decide whether the governorate should join the Kurdistan Region.

In the south of the country, political momentum seems to be moving in the direction of there being perhaps two regions. Whether these would be non-sectarian, as Reidar Visser so persuasively argues as being a possibility, or would be highly sectarian as other commentators expect, remains to be seen. The outcome depends largely on how intra-Shiite political competitions develop and will also be influenced by how the collective Shiite political consciousness adapts in the face of the continued attacks against Shiite communities by Sunni insurgents, and by any heightening of tension between Iran and the US. It is still not possible to say whether the two southern regions identified by Visser will emerge, but it seems that the likelihood gets stronger day by day through the combination of the ongoing civil conflict debilitating the central Iraqi government, with 'localised' powers becoming more prominent because of it, and with the continued pushing of the need to create regions by prominent parties such as SCIRI. When these regions will come to pass is unclear, but political actors promoting the formation of them probably will need the period to April 2008 to prepare. Firstly, they will have to allay fears among their communities that the regionalisation of Iraq equates to the fragmentation of Iraq—it is the case that there exists significant antipathy toward the idea of federalism among great swathes of society in the south (in Wasit, for example), in addition to the tendencies uncovered in Baghdad in this volume. Secondly, there is undoubtedly an element of political preservation and advancement to be factored into how, where, and when southern regions will emerge, with the most prominent political parties needing to use the period to prepare themselves politically and militarily to ensure that they remain leading forces within the new region(s).

If these developments take place, it may become an act of political necessity for the remaining governorates that are not in Kurdistan, nor in one of the two entities to the south of Baghdad, to band together. The alternative, of simply existing as governorates in the Iraqi state, with power woefully limited when compared to the new regions, and answering directly to a central government that will, like it or not, remain dominated by Shiites and Kurds, may be considered a political nonsensical option to pursue. But this will largely depend upon how the relationship between non-federated governorates and the central government is constructed, and how much influence non-federated governorates will enjoy vis-à-vis federal regions. It is highly possible that some governorates that currently display deep animosity toward the idea of federalism may still choose to exist autonomously.

The above (admittedly sketchy) scenario builds upon the expectation that the relevant articles of the constitution, and the appropriate laws, will be followed by all parties. But this cannot be taken for granted. In so far as the constitution of Iraq is upheld and is recognised by all to be the guiding legal document underpinning the design of the state, then federalism will come to pass in Iraq. Yet there is every possibility that the constitution may be revised (particularly as 'anti-federalist' thinking remains prominent among both Shiites and Sunnis as Fanar Haddad and Sajjad Rizvi illustrate), or even ignored (if the perilous situation in Iraq deteriorates into a full-scale civil war). Nothing, it is fair to say, can be guaranteed in Iraq for the time being.

Flashpoints

Constitutionality does not dilute the possibility that serious violence will break out in governorates that are home to 'mixed' populations, whether ethnically or religiously defined, or deemed supportive of federalism or a unitary state. If the currently extant region—Kurdistan—is considered, there is already such serious disagreement over where the border with territories to the south will be that it threatens to undermine the Shiite–Kurdish alliance upon which the Iraqi government is now built. The precedent for a Kurdistan Region in Iraq was set between 1970 and 1974 (when the Iraqi government agreed to Kurdish autonomy), and was further strengthened when the Kurdistan *de facto* state emerged in 1991. But the borders of the territory were a product of the asymmetric balance of power that existed between the Kurds and the Iraqi government. Now, from a position of strength, the KRG *expects* that those areas home to a Kurdish majority will be merged with the Kurdistan Region. Under the terms of the constitution, there is no procedure for the joining together of anything other than 'whole' governorates, with sub-divisions not being discussed. Yet Kurdish maps of 'where' Kurdistan lies—based upon a highly subjective understanding of (a) where the population is predominantly Kurdish, or (b) where the population *was* predominantly Kurdish—cut freely across established governorate boundaries. How to manage this tension is hugely problematic, with Kurdish negotiators already seeking the redrawing of the boundaries of Kirkuk governorate to exclude areas populated by Sunnis and earlier added by the Iraqi government (such exclusion would have a more significant Kurdish majority as its net effect). A stand-off is therefore developing between the KRG and the central Iraqi government over where the southern boundary of Kurdistan shall lie. With a specially-tasked if somewhat awkwardly named Ministry for the Regions Outside 'The Region', the KRG is claiming not only the often-referred-to oil-rich Kirkuk governorate, but also a swathe of land stretching from Mandali on the Iranian border across to Tuz Khurmatu, including not only Makhmur and the Jabal Sinjar region and Talafar (mentioned in the chapter of James Denselow as constituting an integral part of the Jazira region), but also an impressive chunk of that most proudly-recognised part of the map of Arab nationalists—Mosul. Indeed, quoting Khasro Goran, the Kurdish deputy governor of Mosul, Patrick Cockburn noted that 'Mr Goran says that such a poll [the referendum of December 2007] could see all of Mosul province east of the Tigris and the districts of Sinjar and Talafar to the west of the river joining the KRG'.[2] How this could be achieved under the terms of the current constitution is not at all obvious, as there is no provision for districts (*qada*s) to join regions. If the Kurds attempt to disaggregate referendum data, then this would

---

2 Patrick Cockburn, 'Kurds and Arabs vie for control of Mosul', *The Independent*, 27 September 2007.

open a plethora of disputes not only in the north, but across the entirety of Iraq, including heavily-divided Baghdad.

These problems between Kurds and non-Kurds in the north of Iraq are already serious and will probably get much worse before they get better. The disagreements that we see in the north of Iraq exist, however, in a historical context that is quite unique to the interaction of Kurds with the Iraqi government. Memories of oppression and subjugation to Arab nationalist projects resonate strongly in Kurdistan and drive the desire to not only exist autonomously, but to bring all of what is believed to be Kurdistan within the boundaries of the region. It is therefore possible that the problems in the north of Iraq will remain localised, but there is of course a chance that similar disputes could break out elsewhere. If this happens, then even the serious problems in the north will pale into insignificance when compared to any struggle that erupts over Baghdad. The chapter of Fanar Haddad and Sajjad Rizvi emphasises certain facts that have largely been ignored by academics and commentators to date and that are crucial in this regard. First, the idea of 'regionalism' in Baghdad is not one that has any significant amount of support in the capital. This is understandable considering Baghdad's modern history of being the undisputed centre of the political, economic, social, and cultural landscape of Iraq. Perhaps the importance of the city has permeated into the culture of society and how its inhabitants view their fellow citizens across the country. This problem is arguably serious enough to cause significant political headaches when negotiating the relative distribution of powers between regions and the capital, and how Baghdadis themselves should fit into this pattern.

However, there exists a more profound and immeasurably more dangerous problem, and that relates to the identity of Baghdad itself. If the simplistic three-way division of Iraq is considered, Baghdad is more often than not located within the 'Sunni' region, and because, as the capital city of a state that has been politically dominated by Sunni Arabs since its inception (and coloured by them for centuries before it), it stands to reason that the capital is 'Sunni'. This is now a questionable assumption to make, as it is undeniable that since 2003 Iraq's social characteristics have markedly changed. While undermining the idea that there is a strong intrinsic 'Baghdad' city identity in existence, it would appear to be the case that the invigoration of sectarian divisions in Iraq has had the most profound influence on the capital, as people who identify themselves as Shiites now predominate. This, tied with the overwhelming Shiite colouring of the institutions of the Iraqi government, mean that the old 'cosmopolitan' Baghdad identity is now being replaced by something far more 'Shiite' in nature than ever before.

If not regions, then what?

When considering the territorial aspects of regionalism, there are serious problems looming on the horizon if the constitutional requirement of 'governorates' joining together is altered in favour of districts or even sub-districts becoming the base-unit. Not only are the Kurds seeking the redrawing of the boundary of Kirkuk governorate, but there have been occasional Shiite calls to redraw some of the southern governorate boundaries, and evidence of ethnic cleansing in places such as Baquba, Samarra, and, indeed, Baghdad. With the capital becoming increasingly the preserve of Shiites (and especially Sadrists), and the outskirts of the town falling to the control of Sunni insurgents as they seek to isolate the city from the rest of the country, there is a possibility that a pattern of communally defined regions may be appearing, rather than the more geographically-based ones discussed in this book. But, it is important to raise the fact that there exist considerable pressures against this development as well, at least south of Kurdistan. While it is undisputable that ethnic cleansing and forced populations movements are occurring as Sunni and Shiite insurgents and militias terrorise each other, it is still, as yet, not considered acceptable to translate these processes into open ethno-sectarian demands—perhaps due to the fact that combatants and their political fronts on both sides continue to see their actions as being within a wider Iraqi, or Arab, nationalist framework. If the constitutional process fails, or is ignored, or is altered in a way that codifies the building of regions according to identities of ethnicity and/or sect, then the problems now afflicting Iraq will probably be magnified, as there will be absolutely no incentive to view the construction of regions in any way other than through the lenses of communalism. If this comes to pass, there promises to be problems of catastrophic scale over where the lines dividing these regions may fall.

If the 'regionalisation' of Iraq does not occur via the processes mandated in the constitution, then what may happen instead? Would regions form through violence and would their character be influenced to a far greater degree by the polarised identities of sect and ethnicity than the geographic notions we have attempted to describe as 'regionalist'? As discussed above, problems will appear in their starkest and most deadly form in the heavily mixed cities. If the process fails, then it is likely that Iraq's regional framework will be borne from struggle, almost certainly violent, between those who have different visions of:

(a) Iraq's future, whether unitary or federal, or;
(b) their region's future, its geographic parameters, and its political leadership.

Politically, the hardest battles will be fought perhaps within communities as power-holders within region compete over:

(a) whether there should be a region in the first place, and;
(b) which group will predominate in the region.

The aim of this book is to show that there are other ways of conceptualising identity politics in Iraq, by showing that attachment to territory and the influence of space may in fact be seen to override notions of ethnicity and sect in Iraq's history, and even in its contemporary politics. But, to what extent has the rapidly rising and sensitised nature of communal identities in Iraq now pervaded ever-deeper into Iraq's society, and coloured—perhaps irreversibly so at least in the short to medium term—the outlook of Iraqis to those who are now seen as being from a different community or even region? If these dynamics have reached irreversible proportions, then the future of Iraq will be starkly different from what the authors of this book have alluded to as possible—i.e. the emergence of a federal Iraq built on the notion of 'regions'. Rather, Iraq's future will be one of the tearing apart of communities, as is happening now in Baghdad and, to a lesser extent, Mosul and Kirkuk. Predicting how this fighting would then be resolved is impossible due to the manifold variables involved at the domestic, regional, and international levels, but two possibilities warrant mentioning. The first of these would be the emergence of some form of Lebanon-style process whereby political elites of communities recognise that their enemies cannot be defeated, leaving a tortuous mechanism for sharing power within the state as the only option left. The second option would be one whereby a peace is imposed from outside (in a manner similar to the Dayton Agreement in Bosnia), where lines are drawn around communities, producing a map of a complexity only exceeded by the imposed political structures and decision-making processes. Neither of these options is any better than following the regional path as outlined in the constitution of Iraq, but there exists a distinct possibility that they could happen if the cacophony of violence continues unabated. While regionalism may indeed be a (perhaps the only) cornerstone upon which at least stability if not democracy can be built in Iraq, the forces that will break Iraq into pieces are already largely present. Whether Iraqi politicians of whatever ethnicity or religion are capable of withholding and managing the ethno-sectarian pressures that will continue to build between now and April 2008 remains to be seen.

INDEX